D1231093

"Every decade or so a book comes
children's, youth, and young adult ministry really matters. *Growing Young* not only champions the best practices of growing churches everywhere, it also digs deep into the core issues that are crucial for making a forever impact in the heart and soul of young people."

Reggie Joiner, CEO of Orange/rethink,
author of *Think Orange*

"We have all heard the statistics: Americans, especially young ones, are falling away from both the church and personal faith. Amid the handwringing that has understandably ensued, Kara Powell and researchers with the Fuller Youth Institute have found a surprising kernel of good news: hundreds of churches across the country are engaging and retaining young people in real, embodied ways, and they're doing so without using smoke machines or skinny jeans. Chock full of statistics and fleshed out with stories and anecdotes, *Growing Young* is a crucial and hope-filled resource for anyone whose heart beats for the local church."

Katelyn Beaty, managing editor, *Christianity Today*;
author of *A Woman's Place*

"Through research, interviews, observation, and analysis, the authors affirm what pastoral leaders intuitively know—grow young or close up! By identifying six fundamental commitments as well as strategic questions and ideas for action, all anchored in real stories, this book provides a path for adaptive changes in our ministries. The energy and passion of young people can infuse our congregations, creating vibrant disciples of Jesus Christ. Of course!"

Bob McCarty, executive director, National Federation
for Catholic Youth Ministry

"In *Growing Young*, Kara Powell, Jake Mulder, and Brad Griffin have produced probably one of the most thoroughly researched books I have ever come across—but not nebulous research from ivory towers. This research is from on the ground among real-life ministry contexts and communities. It's incredibly insightful, theologically robust, and practically engaging. There's a fine line between catering to young people and understanding the context of our fast-changing culture so that we can engage young people and invite them into discipleship and mission. *Growing Young* is a gift to the wider church."

Eugene Cho, pastor of Quest Church, author of *Overrated*

"If you care about the next generation, this book is for you! Kara Powell and the Fuller Youth Institute understand leadership, culture, and the future of the church. This content is timely, strategic, and helpful."

Brad Lomenick, author of *H3 Leadership* and *The Catalyst Leader*, former president of Catalyst

"This much-needed resource is a wake-up call, urgent challenge, and empowerment tool reminding us how important youth engagement and development is to a thriving church. Allow this book to push you to new levels of youth and family ministry. Let every page cause you to rethink the present and future of your local church, denomination, or outreach ministry."

Efrem Smith, president and CEO of World Impact, author of *Raising Up Young Heroes* and *The Post-Black and Post-White Church*

"Leaders everywhere worry about reaching the youth of today. *Growing Young* is the guide to ease those concerns. Thank you, Kara Powell, for writing this book."

Claire Diaz-Ortiz, author, speaker, and entrepreneur at www.ClaireDiazOrtiz.com

"I remember growing up in my small denominational church and hearing the pastor 'encourage' me and my young adult friends by saying we were the church of tomorrow. Yeah, I never found that to be inspiring. Fortunately, my friend Kara Powell offers some real inspiration and practical guidance in how the church can combat the sin of ageism by showing how church leaders can turn the younger generations' tomorrow into today."

Bryan Loritts, lead pastor of Abundant Life Church, author of *Saving the Saved*

"Every congregation wants to love and be loved by its young people. This book grounds that hope in tangible practices that can actually help make it so. It will give you insights and tools for what matters most, not least just letting your life express the life-giving love of Jesus Christ that holds us all together."

Mark Labberton, president, Fuller Theological Seminary

"Many leaders today can point out what the church is doing wrong with the next generation. Few leaders have taken the time or done the research to discover what churches are doing right. That's why I'm so excited about this book. Kara Powell, Jake Mulder, and Brad Griffin have put together a masterful, accessible work that beautifully documents how churches of all sizes, backgrounds, and denominations are effectively connecting with the next generation. Even better than that, they specifically show what you need to do to become one of those churches. They present their findings in ways that make it extremely easy for any church leader to take action. This is a book filled with practical hope that every church leader will want to read."

Carey Nieuwhof, author of *Lasting Impact*, founding pastor of Connexus Church

"I'm more convinced than ever how important *Growing Young* is for the church today! I'm so thankful that Kara, Jake, and Brad tackled this conversation head-on and have provided amazing insights that can help each of us engage young people."

Tyler Reagin, executive director, Catalyst

"In *Growing Young*, the Sticky Faith team has done it again. This volume takes the conversation up a notch—identifying the factors most commonly found in churches that launch graduates into a lifelong faith. This book breathes with the authenticity and urgency that might only come from authors who, at a passionately practical level, are actively engaged in the business of Christian parenting themselves."

Mark DeVries, founder of Ministry Architects, cofounder of Ministry Incubators, and author of *Sustainable Youth Ministry*

"*Growing Young* provides research that charts the effectiveness of the church's role in the engagement of youth and their families. Church leaders will learn to create and implement strategic steps to strengthen their youth ministry touch. The secret to Growing Young is now out!"

Virginia Ward, Gordon-Conwell Theological Seminary

"The Fuller Youth Institute, the team that pulls together the latest research on the church and young people, has outdone itself in *Growing Young*. It is the culmination of the most comprehensive project to date that seeks to get at what kind of church not only welcomes the young but also includes and empowers them as full participants in the kingdom of God. Perhaps the greatest gift of *Growing Young* is the way that this vigorous research project is delivered—a church can immediately take steps to strengthen not only their ministry to children, adolescents, and emerging adults but the entire community as well."

Chap Clark, Fuller Theological Seminary, author of *Hurt* and *Adoptive Youth Ministry*

"If you care about young people, this book is for you! If your church has ever asked, how can we reach more young people?, this book is for them too. It's packed with practical, proven ideas and supported by top-notch research made user-friendly. I'm certain that *Growing Young* is going to help leaders better reach a generation. This book is for me!"

Doug Fields, veteran youth worker, author, and cofounder of downloadyouthministry.com

"The first rule of successful change is to understand the bright spots where the change is already happening. *Growing Young* reveals the hidden secrets of bright-spot churches that keep their kids engaged. Hint: It's often easier than you think. With this book you can go and do likewise."

Chip Heath, coauthor of *Switch* and *Made to Stick*

GROWING YOUNG

SIX ESSENTIAL STRATEGIES
TO HELP YOUNG PEOPLE DISCOVER AND LOVE YOUR CHURCH

KARA POWELL, JAKE MULDER, AND BRAD GRIFFIN

BakerBooks

a division of Baker Publishing Group
Grand Rapids, Michigan

© 2016 by Kara Powell, Jake Mulder, and Brad Griffin

Published by Baker Books
a division of Baker Publishing Group
P.O. Box 6287, Grand Rapids, MI 49516-6287
www.bakerbooks.com

Printed in the United States of America

Library of Congress Cataloging-in-Publication Data
Names: Powell, Kara Eckmann, 1970– author.
Title: Growing young : six essential strategies to help young people discover and love your church / Kara Powell, Jake Mulder, and Brad Griffin.
Description: Grand Rapids : Baker Books, 2016. | Includes bibliographical references.
Identifiers: LCCN 2016016469 | ISBN 9780801019258 (cloth) | ISBN 9780801072970 (ITPE)
Subjects: LCSH: Church work with teenagers. | Church work with young adults.
Classification: LCC BV4447 .P6526 2016 | DDC 259/.23—dc23
LC record available at https://lccn.loc.gov/2016016469

To protect the privacy of those who have shared their stories with the authors, details and names have been changed throughout the book.

Authors are represented by WordServe Literary Group (www.wordserveliterary.com).

16 17 18 19 20 21 22   7 6 5 4 3 2 1

In keeping with biblical principles of creation stewardship, Baker Publishing Group advocates the responsible use of our natural resources. As a member of the Green Press Initiative, our company uses recycled paper when possible. The text paper of this book is composed in part of post-consumer waste.

To Nathan, Krista, and Jessica Powell;

Will Mulder;

and Anna, Kara, and Joel Griffin.

You inspire us to be better followers of Jesus.

You keep us laughing and humbly seeking God.

Every day you help us grow and keep us young.

Contents

Acknowledgments

As you'll discover in the following pages, remarkable churches never rely on a sole leader to energize their community to grow young. There is always a team.

Always.

We believe the same is true of the best research. In this nationwide study of churches growing young, we've linked arms with an unbelievable cadre of over 60 researchers, leaders, and supporters who believe it's time to change the way the world views young people.

The core of our lineup is the staff at the Fuller Youth Institute (FYI). Steve Argue, Irene Cho, Macy Phenix Davis, Meghan Easley, Johanna Greenway, Tyler Greenway, Jennifer Guerra Aldana, Quinn Harkless, Brian Nelson, Daisy Rosales, and Matthew Schuler, you are the secret sauce of our work and this book.

Every step of the FYI journey is better (and often faster) thanks to our advisory council: Mary Andringa, Jim Bergman, Judy Bergman, April Diaz, Tim Galleher, Cindy Go, Wally

Hawley, Megan Hutchinson, Ken Knipp, Janet Labberton, Mark Maines, Jeff Mattesich, Christa Peitzman, Linda Prinn, Judi Shupper, Albert Tate, Jeremy Taylor, and Jeff Wright.

Our four years of research were made possible by the vision of four foundations who imagine a better future for the church and are giving sacrificially to make that vision a reality. We are forever grateful to the Hanson Family Charitable Foundation, Lilly Endowment Inc., the Tyndale House Foundation, and the Vermeer Charitable Foundation for their financial investment. More importantly, so is every teenager and emerging adult who will be shaped by congregations that gain the help they need to grow young.

The horsepower for our study comes from the world-class faculty members at Fuller Theological Seminary. Chap Clark, Scott Cormode, Jim Furrow, and Cameron Lee, thank you for shaping every methodological decision and every survey question. Our research muscles were also strengthened by these other Fuller faculty members: Justin L. Barrett, Ryan Bolger, Tod Bolsinger, Mark Lau Branson, Warren S. Brown, Kutter Callaway, Mari Clements, Nathan Feldmeth, Ken Fong, Kurt Fredrickson, Oscar Garcia-Johnson, Winston Gooden, Joel B. Green, Benjamin Houltberg, Mark Labberton, Juan Martinez, David Scott, Scott W. Sunquist, and Jude Tiersma Watson.

Three cheers to our research assistants who dedicated countless (well, actually, we counted and it was well over 10,000) hours to survey, interview, observe, describe, analyze, and celebrate all God is doing in amazing congregations nationwide: Arthur Bamford, Brianna Bentley Bleeker, Adam Borozan, Ann-Marie Bradley, Kristin Brussee, Elizabeth Burks, Marcos Canales, Kaitlyn Clark, Jonathan Damiani, Michael DiMarcangelo, Keith Dixon, Maria Drews, Kristopher Fernhout, Stephen Finkel, Denise Flanders, Lorrie Gray, Patrick Jacques, Austin Johnson,

Bryan Johnson, Erika Knuth, Emily Little, Kerri Lopez, Janie McGlasson, Chelsea McInturff, Daniel Mendoza, Christine Merola, Meredith Miller, Sonia Mims, Lauren Mulder, Stephanie Obad, Peter Ou, Rachel Paprocki, Marian Pena, Emily Peters, Christopher Romine, Jill Romine, Aaron Rosales, Kendra Sawyer, Jodi Tompkins, Randel VanDeventer Jr., Jared Votaw, Meredith Votaw, and Sarah Waters.

Along the way, a host of sharp leaders, researchers, visionaries, and parents gave pivotal feedback at various stages in the process, including reading part or all of the manuscript to help us improve it: Abraham Bejarano, Jim Candy, Bill Crawford, Lisette Fraser, Kristen Ivy, Christine Mutch, Sam Park, Christian Smith, Josh Smith, Bill Staffieri, Lawrence Ward, and Glenkirk Church.

We can't imagine a better publisher than Baker Books, and we so appreciate the brilliant and hard work of Brian, Mark, and the entire Baker team.

And Greg Johnson at WordServe Literary Group, hats off to you for forging this collaborative partnership with Baker Books.

To our spouses—Dave, Lauren, and Missy—you make everything we are and do better. Thank you for loving us and patiently enduring the extra work early in the morning (for Kara) and late at night (for Jake and Brad).

To our kids, you fuel our passion for helping the church grow young. We love dreaming about how the church we pray you will grow to love can be changed by Christ to change our world.

1. Growing Young

What Congregations Are Doing Right

A lot of my friends don't really want to go to their church. But we want to be here, and the older people in our church can see that . . . so they want us to be here. Our whole church treats us like we're the church of today, not just the church of the future.

—Ashlee, age 17

Growing old is our default. It happens naturally. And inevitably.

We see the results of growing old when we look in the mirror.

We see the effects of growing old when we look around our congregations.

With age comes great wisdom and beauty. Decades of burrowing in the love and grace of Jesus give the mature members of our faith communities a network of deep roots. Year after year, season after season, their ongoing commitment to love God and others yields a rich harvest.

Old isn't bad. We love old. We just don't think it's the whole story.

If your church is like many, you have bare spots. Holes created by the teenagers and young adults missing from your congregation. You see them on Friday night at the local movie theater and Saturday morning at the neighborhood coffeehouse, but they are absent from your Sunday morning worship services. These bare spots make your church feel incomplete.

Maybe your congregation's bare spots represent more than just missing young people. Perhaps across generations your church isn't growing as you wish. You may be a senior leader trying to hide your disappointment as you stand to preach and think to yourself, "Where *is* everyone?" Or you're a church member noticing it's now easier to find a preferred parking space before your worship services. Regardless of your role, your church's energy and attendance aren't what they used to be or what you would hope.

Those of you who are part of a growing church likely wish it was growing faster. And yet with that growth, you still want your congregation to feel close and intimate. You are thrilled with the new faces, but you don't want to lose the relational glue that drew you all together in the first place.

Or perhaps you are blessed to be in a congregation bursting with young people. You love how the Spirit is drawing them. But you want to make sure that they don't merely consume what you offer. You want them to be unleashed to join—and help lead—God's redemptive work in the world.

The truth is, every church needs young people. Their passion enriches the soil around them. The curiosity they bring to Scripture and the authenticity they bring to relationships keep your church's teaching fresh and fellowship fruitful.

Young people also need a thriving church. A thriving church both grounds them in community and sends them out to serve.

Your church needs young people, and they need your church. One without the other is incomplete.

The Alarming Reality of Congregations in America

If you're wondering why your congregation is aging, shrinking, or plateauing, you're not alone. Almost weekly, someone at Fuller Theological Seminary quotes this powerful axiom from beloved senior trustee Max De Pree: "The first job of a leader is to define reality."[1] The unfortunate reality is that most churches are not growing, and they aren't getting any younger.

Church Attendance Is Declining

According to an extensive survey by the Pew Research Center, the share of adults in the US who identify as Christians fell from 78 percent to 71 percent between 2007 and 2014. The corresponding increase in those who identify as "religiously unaffiliated" (meaning atheist, agnostic, or "nothing in particular") jumped by almost seven points, from just over 16 percent to 23 percent.[2]

This well-publicized "Rise of the Nones" varies by denomination. Mainline Protestantism, including the United Methodist Church, the American Baptist Churches USA, the Evangelical Lutheran Church in America, the Presbyterian Church (USA), and the Episcopal Church, has experienced the

RELIGIOUS AFFILIATION IN AMERICA 2007–2014

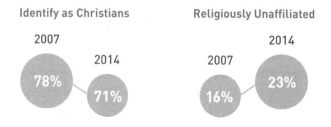

15

greatest dip in numbers. From 2007 to 2014, mainline Protestant adults slid from 41 million to 36 million, a decline of approximately 5 million.

Roman Catholic adults fell from 54 million to 51 million, a drop of nearly 3 million.

Adults in evangelical denominations (such as the Southern Baptist Convention, the Assemblies of God, Churches of Christ, the Lutheran Church–Missouri Synod, and the Presbyterian Church in America), as well as adults in nondenominational churches with evangelical leanings, grew from 60 million to 62 million. While that might seem like something to celebrate, we should hold our kudos. Although the total number of evangelicals has increased, the percentage of Americans who identify as evangelicals has actually decreased almost 1 percent from just over 26 percent to just over 25 percent.

Even though these shifts represent major downturns in three of our nation's largest Christian traditions, not all denominations are experiencing a slump. Historically black Protestant denominations, such as the National Baptist Convention, the Church of God in Christ, the African Methodist Episcopal Church, and the Progressive Baptist Congregation, remain relatively stable at almost 16 million adults.[3]

To summarize, *no major Christian tradition is growing in the US today*.[4] A few denominations are managing to hold steady, but that's as good as it gets.

Congregations Are Aging

Those who study demographics believe the decline in overall church attendance is linked with young people's religious practices, or lack thereof. According to 2001 US Census Bureau data, adults ages 18 to 29 comprised 22 percent of the adult population. Yet that same age group represents less than 10 percent of church attendees nationwide. Evangelical Protestant congregations have the highest concentration of young adults at 14 percent, followed by Catholic parishes at 10 percent, and mainline Protestant congregations at 6 percent.[5]

The last handful of years has brought major changes to the faith of young Latinos, one of the fastest-growing ethnicities in the US. From 2010 to 2013, the number of 18- to 29-year-old Latinos who identified as Roman Catholics dropped from 60 percent to 45 percent, while those who identified as "religiously unaffiliated" skyrocketed from 14 percent to 31 percent.[6]

Another fast-growing group in the US, Asian Americans, is experiencing its own faith struggles. While the "Rise of the Nones" cuts across ethnicities, Asian Americans are 7 percent more likely to be "religiously unaffiliated" than the general population.[7]

Across cultures, a major turning point for young people's faith seems to be high school graduation. Multiple studies highlight that 40 to 50 percent of youth group seniors—like the young people in your church—drift from God and the faith community after they graduate from high school.[8]

YOUNG ADULTS AGES 18–29 AS A PERCENTAGE OF OVERALL POPULATION

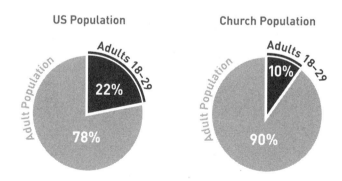

US Population   Church Population

"Right now, in this season, we have a youth group that is very centered on going outside of our doors. These students are taking our congregation back to the type of service in our community that helped our church get started. They are breathing fresh air into our church and lighting our passion again. They are modeling for older generations what it means to be a light and glorify God." —Colette,[9] age 27.

Let's make that statistic a bit more personal. Visualize a photograph of the young people in your congregation. Now imagine holding a red pen and drawing an X through almost 50 percent of their faces. That many will fall away from the faith as young adults.[10]

Some—perhaps more than half—of those who drift from the church end up rejoining the faith community, generally when they get married and have children.[11] But that leaves close to 50 percent still adrift. Even those who return have made significant life decisions about worldview, relationships, and vocation—all during an era when their faith was shoved aside. The consequences of those lasting decisions are often tough to erase.

As followers of Jesus, parents, and leaders who have been in student and pastoral ministry much of our adult lives, we aren't satisfied with the shrinking and aging of congregations. We bet you aren't either.

From Bare Spots to "Bright Spots"

Thankfully, the news for the church is not all gloom and doom. Despite the cloudy sky, light is breaking through here and there. Our team calls these "bright spots."[12]

All around the country, these hundreds of "bright spot" congregations are effectively loving and serving young people. Some of them quietly and without flash. Others with great magnetism and fanfare. We call these churches that *grow young* because

1. they are engaging young people ages 15 to 29; and
2. they are growing—spiritually, emotionally, missionally, and sometimes also numerically.

Thanks to these remarkable congregations, tens of thousands of young people can't stop talking about how "known" they feel in their church and how, no matter what happens, their church feels like "home."

Like the 1,000-member Presbyterian church on the East Coast that developed a long-term high school ministry team that pours into volunteer adult leaders, who in turn build a web of support around students.

Or the 100-member midwestern rural Reformed church that has become so hospitable to teenagers and young adults that being at church is now the highlight of their week.

Or the 1,500-member urban multiethnic congregation in the South that was so passionate about investing in young people's growth that it launched not one but *two* leadership training programs for young adults in its city.

Or the 5,000-member nondenominational church that responds to young people's core questions and struggles with an authentic journey of faith rooted in the grand narrative of the gospel rather than pat answers.

Or the 200-member urban Baptist Latino congregation that chose to integrate English into its worship services because it places such a high priority on young people. This church is literally learning a new language in order to grow young.

Four years ago, we launched an investigation into what these sorts of innovative churches are doing right. We conducted this research because we wanted to give you access to what's actually working. This book describes what we found. It spells out the *core commitments* of churches that are not aging or shrinking but growing young.

The data detailing the decline and "graying" of congregations is convincing, but it's *not the full story*.

And it doesn't have to be your story.

It Might Feel like the Sky Is Falling, but There Is Hope

One of the teenagers in our study, Isabella, was changed because 50 years ago, her church decided to live a new story. In the 1960s, this southern church was on the brink of shutting its doors. But instead of going dormant, the congregation resolved to grow young. The church recruited Roger, a new senior pastor who valued young people and their families. Roger emphasized safe and appealing facilities for children and also hired staff specifically devoted to children, teenagers, and their parents. Under Roger's leadership, the church involved children, senior adults, and everyone in between in local and global intergenerational mission trips. The congregation worked together to help young people feel included and represented across all departments of the church. It was hard work, but eventually that effort led to growth, as well as a long-term commitment to prioritize young people.

Fast-forward to 2014. Isabella, a high school sophomore, found she had no place to go. Kicked out of her house by her drug-addicted mom, Isabella ended up wandering the streets of her town, looking for someplace safe to spend the night.

Desperate, Isabella remembered Dale and Kathy, a couple who had already welcomed a homeless classmate of Isabella, named Emily, into their home. Isabella didn't know that Dale and Kathy followed Christ. Or that the couple was part of this church with a 50-year legacy of living out Scripture's mandate to care for all young people, including orphans.

All Isabella knew was that Dale and Kathy had already said yes to Emily. If she was lucky, they would accept Isabella also.

Dale and Kathy were overwhelmed with Emily. Self-employed and strapped financially, they felt stretched thin in every way. But they knew Isabella needed a family and had a strong hunch they could be family for her.

It wasn't all sweetness and light. Far from it. Isabella could be moody, angry, and downright mean. Dale and Kathy knew this was normal teenage rebellion on steroids thanks to Isabella's turbulent childhood. They were committed to loving her unconditionally, but the slammed doors and sulking didn't make it easy.

Isabella certainly wasn't excited about attending the church's worship services with her new family. Hank, the youth pastor, recalled that on Isabella's first Sunday morning in youth group, she was a "pretty dark thundercloud." Seeing Isabella standing in the back, one of the youth leaders, Tori, approached and started a conversation. Or rather, *tried* to start a conversation. Isabella responded to her questions with the shortest answers possible. (If you've ever tried to talk to a surly teenager, you know what we mean.)

At the end of that morning, Tori told Isabella, "I hope you come back next week."

Arms crossed, Isabella mumbled, "I probably will. Because my new parents will make me."

Isabella's grumpiness would have been too much for many leaders, but not Tori. Every week that Isabella was forced to come to church with Dale and Kathy, Tori tried to start a conversation. Eventually, Isabella's responses went from a few words to a few sentences. And then a few stories.

Isabella loved to play guitar, so Tori invited her to join the youth ministry's worship team. Since Dale, Isabella's adoptive dad, was also a musician, he and Isabella would practice together in the evenings at home. Despite their financial challenges, Dale would take time off work to watch Isabella rehearse and play at church.

A few months later during a youth group retreat, Isabella pulled Tori aside and confessed, "I feel dirty. And like something is missing in my life." Isabella shared more with Tori about her sexual promiscuity, as well as how she had been cutting herself to try to relieve some of her pain.

Wide-eyed, Tori responded, "Well, would you like to trust Christ and experience his love?"

Isabella broke down in tears. "That's all I want." After months of being loved by a new family and church that didn't abandon her, Isabella decided she was ready to follow Jesus.

According to Hank, "Isabella went from being a dark, scowling thundercloud to telling everyone she couldn't stop smiling."

Isabella remembers that her friends at school noticed (and were a bit "weirded out") by the "new me." She stopped cutting and developed healthier relationships with guys. When our team visited this church and met Isabella, she told us with tears in her eyes, "One of the families here took me in and adopted me. You *have* to understand how loving this church is. This church has changed my life."

Seventeen-year-old Isabella was changed by *Roger*, the senior pastor she never met but who God used to change the trajectory of the church 50 years ago, which eventually inspired . . .

Dale and Kathy, two "regular" church members who realized they couldn't turn away a young person who needed love and a safe place, a decision that connected Isabella to . . .

Hank and Tori, two church leaders who didn't give up on Isabella and helped her experience the embrace of a loving God who doesn't give up on anyone.

If You Care about Young People, This Book Is for You

Isabella was changed because of a team of adults—adults who played different roles in her life and her church. Just as young people need a team of adults, in no "bright spot" church did we find one person who was the sole spark that helped the congregation grow young.

Growing young takes everyone. Always.

Senior pastors, you are almost always the most vocal and visible spokesperson for your congregation's vision. If your church is on a rafting expedition, usually you are the raft guide; typically, no one influences the direction and progress of your church more than you.

We realize you juggle many tasks and priorities. Too many to count. All of them important. You barely have time to read this book, let alone spend the additional time to put its principles into action.

Our research revealed that growing young can energize your entire congregation. As you navigate the waters of growing young, your other priorities (like effective evangelism, dynamic worship services, powerful service and missions, and authentic community) will gain momentum. If your overall hope and prayer is to have a vibrant congregation, there is arguably no better starting place than the contagious passion of teenagers and young adults.

Associate pastors, executive pastors, family ministry pastors, and youth pastors, you often steer the raft, providing your senior leadership with navigational information, encouragement, and warnings about rocks ahead. The raft would be lost without you.

As a key member of your church's leadership team, you have dreams for your congregation and ideas for how to make those dreams a reality. But sometimes you may feel like your input and expertise aren't valued. This book can help you determine if your instincts are on track; our research gives you more credibility as you help point your church toward an even more promising future.

Ministry volunteers, leadership team members, and parents, you sit in the front of the raft and help guide it to the best possible waters. Without your ownership, dedication, and hard work, the raft would run aground.

Pastors may come and go, but you don't. You love your church, and you want to see it reach its potential. You're willing to work hard and volunteer long hours. You're probably reading this book because you want the time and energy you devote to make the biggest difference possible.

Teenagers and young adults, your creativity and authenticity bring lifeblood to the journey. Let's be honest—the whole rafting journey would be downright boring without *you.* More than this, you take up the oars and keep the raft moving forward. Without you, the raft would flip over.

You are remarkable. You are made in God's image and have unique passions, gifts, and talents—all of which are waiting to be unlocked and explored through your local congregation. This book is geared to help you know how to step out of the shadows and play a leading role in your church's present and future.

Regardless of your age or role in your church, *you have a vital role* to play in helping your congregation grow young. Churches today navigate rough waters. Your church needs *you* to pay attention to what we discovered is working in other congregations. Young people need *you* to dream new dreams that affect this generation and, in the case of Isabella and thousands of others, future generations to come.

10 Qualities Your Church Doesn't Need in Order to Grow Young

Whether you're a senior pastor, church staff member, ministry volunteer, parent, teenager, or young adult, if you are like us, you may be hindered by your preconceived image of what it takes to grow young. Odds are good that your picture of a thriving congregation has had branch after branch grafted on to it over time. Most of these branches stem from the experience of one person—either you or another (likely well-known) leader.

Even your images of successful ministry that are rooted in broader research are often several years—or decades—old. At this point, it's hard to tell which branches have the potential to bear fruit and which are dead weight that drain the life from your congregation. Your ministry efforts are left wilting under the heavy burden of too many unrealistic expectations.

We need to prune the distractions so the only branches remaining are those that help our churches grow young. Thanks to our research team's surveys, interviews, and site visits with churches across the US, we can cross off these 10 qualities from our list of what churches need to grow young.

1. *A precise size.* Don't buy into the Goldilocks fantasy that some churches are too big, others are too small, and some are "just right." We saw no statistical relationship between church size and effectiveness. Size doesn't matter.

2. *A trendy location or region.* Did our data unearth churches flourishing near bustling urban centers and dynamic college campuses? Sure. But we also uncovered equally robust

ministry in rural one-stoplight towns and middle-class suburbia. Your location does not have to be a limitation.[13]

3. *An exact age.* We applaud how God is working through new church plants. We love what we learned from churches that are less than five years old. But we learned just as much, and recorded just as much life change, in churches over a century old. When it comes to churches that grow young, there is no age discrimination.

4. *A popular denomination . . . or lack of denomination.* When we started our study, we wondered if the churches that rose to the top would skew toward particular denominational, or nondenominational, leanings. While it's true that some denominations are shrinking or aging faster than the average, our fear was unfounded. No need to apologize for your tradition or the fact that you are part of a denomination at all. God is working powerfully through churches of all stripes (and plaids too).

5. *An off-the-charts cool quotient.* Granted, several of the congregations and leaders bubbling to the top of our research have a certain hip factor. But those were in the minority. For young people today, relational warmth is the new cool.

6. *A big, modern building.* Some of the congregations that are most effective with young people have new, state-of-the-art facilities. But not all. The majority of the effective churches we studied gather in decent, but not spectacular, spaces. Some don't own their facilities and are creatively meeting in local schools, community centers, and living rooms. For teenagers and young adults, feeling at home transcends any building.

7. *A big budget.* Churches that grow young intentionally invest in young people, and most often that translates into

a financial investment. But not always. Less resourced congregations creatively support young people in other ways, proving that a small budget does not have to mean small impact.

8. *A "contemporary" worship service.* Our data indicated that while many young people are drawn to "casual and contemporary" worship, others are drawn to "smells and bells" high-church liturgy and everything in between. While the churches we visited were likely to prefer modern worship in some or all of their worship contexts, they didn't depend on that alone as a magnet to draw young people.

9. *A watered-down teaching style.* It's often assumed that we have to whitewash the teachings of Scripture and somehow make them seem less radical in order to appeal to teenagers and young adults. That's not what we found. For today's young people, growing young doesn't mean we talk about Jesus or the cost of following him any less.

10. *A hyper-entertaining ministry program.* The entertainment options available to young people in our culture are endless. We don't have to compete. If we try, we will almost certainly lose. Our research highlighted that faith communities offer something different. Slick is no guarantee of success.

The Vision That Fueled Our Research

The spark that ignites both our research team's passion for growing young and our research engine is our mission. The mission of the Fuller Youth Institute, which is embedded in Fuller Theological Seminary, is to equip young people with the faith they need. To accomplish this goal, we *leverage the*

For more on the mission, strategy, and resources of the Fuller Youth Institute, please visit FullerYouthInstitute.org. For resources for leaders and families on Sticky Faith, see StickyFaith.org. For the research methods and procedures used in the study that fueled this book, see the appendix and ChurchesGrowingYoung.org, where you can also access a free church assessment tool to help your church identify next steps beyond the book.

best research that Fuller and others are conducting *into practical resources*. Through all of this, we hope to change how the world sees young people.

Since 2004, we have had the unbelievable honor of dreaming with leaders and parents about how teenagers can develop a lifelong relationship with Jesus, or what we call Sticky Faith. We studied over 500 youth group graduates during their first three years in college, as well as 50 families who are particularly effective at building long-term faith. From that and other data, we've been able to share our Sticky Faith findings and implications with hundreds of thousands of leaders, parents, and grandparents.

During a rare lull in the 12 years that we have pioneered Sticky Faith research and writing, our team started praying about new ministry frontiers. One morning as I (Kara) was praying and journaling about our future, I wrote this phrase: "Sticky Faith studied young people themselves. Now we need to study congregations that are really good at reaching young people."

That fairly vague phrase penned on a yellow tablet on the navy blue couch in my living room evolved into a four-year interdenominational research effort called the Churches Engaging Young People (or CEYP, pronounced "keep") Project. Funded by four amazing foundations, this initiative had the goal of understanding how and why exemplary churches are effectively engaging 15- to 29-year-olds. Our dream is that what we learned from these highly effective congregations will help congregations nationwide advance into new territory.

Why We Studied 15- to 29-Year-Olds

The majority of the Fuller Youth Institute's prior research focused on teenagers. Given the lengthening of adolescence we will further describe in chapter 3, we believed it was important to zoom out beyond teenagers to include the malleable stage of early adulthood commonly referred to as "emerging adulthood."[14]

While there is ongoing debate in the academic and ministry communities about terms and respective age divisions, in this book we opt for the following phrases:

Teenagers or *adolescents* refers to 15- to 18-year-olds.[15]

Emerging adults or *young adults* indicates 19- to 29-year-olds.

A term we won't use as often for the specific subset of emerging adults who are 19 to 23 years old is *college students* or *college-age young adults.*

Young people is an umbrella term that includes everyone from ages 15 to 29.

The lengthening of adolescence is shown in the delayed timing of five traditional demographic markers of adulthood (leaving home, finishing school, getting married, having a child, and becoming financially independent). In 1960, 66 percent of American men and 77 percent of American women had completed all five of these milestones by age 30. In 2010, only 28 percent of men and 39 percent of women had done so at age 30.[16]

We realize that the wonderfully diverse churches in our study, as well as the equally wonderfully diverse readers of this book, use different terminology in describing their faith communities. Some of you are devoted to your "church," while others of you are committed to your "parish." Many of your congregations are led by "pastors," but others are led by "reverends," "rectors," or "priests." As much as possible, during our research project and in this book, we used language that is broadly common across Christian traditions. Please read between the lines and adjust to whatever leadership and community language best fits you.

How We Selected Leading Churches

Working largely through Fuller Seminary's vast network, we solicited names of vibrant congregations from over 35 nominators who fell into three categories:

National denominational leaders from 13 Protestant denominations[17] as well as the Roman Catholic Church and Greek Orthodox Church.

Respected scholars from seven educational institutions: Fuller Theological Seminary, Princeton Theological Seminary, Wheaton College, North Park University, Gordon College, Trinity Evangelical Divinity School, and Luther Seminary.

Other experts in ministry to young people outside of specific denominational channels, including the Willow Creek Association, Orange, the Youth Cartel, Catalyst, and our own Fuller Youth Institute team.[18]

We asked these nominators to identify congregations that have ministries with young people that are numerically growing, are engaging a large number of young people relative to the size of their congregation, or have something "exciting or missional" going on with young people. Using this list of criteria, nominators identified a total of 363 congregations.

Our Research Journey

We divided our research journey into three stages, each of which used the previous stage as a springboard to dive progressively deeper.

Stage 1 consisted of two steps, the first of which was completing a thorough review of over 80 books and articles containing academic research and popular writing about both young people and church health. The second step was an extensive online survey about church demographics and ministry qualities completed by the senior leader and youth/young adult director at 259 of the 363 congregations.

Working from that evaluation, we chose 41 of the most noteworthy churches to participate in *Stage 2* interviews.[19] Almost always by telephone, our research team conducted one-hour interviews with a total of 535 young people, parents, church staff, and volunteers across these congregations, yielding nearly 10,000 pages of interview transcripts.

Given overall themes and individual churches' responses to Stage 2, in *Stage 3*, we sent teams of two or three researchers to visit 12 of the 41 congregations. By spending a handful of days at each congregation, we were able to experience both their congregational worship services and their age-specific ministries, as well as conduct in-person interviews and focus

"Younger folks like me tend to prefer different worship styles than previous generations. In our church, those of us in our twenties are introducing new worship styles that are stretching for more traditional folks. But by worshiping in the same space as older folks, we've come to appreciate what they love about worship. I think my church is realizing that for a 140-year-old church to keep going, younger folks need to feel included." —Cody, age 25

If it's God who causes all growth to happen, why do research at all?

As committed as we are to translating research into practical resources, we are even more committed to seeking God for vision, wisdom, and strength. One of my (Kara's) favorite Scripture passages is John 15:4: "Remain in me, as I also remain in you. No branch can bear fruit by itself; it must remain in the vine. Neither can you bear fruit unless you remain in me." I have tried to make this passage a core tenet of my life and ministry, so much so that my husband, Dave, and I included it in our wedding ceremony.

But just as the Spirit inspires you and me through times of prayer, Scripture study, and journaling, the Spirit also teaches us through others. The wise comments of a friend over coffee or the vivid insights from a speaker at a conference can alter our lives and ministry trajectories. Instead of asking you to devote years of your life to listen to the stories of over 250 churches, we have done it for you.

So while Scripture doesn't change, the world around us does. Research like ours helps make sense of our changing world.

As much as we love research, we need to be clear: there is no formula for growing young. Our research shows correlations, not causation. The more the congregations we studied *tended to* demonstrate six core commitments, the more they *tended to* effectively engage teenagers and emerging adults. But just as the Spirit empowers us each to grow individually, it's ultimately the Spirit who empowers churches to grow young.[20]

groups with young people, parents, volunteers, congregational members, and leadership staff.

In all, these three stages of research totaled over 10,000 hours of research personnel time and involved interviews or surveys with 474 young people and 799 adults.

The Diversity of Churches Growing Young

Wondering if any of these churches are similar to yours?

Almost certainly.

Since the launch of the project, we have been pleased by the rich diversity of churches that graciously accepted our invitation, responded to online surveys, answered questions by phone, and opened their doors (literally!) to us. Here's a snapshot of how the 259 churches that chose to participate in Stage 1 describe themselves.

Church body/denominational affiliation	Percentage
No denominational affiliation	17%
Presbyterian	12%
Baptist	12%
United Methodist	10%
Evangelical Covenant	7%
Roman Catholic	6%
Reformed or Christian Reformed	4%
Nazarene	4%
Anglican or Episcopal	4%
Assemblies of God or Pentecostal	4%
Christian & Missionary Alliance	4%
Lutheran Church–Missouri Synod	3%
Evangelical Lutheran	3%
Church of Christ or Disciples of Christ	3%
Church of God in Christ	2%
Greek Orthodox	2%
Other	3%

CONGREGATIONAL SIZE[21]

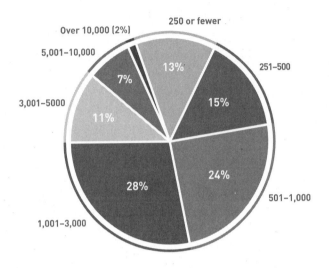

250 or fewer — 13%
251–500 — 15%
501–1,000 — 24%
1,001–3,000 — 28%
3,001–5000 — 11%
5,001–10,000 — 7%
Over 10,000 (2%)

REGION OF THE US
IN WHICH CONGREGATION IS LOCATED

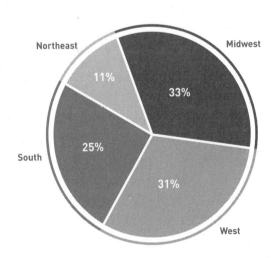

Northeast — 11%
Midwest — 33%
West — 31%
South — 25%

AGE OF CONGREGATION

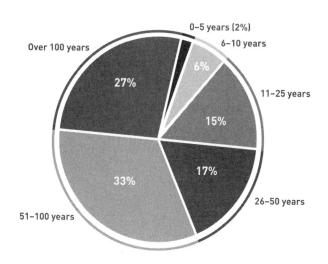

0–5 years (2%)
6–10 years
Over 100 years
6%
27%
11–25 years
15%
17%
33%
26–50 years
51–100 years

TYPE OF COMMUNITY
IN WHICH CONGREGATION IS LOCATED

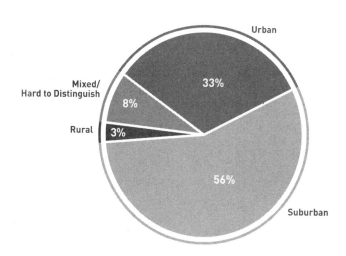

Urban
Mixed/
Hard to Distinguish
33%
8%
Rural
3%
56%
Suburban

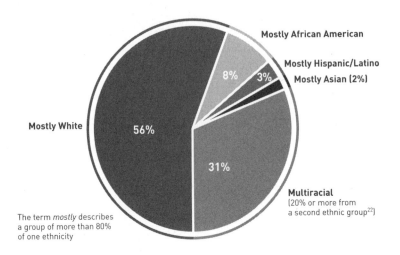

STAGE ONE
CONGREGATION'S ETHNIC DIVERSITY

Mostly African American

Mostly Hispanic/Latino

Mostly Asian (2%)

Mostly White

56%

8% 3%

31%

Multiracial
(20% or more from
a second ethnic group[22])

The term *mostly* describes
a group of more than 80%
of one ethnicity

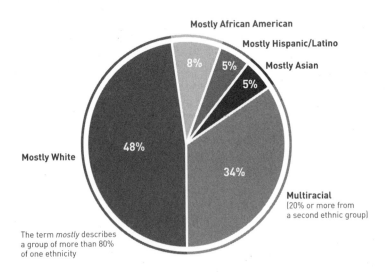

STAGE TWO
CONGREGATION'S ETHNIC DIVERSITY

Mostly African American

Mostly Hispanic/Latino

Mostly Asian

Mostly White

48%

8% 5%

5%

34%

Multiracial
(20% or more from
a second ethnic group)

The term *mostly* describes
a group of more than 80%
of one ethnicity

While we were unsatisfied with the representation of predominantly Hispanic and Asian congregations in Stage 1, ethnic diversity increased in churches included in Stages 2 and 3.[23]

**STAGE THREE
CONGREGATION'S ETHNIC DIVERSITY**

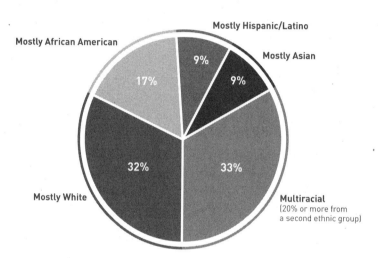

Mostly Hispanic/Latino

Mostly Asian

Mostly African American

9%

9%

17%

32%

33%

Mostly White

Multiracial
(20% or more from
a second ethnic group)

The term *mostly* describes a group
of more than 80% of one ethnicity

Our Advisors

At the Fuller Youth Institute, our aim is that everything is done through partnerships. This four-year project has been no exception. In fact, it's been our most stellar example in our 12-year history. Like a good church potluck, everyone involved brought their best fare to the table.

Four key Fuller faculty members (Chap Clark, Scott Cormode, Jim Furrow, and Cameron Lee) served as our senior research advisors, bringing research validity and reliability throughout all

Our partners were crucial in helping us define a handful of terms we will use throughout this book, such as:

Effectively engaging young people, which we conceive as "churches that are involving and retaining young people in the congregational community, as well as helping them develop a vibrant faith in Jesus."

Faith vibrancy and maturity, which we define through both individual and corporate practices commonly held as markers of faith development.[24]

For those of you craving more details about our research terms and methods, please see the appendix and ChurchesGrowingYoung.org.

three stages of the project. At various points, we consulted with an additional 21 Fuller faculty members whose various fields of scholarship flavored our research design. (We know, you're wondering, "How many PhDs does it take to do a four-year research project on congregations today?" Apparently the answer is, "Quite a few!")

Sixteen additional researchers and nationally recognized thought leaders in youth ministry and church leadership shared their collective wisdom by joining our Expert Advisory Council. By meeting in person for a three-day summit, as well as providing regular input by phone and email, this team made sure we were asking the most pressing questions and following the right recipe to get the best possible answers.

In order to translate our research into practical resources that are valuable to congregations of all shapes and sizes, we also formed a 10-member Pastor Advisory Council. These senior leaders teamed with us in the latter stages of the project to help ensure that this book and our additional writing, training, and online tools meet the needs of churches thirsty to grow young.

We are grateful to each of our world-class Expert Advisory Council
members for the hours and hours they spent reviewing our survey
drafts and interview questions, as well as processing our findings
and dreaming with us about implications.

Steve Argue, Fuller Theological Seminary

Andy Crouch, Christianity Today

Kenda Creasy Dean, Princeton Seminary

Mark DeVries, Ministry Architects

Reggie Joiner, Orange and reThink Group

Pamela King, Fuller Theological Seminary

David Kinnaman, Barna Group

Terry Linhart, Bethel College

Brad Lomenick, BLINC

Bob McCarty, National Federation for Catholic Youth
Ministry

Amy McEntee, National Catholic Young Adult Ministry
Association

Soong-Chan Rah, North Park Theological Seminary

Dave Rahn, Youth for Christ

Tyler Reagin, Catalyst

Andy Root, Luther Seminary

Virginia Ward, Gordon-Conwell Theological Seminary

Why Bother? What Young People Can Add
to Your Congregation

In the midst of reading about our exhaustive research process,
you might wonder whether it's worth all this effort to help

your congregation grow young. They don't tithe much. They can be a bit flaky. They prefer different—and way louder—music.

Teenagers and emerging adults, we know that you have concerns about your church too.

When we started our research, we wondered if growing young was worth the effort. So in every stage, we explored the specific contributions that young people like Isabella make to churches and parishes that have successfully grown young. The term we heard more than any other was "vitality." Young people infuse congregations with energy and intensity. As we peeled back the layers to further understand how young people contribute, we realized they add *more* to congregations.

Each member of our Pastor Advisory Council helped design the right menu of resources for adults and congregations needing answers.

Eugene Cho, Quest Church, Q Cafe, One Day's Wages, WA

Sergio De La Mora, Cornerstone Church, CA

Erwin Raphael McManus, Mosaic, CA

Brenda Salter McNeil, Quest Church and Seattle Pacific University, WA

Carey Nieuwhof, Connexus Church, Ontario, Canada

Perry Noble, formerly of NewSpring Church, SC

John Ortberg, Menlo Church, CA

Efrem Smith, World Impact, CA

Jill VerSteeg, Reformed Church in America, MI

Len Wenke, Holy Family Church, Catholic Archdiocese of Cincinnati, OH

"A few weeks ago, I met a woman who is new to our church. She started coming because her son started to attend our youth group. Because of how much he's loved the youth ministry, she is now an active member of our church. Her journey to join our faith community started with her 16-year-old son." —Maggie, parent

More service. The most dominant theme in the descriptions of what young people add is that they help congregations accomplish their mission. Church leaders are quick to value how young people serve in their worship services, as well as outreach and discipleship ministries. But leaders are not myopic in their appreciation of young people's service; they are just as likely to appreciate young people's service inside the church as their service outside the church through community-based and global organizations.

More passion. When adults describe how young people improve the tenor of the overall congregation, the quality they emphasize more than any other is that young people add passion. They pour themselves wholeheartedly into what they do, which energizes those around them and increases what's possible.

More innovation. The fresh spin young people bring to life and ministry is often appreciated by leaders whose entire congregations have been infiltrated by the creativity all too often bottled up in youth ministry. Churches willing to twist off the cap release innovative energy that can transform their communities.

More money. When we asked leaders at churches growing young how teenagers and young adults contribute financially to their church, they generally chuckled and responded, "Not much." But usually those same leaders quickly added that young people's energy attracts older adults with more financial resources, who in turn generously support the ministries of their church. Plus, eventually those young people gain more vocational stability and can become part of their church's financial backbone.

More overall health. As we discussed our findings with our advisors, many commented that young people seem to be a barometer of the overall health of a church. According to FYI advisor and lead pastor Erwin Raphael McManus, "Healthy churches reach young people, and young people make churches healthier. If your church is reaching 20-year-olds, your church will reach 60-year-olds."[25] John Ortberg, also a research advisor and senior pastor, added, "You can't build a great church with a bad student ministry, and you can't build a great student ministry with a languishing church." For those wondering if churches that grow young inevitably reach other generations less effectively, the answer is an emphatic no. In a kingdom win/win, stronger ministry to young people bulks up the ministry muscles of the entire congregation, and vice versa.

The Six Core Commitments Your Church Needs to Grow Young

Our deep and wide analysis of some of our nation's most innovative churches unearthed a Growing Young Wheel and six core commitments. While there is no guarantee that enacting these six commitments in your congregation will produce better engagement with young people like Isabella, they are the most universal commitments in churches with the greatest proven effectiveness. The rest of this book fleshes out each commitment in detail.

1. Unlock keychain leadership. Instead of centralizing authority, empower others—especially young people.

2. Empathize with today's young people. Instead of judging or criticizing, step into the shoes of this generation.

3. Take Jesus' message seriously. Instead of asserting formulaic gospel claims, welcome young people into a Jesus-centered way of life.

4. Fuel a warm community. Instead of focusing on cool worship or programs, aim for warm peer and intergenerational friendships.

5. Prioritize young people (and families) everywhere. Instead of giving lip service to how much young people matter, look for creative ways to tangibly support, resource, and involve them in all facets of your congregation.

6. Be the best neighbors. Instead of condemning the world outside your walls, enable young people to neighbor well locally and globally.

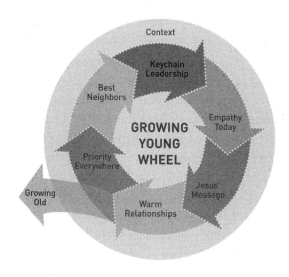

The Ground Rules of Growing Young

Having studied congregations like yours, we identified a handful of ground rules that guide these six core commitments and we hope will guide your church.

The order is flexible. The Growing Young Wheel follows the chronological sequence we saw most commonly. In other words, more congregations start growing young by beginning with keychain leadership than any other core commitment. But some congregations inaugurate the process through other portals (most notably, through warm community and prioritizing young people). Like a child building a Lego masterpiece, your congregation might unsnap a few of these core commitments, arrange them in a different order, and try again.

The boundaries are permeable. The distinction among the core commitments isn't always clean. Dotted lines separate them because they often (beautifully) bleed into each other, infecting each other with new priorities and practices.

The turning point is priority. A large swath of our nation's congregations can, and do, foster many of these core commitments. They are filled with lovely people doing lovely ministry. *They just aren't reaching young people.* For many congregations, making the intentional decision to disproportionately prioritize young people (within the context of their families) is the inflection point between growing young and growing old.

The context is pivotal. Thanks to our own and others' research, we feel like we know young people. But we don't know *your* young people or the particular dynamics of *your* community. The six core commitments are surrounded by a layer of context because you need to listen and adapt constantly to the teenagers and emerging adults in your family, congregation, and city.

The pursuit of Jesus is the overriding motivation. As with other pursuits, a church's passion to grow young is motivated primarily by members' dedication to walk in the way of Jesus and invite young people to join them. The life, death, and resurrection of Jesus Christ are what distinguish congregations from community centers or country clubs. Imagine the Growing Young Wheel as a set of commitments orbiting the core of Jesus-centered communities.

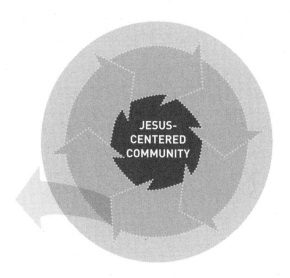

Findings and Ideas: A Dynamic Duo

As much as we applaud the data that helped us develop this Growing Young Wheel and six commitments, we cheer even more enthusiastically when that data is translated into practical ideas. We believe it is the application of research that helps you develop a unique strategy that fits your distinct vision and philosophy.

In the first sections of most chapters, you will get a front-row seat to a powerful story of these core commitments lived out in churches we studied, as well as *research findings* that help you embody them. While the bulk of the data stems from our research, it would be both naïve and arrogant for us to assume that our work is the only—or most important—research on the faith development of teenagers and emerging adults.[26] So we also draw from leading theologians and researchers—hopefully making this book a "one-stop shop" for your toughest questions about both your church and young people.

In the *ideas for action* section of each chapter, ideas from congregations we studied will take the field. Since no two towns, congregations, or leadership teams are identical, it's impossible for us to give you a foolproof, step-by-step blueprint to build a church that grows young. These examples from inspiring congregations, along with a handful of *strategic questions* that conclude each chapter, are like scaffolding. Whether you're a senior pastor, associate pastor, ministry volunteer, parent, or young person, our hope is that you and others reading along with you can use these ideas and questions to build a plan tailored to your unique church.

As we showcase over 250 amazing congregations in this book, we are concerned that you might end up feeling worse about the current state of your congregation. *Please don't compare the best of what we share about these churches with the worst of what you know about your own.* Instead of comparing yourself to others, please remember that *growing young means starting where you are.* For all of these churches, it's been a multiyear (and sometimes multidecade) process involving a complicated interplay of forward momentum and setbacks of all sizes. While we've chosen to focus on what's positive and hopeful about these churches, so many leaders we interviewed wanted to make sure we heard the negative, including their pain and struggle. We could have written several books on their trials and challenges alone. So we don't want you to feel discouraged about the gap between where you are and where you hope to be. When you take three steps forward and then fall two steps back, celebrate that at least you're one step closer to your goals.

Growing Young Can Change More Than Just *Your* Church

Throughout our research, we kept you and your church in mind.

But we also had a bigger dream in mind. *Growing young can change more than just* your *church*. We love the church. So much so that we are convinced that the best way to change a society, or even the world, is through congregations dedicated to living out Jesus' commands to love God and love others. (If you also believe in the church, we know you're nodding along with us.)

We believe that congregations stand the greatest chance of living out these commands when they are ignited by passionate young people.

As the nearest middle schooler will remind you, if $A = B$ and $B = C$, then $A = C$. In other words, if we transform a country by transforming our churches, and if we transform our churches by transforming our work with young people, then transforming our work with young people can transform our society and even our world.

In remarkable churches nationwide, this vision to change congregations, communities, and our culture is a reality. It could be your reality too.

Chapter Highlights

- Shrinking and aging are the default for the vast majority of denominations and congregations in the US today.

- In order to understand what's working in churches that grow young, we launched a four-year project examining over 250 churches and parishes that are especially effective with 15- to 29-year-olds. Our hope is that studying these "bright spots" will catapult other congregations forward into more innovative ministry.

- Whether you're a church with bare spots because you are missing young people or a congregation that's thriving and wants to stay on that trajectory, we must all prune away our preconceptions of what churches need in order to grow young. Our research unearthed a treasure of compelling ministry happening in congregations of all sizes, denominations, locations, buildings, and budgets. The good news is that according to our data, any congregation can grow young.

- Based on our research, we believe congregations are most likely to grow young when they embrace the six core commitments in the Growing Young Wheel:

    Unlock keychain leadership.

    Empathize with today's young people.

    Take Jesus' message seriously.

    Fuel a warm community.

    Prioritize young people (and families) everywhere.

    Be the best neighbors.

- Young people add great vitality to their faith communities by increasing their churches' service, passion, innovation, financial resources, and overall health.

Strategic Questions to Help You Grow Young

1. What motivates you to read a book geared to help churches grow young?

2. How, if at all, have you seen signs of aging or shrinking in your congregation or other congregations?

3. Which of the 10 things your church doesn't need in order to grow young on pages 25–27 have you tended to believe?

4. Based on your first look at the six core commitments briefly described on page 43, which are most prevalent in your congregation? Which are missing?

5. How have young people added vitality to your life and congregation?

6. Who else needs to join you on your journey to help your congregation grow young? What dialogue partner, small group, or team in your church can help you with your discoveries and dreams?

2. Unlock Keychain Leadership

Sharing Power with the Right People at the Right Time

Our pastor has been transformed by Jesus, and now he's the definition of authentic. In fact, he's the most authentic person I know. And he doesn't treat us like we're kids. . . . He treats me like I'm his younger friend. —Mark, age 23

Remember your first set of keys?

Stephen—who goes by "Stretch"—received his first set of keys when he was 16. His town handed him a driver's license, and his parents handed him the key to the family car. Heart pounding with excitement, he climbed behind the wheel and pulled out of his driveway for the first time on his own. Stretch couldn't believe the newfound freedom and responsibility he had been given. He took a step away from childhood and a step closer to adulthood.

As Stretch pulled onto the street and began to accelerate, he faced an important and practical question. *Where should I go?* Within a moment he knew the answer. Over the past several years, his church had become like a second home to him. There he felt known, accepted, and valued. So naturally, he headed in that direction.

As he drove into the parking lot, the church's childcare was wrapping up for the day. One of the coordinators who knew Stretch noticed him driving the car. Given a recent shortage of childcare workers and seeing that he now had transportation, she asked if he was interested in helping after school.

She was only halfway through the question before Stretch knew his answer. He would get to hang out at the church, spend time with kids, and on top of it all . . . he would get paid. *This day couldn't get any better!*

Until a few minutes later, when she returned from the church office and handed him a key to the church. "If you're going to help us, there will be times when we'll need you to lock up," she explained.

Stretch was staring so intently at the key that he barely heard her words. The pastor had this key. His Sunday school teacher had this key. Other adults who were mature—who had power—had this key. But *him?* It was like he had been waiting on the sidelines during the big game and was now being called to step onto the playing field.

Life was truly as good as it could be. Until it got even better.

A week later, while Stretch was working in the childcare center, the youth pastor dropped by. "You know, Stretch," he said, "if you have your license and are already at the church, would you be willing to stock the soda machine for me? The job comes with all the Mountain Dew you can drink."

Key to the car. Check.

Key to the church. Check.

Key to the soda machine. Check.

Stretch knew he had arrived.

Later that night, Stretch received the final "key" that forever changed the course of his life. Standing alone in the empty church, he heard God speak to him—not audibly but distinctly.

"You like to be here, don't you?" God asked.

"Yes, I do," Stretch answered.

"Well, get comfortable, because you're going to be here a lot."

From that day on, Stretch knew that both his future and his vocation were closely tied to church ministry. Leaders he deeply respected had entrusted him with access and authority by giving him keys, both literally and figuratively. In the several decades that followed, others continued to entrust him with the keys of leadership, and he's now been a youth pastor for over 20 years. Today Stretch, his senior pastor, and the culture of Immanuel Church of the Nazarene exemplify a powerful kind of leadership pervasive in churches and parishes that grow young—a type of leadership that can unleash the limitless potential of young people and infuse your entire congregation with new life and energy.

CORE COMMITMENT:
UNLOCK KEYCHAIN LEADERSHIP

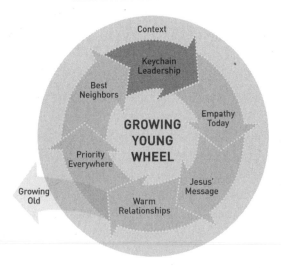

Churches that grow young are brimming with staff, volunteers, and parents who demonstrate *keychain leadership*. Whoever holds the keys has the power to let people in or to keep people out. Keys provide access to physical rooms, as well as to strategic meetings, significant decisions, and central roles or places of authority. The more power you have, the more keys you tend to possess.

When we refer to *keys*, we mean the capabilities, power, and access of leaders that carry the potential to empower young people.

By *keychain leaders*, we mean pastoral and congregational leaders who are

- acutely aware of the keys on their keychain; and

- intentional about entrusting and empowering all generations, including teenagers and emerging adults, with their own set of keys.

Beyond simply the launching of a student leadership team, keychain leadership is a spirit and commitment demonstrated by both paid and volunteer leaders that permeate every area of the church.

How Keychain Leadership Helps Your Church Grow Young

Like so many teenagers and emerging adults we studied, Stretch moved from being a satisfied participant to a contributing partner once keychain leaders gave him the right keys at the right time.

But we know it's not always that simple.

If you're on staff with a church as a senior pastor, executive pastor, associate pastor, family pastor, or youth pastor, you are doing incredible—and hard—work. We know because all three of us have served on pastoral staff for churches in California, Kentucky, and Michigan. In every church we served, we (like you) were sometimes given and other times had to earn keys—both literally and metaphorically.

As a pastoral leader, you may physically unlock the church doors early in the morning or lock them long after sunset. Even if you're not the one unlocking the church doors, perhaps week after week you invite all generations to take up the keys of leadership, but the only ones willing to work are the same group of volunteers.

Maybe there are keys you were given or earned, but they no longer grant you the access you need to get the job done. Instead of trusting you or listening to your perspective, dozens of congregational voices advise you about how best to lead. The majority of the time their input is helpful, but at times you feel like they are critically pointing out where the church *should be* heading or loudly wondering why your ministry is not as large or exciting as the church down the street. You're *supposed to be* the one with the keys, but at times it feels as if someone has changed the locks without telling you.

The great news is that you're probably already closer than you think to keychain leadership. This chapter (and indeed this entire book) can support what you're already doing by reducing the guesswork, removing the guilt, and helping you return to what you loved about ministry in the first place. With just a few intentional decisions, you can add new keys to your keychain, better understand why some doors won't seem to open, and increase your ability to pass off keys to others.

If you're a ministry volunteer, member of a leadership team, or parent, the number of keys on your church leadership keychain might be fewer than for those on staff. In reality, other leaders may make the primary decisions for your church and you're not always sure how to shape those discussions. You might think this means you'll have less impact on helping your church grow young or that your church can't grow young unless the head pastor or overall church leadership team is on board.

Think again.

Notice in Stretch's story that the *first people* to give him a set of keys were his parents and the childcare coordinator. Our interviews uncovered that keychain leaders can be found in any area of the church—from a college student working in the nursery to a 90-year-old church secretary. The three of us and our spouses have served in multiple roles, from volunteer small group leader to church chairperson, and we've seen this truth firsthand. Whether you're reading this book because you don't want your church to die or because your own life is ignited by the passion of young people, you can unleash the power of these leadership concepts in any and all facets of the church.

No matter your role, here is what we want you to know: if you are willing to entrust your keys to young people, they will trust you with their hearts, their energy, their creativity, and even their friends. Yes, it can sometimes seem like more work than it's worth—but if you give them your access, you have the opportunity to touch a whole generation.

Research Findings

The "Priesthood of All Believers" Doesn't Mean Leaders Are Absent

Because we so value the priesthood of all believers, we began our research somewhat hoping that we wouldn't find a leadership-driven solution. We initially theorized that maybe churches that grow young share such collaborative leadership that it might be difficult to identify who was the clear leader. Our hunch was wrong.

Both leadership in general and specific leaders were mentioned in every stage of our research as principal contributors to

> The *priesthood of all believers* is a term commonly attributed to the sixteenth-century German theologian and Reformer Martin Luther. When we use it, we are referring to the idea that all Christians are "priests" and are called to serve God meaningfully (see 1 Pet. 2:9). The implication is that those who attend churches need not passively watch while one qualified leader dominates. In fact, the priesthood of all believers doesn't mean there are no leaders—just that leadership, in the church and especially with young people, is different than many people think. All people have an important voice and responsibility. Everyone has gifts to contribute to make the church complete (1 Cor. 12:1–31).

churches that grow young. When pastoral leaders were asked to describe what accounts for their success with young people, the highest response (mentioned by 48 percent) was *church leadership*. Church leadership ranked ahead of worship style, emphasis on social justice, and utilizing the latest technology.

Congregation members were *even more likely* to attribute their church's effectiveness to leadership. Over 77 percent highlighted leadership, using statements like:

I chose this church because of the leadership. (Jerome, age 21)

The biggest thing is our ministers. They are excellent and that has helped more than anything. (Karen, parent)

There is a commitment to young people at our church, but our youth pastor is the secret sauce. (Jim, elder and youth ministry volunteer)

What Makes Keychain Leadership Unique

Why call it keychain leadership? Aren't there already plenty of popular leadership mantras or models to draw from?

We've coined the term *keychain leadership* because it is different from many popular and recent leadership paradigms.[1] While every leader has keys on their key ring, not every leader uses those keys in the same way. Some leaders cling to their keys tightly and refuse to share them even for a moment, but keychain leaders model a posture of giving away access and authority. This posture not only empowers others but also meaningfully links them to the life of the congregation.

Based on our research, we've identified four types of key leadership ranging on a continuum from key-less leaders to keychain leaders.

Key-less leaders: Often young and inexperienced, without much authority or access, these leaders spend their time proving they're worthy to possess keys. This could be a high school student ready to volunteer in the children's ministry—full of potential and passion as he begins his leadership journey. It may also represent an older congregant who feels as though she lost access to keys—and her voice in the church—a decade or two ago.

Key-hoarding leaders: Always holding the keys and refusing to give others access, they run the show. This might include an outgoing, extroverted ministry leader who draws a crowd through sheer personality and ends up driving away others who offer to help (we won't ask you to name any names but would wager you could name a few leaders in this category pretty quickly).

Key-loaning leaders: Often taking keys off the keychain and letting others borrow them temporarily, they make sure the keys are returned quickly. One example might be a pastor of a fast-growing church plant who knows the contribution of others is important—but also believes others won't do as good of a job as he or she will.

Keychain leaders: Very aware of the keys they hold, they are constantly opening doors for some while training and entrusting others who are ready for their own set of keys. This could be a long-standing senior leader, associate pastor, or trusted volunteer who young people, staff, and congregation members turn to for advice or to be sharpened in their ministry skills. *Everyone* seems to get better when this leader is involved, and a long list of people can point to this leader as the reason they serve in the church today.

When comparing keychain leadership to some popular models of church leadership, you might wonder if it is easier or requires less skill. We think the exact opposite. The leaders we've studied don't share the keys of leadership with others because they are *less* talented or visionary. These capable leaders have a keen sense for where God is leading but leverage their strengths for the good of the overall church. They understand that young people like Stretch don't want to sit passively on the sidelines but are drawn to churches and leaders who help them get in the game.

However, sharing leadership with others will likely be more challenging (at least in the short term) than leading alone. When my (Jake's) wife, Lauren, and I moved to the pedestrian-friendly town of Pasadena, we decided that we could get by with one car instead of two. While that has simplified life in some ways, it has also made it more complicated. We share the same set of keys, so when each of us drives, we have to adjust the seats, mirrors, and more. Lauren and I also have to coordinate schedules closely, because if we miscommunicate, one of us may end up

"There is just no escaping the fact that the single biggest factor in determining whether an organization is going to get healthier—or not—is the genuine commitment and active involvement of the person in charge."[2] *—Patrick Lencioni, management expert*

stranded. Similarly, sharing the keys of leadership requires constant adjusting, staying in touch, and being willing to persevere even if someone feels stuck. This is complicated enough with two experienced drivers but becomes even more complex when journeying with a young person who is a driver in training. While keychain leadership requires close collaboration and hard work, the long-term payoff of growing your church young is worth it.

In the following pages, we reveal the six essentials of keychain leadership that dominated our research. Toward the end of the chapter, we shed light on several "ideas for action" that can be contextualized to empower your church to unlock keychain leadership—whether you're just beginning that journey or are miles down the road.

Keychain Leaders Are Mature . . . Not Always Young

I (Kara) was recently sharing our research about effective leadership with a pastor who pushed back: "Now really, tell me the truth. Don't all young people want a hip 25-year-old pastor who rides a motorcycle and sports the latest fashion? If I want my church to grow young, I'll need a bunch of young leaders, right?"

Wrong.

At least in most cases.

While there is certainly some value in having young leaders who can connect with young people, it's not the whole story. When interview participants from our study were asked why their church is effective with young people, only 1 in 10 mentioned having younger leaders. Further, when asked why they stay involved in their church, *almost no one* talked about how their leaders or their overall church is exclusively young. In fact, many of the teenagers and emerging adults interviewed wish they had more connection with those in older generations. Although in theory it might be *fun* for a teenager to learn to drive a car from their friends without licenses, most we talked to seemed to understand that it's *better* to learn from a more experienced driver.

When keychain leaders were asked *how* they had moved from being a key-less, key-hoarding, or key-loaning leader to keychain leadership, they often shared that their maturity was born out of difficult personal and professional experience, failure, and other struggles. No keychain leader we met acquired or learned to use their set of keys overnight, even when that wasn't apparent to others. Indeed, keychain leaders needed someone to teach them to drive, to entrust them with the car, and yes, to forgive them and continue to instill confidence even after a few wrong turns.

For example, the pastor of a fast-growing church of young professionals in Washington, DC, shared how he grew up as a Baptist missionary kid in Kuwait and Liberia and was once held hostage during the Persian Gulf War. While his family's focus overseas in Liberia was ministry with the poor, his dad eventually took a job as a pastor in an affluent suburban church in the US. Understandably, the son found it difficult to navigate the contrast between his previous world of risk and poverty and his new world of comfort and plenty. Later in college, his worldview was stretched even further when two charismatic inner-city pastors (one white and one African American) mentored him, a white 20-year-old. They eventually helped him learn how to balance a life of privilege with the surrounding brokenness. This DC pastor shared how these wildly contrasting experiences (along with pastoring an African American church in the inner city of Boston for five years) formed him to read the needs in his context and speak to people from varied backgrounds. Such diverse interactions proved the perfect preparation for leading a church that is both growing young and changing its community in our nation's capital.

Keychain Leaders Are Real . . . Not "Relevant"

Picture a 50- or 60-year-old pastor purchasing a hip and trendy new wardrobe to mimic the clothing styles that most twenty-somethings wear today. While the attempt to relate to a younger audience is admirable, is that sort of style change needed to help congregations grow young? The good news is that it's not.

Pastors everywhere can leave their skinny jeans at home.

When parishioners were asked why they attend their church, many talked about the qualities of their leaders. Of those who did so, only 13 percent focused on how their leaders are relevant, while 87 percent talked about authenticity or other qualities unrelated to relevance. Further, surveys completed by leaders show that a pastor's transparency in decision making is positively related to both vibrant faith in young people and measures of church health. In other words, the more transparent the leader is personally and the church is organizationally, the better positioned the church seems to be to grow young.

The implication is that young people like Stretch aren't looking for leaders who frantically change their wardrobe or their lingo in order to connect. Young people want leaders who are honest and comfortable being themselves. Keychain leaders understand that this younger generation has a sixth sense for authenticity and intuitively knows whether or not leaders are genuine.

Metro Community Church, a multiethnic church in New Jersey that was planted about 10 years ago, understands this well. Talking about her pastor, a 22-year-old college student said, "The main draw is how transparent our senior pastor is. It's the only church I've ever been part of where the pastor shares how he feels and even shares his mistakes. This helps you feel like you can come in your brokenness and can walk with people when they're going through stuff without any judgment."

First United Methodist Church, a large church in Tulsa, Oklahoma, has also tapped into young people's desire for leaders who are real. Prior to our team's visit, we interviewed several people who spoke highly of one pastoral leader in particular. While in Tulsa, sitting across the table from him, we eagerly asked what advice he would offer to pastors who want to strengthen their ministry with teenagers and emerging adults.

We were prepared to walk away with insightful programming ideas or perhaps something about the need for a robust theological education. Maybe even some great quotes from John Wesley, the eighteenth-century pastor and theologian whose teaching gave rise to the Methodist Church.

Instead, this 30-year ministry veteran paused, lowered his voice a bit, looked at us intently, and advised, "Don't neglect your heart. Spend time in the Word, pray, and let God speak to you. Carve out time each day for this, listen to wise people, and take the long view." There was no air of false spirituality here. As researchers, we were struck by this leader's willingness to ruthlessly shelve the daily tasks of ministry in order to stay centered in Jesus and vital relationships. As a result, the pastor's visible love for people, spiritual depth, and authenticity were mentioned by nearly every young person we talked to at the church.

Keychain Leaders Are Warm . . . Not Distant

It is possible to be real from a distance but still not connect in relationship. While teenagers and emerging adults might sometimes project that they have their act together or want complete independence, those we met desperately want keychain leaders who understand them, mentor them, and personally hand them keys as they're ready. When young people were asked what made their church effective, 43 percent pointed to the relational nature of their leaders, specifically that they were caring, accepting, or enjoyable to be with. Being relational doesn't mean leaders jettison their boundaries and try to be a "best friend" to everyone in their congregation. But it does mean that leaders are approachable and genuinely care and connect.

In chapter 5, we'll further explore the concept of warmth. While it stood out as a core commitment of the whole church community, warmth was also named as a distinct characteristic of keychain leaders.

Being a warm leader doesn't mean being a pushover. In our first interaction at an African American congregation near Chicago's Hyde Park neighborhood, we were surprised by the pastor's gruffness with teenagers during a church basketball game. He almost didn't let one of the boys play because he arrived a few minutes late. Then the pastor threatened to end the game early after a minor argument broke out over a foul. But when we witnessed the teenagers, some of whom come from broken homes or have been involved in gangs, verbally push back and joke with him in a friendly manner, we realized this leader's firmness matches his context.

In our interviews with teenagers afterward, they told us how this same pastor sometimes calls them out from the pulpit for wearing their pants too low or using their phones in church. But his actions don't offend them, because he has a relationship with them. The pastor regularly spends time in their world outside the church walls, treats them with respect, and demonstrates that he cares about them as individuals. It also didn't hurt when, during a high school Bible study, he made a striking analogy linking mistakes, NBA all-star LeBron James, grace, and the Trinity. We were pretty impressed too.

Warm leadership is not limited to churches of a particular size; we found it alive and well in churches both large and small. During our visit to Trinity Church, a 5,000-attendee Assemblies

"I really believe that the leaders are investing in our kids not for any other type of outcome than simply to get to know them and learn who they are. And that seems to resonate with them. They know that they are truly being cared for, and that opens them up to listen to the gospel. They are not preached at in a condescending manner or given a set of rules to follow. They are just loved on." —Andrea, parent

of God congregation in Miami, nearly everyone mentioned the relational warmth of the church and attributed this tone to the pastors. When we asked these pastors how they relate to so many people, they shared that it starts with a commitment to be with people rather than remain cloistered in an office.

Beyond this, they strategically invest in other leaders who carry the relational load. As one example, every Monday nearly 100 core volunteers and staff gather for a chapel service that includes worship, testimonies, a devotional, birthday celebrations, and prayer for the congregation. Rather than try to connect with thousands in the same way, these keychain leaders strategically infuse this smaller group with a relational warmth that spreads to the rest of the congregation.

While young people may be able to find great preaching online, many told us they're aching for more than that. They want to be in relationship with leaders who know their name and model a life of faith. These young people look to Christian leaders in their community and ask, "Are you the real deal?" and then watch closely to see the answer.

As eloquently stated by Dr. Virginia Ward, a research advisor to our project and Director of Leadership and Mentored Ministry at Gordon-Conwell Theological Seminary, "Effective leadership is about much more than just the sage on the stage."

This was demonstrated at a predominantly Asian church overflowing with teenagers and young adults. Person after person shared that the Bible is taken seriously in this church and that the pastor is the linchpin of that emphasis. Hearing that, we anticipated this pastor might spend the majority of the week in his office crafting a perfect sermon for Sunday morning or making sure small groups are set up just right.

Once we spent time with the congregation, it was evident that the preaching and programming were important. But instead of the pastor sequestering himself in his office, he spent almost the entire weekend with a group of 25 church leaders on an intensive discipleship retreat. Most of the leaders were under age 30. These retreats take place two or three times per year and are an opportunity for the pastor to inspire church leaders with what matters most. Rather than being spent discussing the church calendar or other business items, retreats are dedicated to utter honesty and vulnerability about each person's faith journey. The pastor *models* a life of faith through relational warmth rather than just talking about it. As a result, their church continues to grow young.

Keychain Leaders Know What Matters to People . . . Not Just to Other Pastors

While many pastors are good listeners, they often find themselves influenced the most by their peer group—other pastors. In many ways this makes sense, as their closest friendships may have been developed in seminary, the books they read are often written by other pastors or theologians, and most training they attend also involves other church leaders. The downside is that this can leave some leaders disconnected from what matters most to those in the pews.

Robert Wuthnow, a leading sociologist of religion from Princeton University, asserts that clergy do not focus on the issues that matter most in the everyday lives of their congregants;

instead, they talk about culture wars and minute distinctions of doctrine.[3]

To avoid this disconnect, the keychain leaders in our study value, and regularly practice, listening to their congregants in order to understand what matters most. This helps them develop an adept understanding of which doors to unlock and when to give away particular keys. It also informs how they lead, preach, and structure ministries. Instead of adding more and more activities to their already busy calendar, these leaders strategically prioritize listening to congregation members of all generations.

Keychain Leaders Entrust and Empower Others . . . They Don't Try to Be a "Superpastor"

Perhaps the most important choice that moves a leader from key-loaning to keychain is that of entrusting and empowering others. All too often a mythical but popular church hero, the so-called Superpastor, interferes with the development of this carefully honed skill.

If you're a ministry leader, you know about the Superpastor (picture Superman or Superwoman, but then add a Bible). In too many churches, this is who the congregation expects their pastor (and youth pastor, and children's pastor, and fill in the blank with most any pastoral or volunteer role) to be.

A Superpastor is a key-hoarding leader who never shares the keys of leadership with others because they believe others are not as capable. Donning their metaphorical capes, Superpastors

"I think we have produced a generation of leaders who are preaching the gospel, but they forget that they are dealing with people. This does a disservice to the gospel because it results in people not leading well." —Tyler Reagin, president of Catalyst

are pressured to be (or maybe believe they are) faster than the nearest church board, more powerful than the rest of the pastoral team, and able to leap over pulpits in a single bound.

All kidding aside, perhaps there's been a time when you've pressured your own pastor to be a Superpastor. Or maybe there's a lot of pressure on *you* now to be the Superpastor.

While hints of a Superpastor are common in churches and parishes nationwide, churches that grow young tell a different story. When we asked hundreds of leaders what accounts for their effectiveness with young people, over 30 percent mentioned that they entrust young people with opportunities to lead and contribute. This was one of the highest responses, behind only a focus on relationships, prioritizing young people, and the overall church culture (each of which will be further analyzed in future chapters).

One nondenominational church of over 1,000 members in the Northeast understands young people like Stretch don't just want to fill space. They want to be given keys to responsibilities that matter and make a difference. Every fall, the church celebrates its volunteer small group leaders through a commissioning service. Rather than patronizing or "honoring" them with a certificate or token gift, the pastor passionately shares how they are the "real pastors" of the church. Last year, he went so far as to claim the church would get by just fine without *him*, but the doors of the church would close if *these volunteers* ever

"The leadership style of our pastor has had a big impact on younger generations that have come out of dysfunctional churches, myself included. We've all been at the place where we've said, 'I will never step foot into church again.' But because of the patience, love, and mutual trust of our pastor, we have become a sanctuary for those people." —Peter, age 26

went away. The small group leaders shared with our team how meaningful the experience was and that they'll gladly sacrifice their time and energy to lead again.

When we interviewed parishioners in other churches growing young, they described their pastoral leaders as being generally competent in their responsibilities, or what some participants named as "good enough." These leaders typically don't hit a homerun in *every* area of their job. While they are outstanding in maybe one or two areas, they develop enough competence in the rest to get by. That doesn't mean the church settles for mediocrity. Rather, these leaders focus on building a team of other capable leaders who have strengths that they lack. As a result, the appropriate keys are taken off *one* leader's keychain and given to the leaders best suited for particular roles or responsibilities.

Further, when interview participants were asked why they stay involved with their church, only 1 in 20 pointed to a particular leader. The implication is that while your leadership is likely critical for a few areas of the church, you don't have to be the Superpastor who is the face of every event, agrees to every invitation to meet in person, or continually reaches out on social media.

How are churches ditching the Superpastor syndrome and sharing the keys with young people? While most leaders don't *want* to clutch all the keys to their church and be a Superpastor, several told our team that it often feels like the only option to move forward. Reflecting on this conundrum, we've found Lee Bolman and Terrence Deal's work on leadership frames helpful in understanding how to share keys and with whom.

Bolman and Deal define a *frame* as "a mental model—a set of ideas and assumptions—that you carry in your head to help you understand and negotiate a particular 'territory.'"[4] Formed by our unique experiences, these frames influence what we see—and don't see—in our church.

Leaders in any role often default to one frame that feels most natural, causing confusion or frustration when others don't "get it" or see things their way. This makes it hard to share keys and easy to conclude they should just lead on their own.

Consider how one (or more) of the following frames might describe the way you understand and use the keys of leadership.[5]

The *structural frame* views the church primarily through its roles and responsibilities. Church leaders operating out of this frame might see themselves as the CEO of the church. They can be task oriented rather than people oriented, eager to develop plans and assign roles. At one multisite church we visited, the small group pastor gave a 10-minute description of the leadership structure, volunteer training, and curriculum selection process for the church's exceptionally well-run small group ministry. She is heavily oriented toward the structural frame.

The *relational* or *human resource frame* understands the church primarily through personal relationships, or like a family comprised of individuals with distinct skills, feelings, and needs. Church leaders operating out of this frame might picture themselves like a mother, father, or best friend. They want to get to know people and *do life together*. During our visit to a multigenerational church, nearly every teenager and emerging adult talked about Arthur. Arthur had recently been to their basketball game, dance recital, or some other activity. When we interviewed Arthur, a grandfather in his seventies, he expressed the joy he feels by making sure young people know they matter. He operates out of a relational frame.

The *symbolic frame* views the church primarily through its stories, rituals, sermons, and spiritual practices. Church leaders operating within this frame might picture themselves like a sage, prophet, or spiritual guide. They want to spend time discussing theology or otherwise focusing on the deeper meaning of the work of the church. When we interviewed the senior pastor of a church that was nearly 150 years old, he somehow ended up answering every question by telling us a story—most often a story from Scripture. This pastor is strongly oriented toward the symbolic frame.

Each of these frames has obvious strengths and weaknesses when it comes to church life. Imagine your church board or leadership team discussing the future of your congregation and creating a plan for growing young. Someone who lives in the structural frame will likely want to lay out a step-by-step process or examine the potential impact on the church's budget. Someone from the relational frame might contemplate how the process will make people feel or if it will result in deeper personal connections. Another leader operating in the symbolic frame might want to know how the decision fits theologically or might even cast a compelling vision of what the future could look like if the church grew young.

These three perspectives can evolve into meetings and ministries marked by a beautiful diversity or meetings and ministries that devolve into an ugly mess. Further, if a majority of your church tends too much toward any one particular frame, the other two may be neglected and your church could end up unbalanced (in fact, you might be thinking about how it's unbalanced right now). Instead, the best teams intentionally incorporate leaders from each frame, while the best leaders learn to be good enough in their less natural frames.

Awareness of these frames and the ability to apply each at the right time can enable your church to ditch the Superpastor syndrome and effectively share the keys of leadership with young people like Stretch. To help you gain this awareness, we've provided several reflection questions on pages 75–76.

Keychain Leaders Take the Long View . . .
Not Shortsighted Steps

Across the board, our surveys, interviews, and church visits all highlighted the importance of consistent and long-term leadership—in both the youth ministry and the overall church. In particular, our analysis of surveys found a positive relationship between the longer senior pastors served at a particular church and overall church health.

That makes sense given that moving from key-less, key-hoarding, or key-loaning to keychain leadership simply takes time, especially in youth and emerging adult ministry. Young people are already going through significant developmental changes in their friends, schools, and physical bodies. Relationships at church have the potential to be a rare constant. One volunteer from a church in Michigan shared, "In fifth grade, we pair students with leaders, taking into account the school that they attend or where they live. Then we put them in a group to ideally stay with the same kids and leaders through high school so they have long-term care."

The impact of the long view is not limited to youth ministry. Bonnie, a senior adult from Volga Christian Reformed Church, a small congregation in rural South Dakota, shared how a tumultuous period of pastoral transition began with several interim pastors who each stayed less than two years. When they hired their current pastor, Bonnie passed by his house and noticed he was planting asparagus. "Asparagus can take three years before it produces a crop!" she explained. "Once he did that, we knew he was here to stay."

Later in the visit, we interviewed this pastor and asked him about the asparagus. Laughing, he affirmed it has become an iconic moment in his congregation. While he didn't originally mean to make such a statement, he noticed a tangible difference in the congregation's trust in him.

71

Is preaching still important in the age of downloadable sermons and social media?

Overall, preaching was not mentioned nearly as often as we anticipated in parishioners' descriptions of why or how their church was growing young. When we asked what keeps people involved in their church, preaching was only the sixth highest response (mentioned by 12 percent of people). This was far behind the top responses related to personal relationships, the general sense of community within the church, activities such as small groups and retreats, respondents' personal involvement, and a sense of calling or loyalty.

This data does *not* lead us to conclude that preaching is unimportant. During our 12 site visits, we experienced a range from excellent to "good enough" preaching skills but no bad preaching. Our hunch is that even though young people don't highlight preaching as a magnet that draws them to church, bad preaching could easily repel them.

Having said that, we wonder if sermon preparation and preaching is an area in which some leaders could invest less time. While we hold the Word of God with the highest value and respect, we believe that verbal proclamation is *one* (albeit one very important) form of expression. Given that young people are especially dialed in to relationships, might your time crafting a gospel-centered community be worth as much attention as preaching? Could you perhaps exhibit keychain leadership by sharing the pulpit and training other (maybe younger) teachers and preachers? After all, young people who want top-notch preaching can download sermons from amazing communicators nationwide. But they can't download a vibrant community.

While long-term pastoral leadership is usually preferred, churches that grow young manage to thrive even in the midst of senior leadership transitions. This health seems to stem from senior leaders sharing the keys with congregation members and church board members, thus developing a leadership team that stays consistent even when pastoral staff leave.

Ideas for Action

What follows are practical ideas for action that you can implement as you unlock keychain leadership. Please keep in mind that not every idea will apply to your church or your particular role. Please also remember that we are not suggesting any church try all (or even most) of these ideas—the last thing we want is to overwhelm you with an overly long to-do list. We provide multiple ideas because every church is different, and it takes a team of leaders to grow young.

As you review this part of the chapter, perhaps make notes in the margin about

- whether or not the particular idea is a fit for your church;
- if you should implement it now or later; and
- if the idea might best help you or another leader in your church (if the latter, write down that person's name so you'll remember to share the idea with him or her).

Aim for two or three ideas that *you* want to act on now. Then at the end of the chapter, you can answer strategic questions to guide your church toward a specific plan to unlock keychain leadership.

Evaluate Your Own Keychain Leadership

In order to share the keys of leadership, your first step is to make sure you are aware of the keys you actually hold. Whether you serve in a paid or volunteer role, begin by looking at your job description—if it has actually been updated in the last five years! (If not, that might be step one.)

Working with or without a job description, list your major responsibilities in a single column. Then in a second column, note whether you hold the keys to that area, have shared the keys to that area, or have given away the keys to that area. For those responsibilities in which you hold or share the keys, consider whether it is possible for you to train someone and hand over the keys, or if it's an area you absolutely must hold on to (at least for now). Circle your next few key-sharing goals. You might even take a step further by seeking feedback from one or two trusted leaders about how well you share the keys of leadership.

Evaluating your own keychain leadership also means asking why you have keys in the first place. Examine your own theology of leadership by meditating on or discussing relevant Scripture passages (possibly with your leadership team). Spend time reflecting on powerful scriptural examples including Exodus 18:1–27; Joshua 1:1–18; 1 Samuel 8:1–22; Jeremiah 1:4–19; John 13:1–17; 15:1–17; 1 Corinthians 12:1–31; Ephesians 4:11–16; and Philippians 2:1–18.

Conduct a Young Leader Assessment

Instead of starting with the keys you hold, a second strategy is to start with actual young people. In the spirit of helping your church grow young, list teenagers or emerging adults who already hold, or could receive, the keys of leadership in your congregation. Like Stretch, many of them may never have received a set of keys and are simply waiting to be entrusted.

For each person, write out the type of key (meaning the area of responsibility) that might fit them based on their skills, gifts, or passions. Then write out potential next steps you could take to help them get ready to handle each particular key. After you try this exercise on your own, invite other volunteers, staff, Sunday school teachers, or leadership groups to join you in dreaming about the future potential of your church's young people.

Ditch the Superpastor and Find Your Frame

As your church contemplates how to help leaders move away from the Superpastor syndrome and share keys with young people, ask these three questions based on the description of frames on pages 69–70.

In which frame am I most comfortable? This is likely the area in which you are best positioned to identify and equip young people with their own keys. Rather than throw young people into difficult situations before they're ready, one church leader who operates in a relational frame and excels at leading small groups invites specific young people to spend time learning alongside him. Bit by bit, he gives them increasing levels of responsibility until they're ready to lead a group on their own. Another very talented preaching pastor who is most comfortable in the symbolic frame intentionally preaches only three Sundays each month so that he can provide regular speaking opportunities to younger leaders.

Which frames are least natural for me? These are the domains in which you need to identify other leaders who can take the keys and provide leadership. If particular ministries or your overall church is lacking particular frames, consider how you might invite one or multiple volunteers to lead (or even hire someone) to provide greater balance. Sharing the keys with leaders from another frame may be uncomfortable and will require both determination and a heavy dose of listening. As you build partnerships, encourage these leaders to identify young people with great promise in those particular frames whom they can train.

How can I grow in my less natural frames? Just because you may not feel comfortable in a particular frame does not mean you can ignore it. Most church leaders need to develop threshold competencies (meaning they need to be "good enough") in multiple areas. Perhaps make a list of the areas in which you know you need to develop a threshold competency but aren't quite there yet. You could ask another leader (inside or outside your church) who is strong in that area to coach you. We'd love to be able to suggest a comprehensive list of the areas in which keychain leaders need threshold competencies and a second list of areas in which excellence is required. However, we found it varies based on your context and unique role, which means it's critical to listen to and know your congregation.

Make Sure Young People Are Trained before Giving Them Keys

If you've ever asked a young person to house-sit while you were on vacation, you probably didn't completely pass off the key until you knew they were ready for tasks like watering the plants or feeding and walking the family dog. Chances are good that you guided them through your house, taking the time to clarify any area of confusion. No way would you hand over the key to your home until that young person was trained.

The same is true with your church. Even more so.

Once you've done the work of identifying your leadership frames, envision how you and your church can invest in developing young leaders. Is there a training plan to make that vision a reality? Is there a specific line item in the budget to make it possible?

Over this next year, implement a few of the following methods for training the young people on your team:

- Read through a book together. Select a strategic topic that's relevant to your team and spend one hour each month discussing it.

- Invite a young person to preach or lead a small group and help them craft their sermon or lesson.

* Send a promising young church leader to seminary. That person doesn't even have to leave your community. Multiple online education options allow your team members to stay in their current roles while sharpening their skills.

* Ask young leaders in your church about an area in which they'd like training. Then invite an expert from that field (maybe even someone who attends your church) to lead the training. For example, if young people want to learn more about communication, there may be a professor or business executive in your congregation with relevant insights to share.

* Partner with several churches in your area to host a staff or volunteer training together. Maybe even bring in a nationally recognized expert on a particular topic and invite more organizations and churches in your community.

* Create an internship program. Several churches in our study offered one or a handful of young people opportunities to serve through volunteer, part-time, and full-time internships.

Conduct a Time Inventory

Sometimes our picture of how we spend our time isn't just blurry; it's plain wrong.[6] In order to get an accurate understanding of time usage, our Fuller Youth Institute team has benefited greatly from conducting time inventories.

Begin by dividing your responsibilities into logical categories (for example, prayer and Bible study, sermon preparation, relationship building, meetings, event planning, and administrative tasks like answering email).

Second, spend at least one week tracking your time, allocating every hour to those categories.

"One of the things that I tell all of our small group leaders is that if you want to build community, it is going to take vulnerability. If you as a leader model vulnerability, then people will be more comfortable sharing their own lives with each other. So anytime I preach, anytime I counsel, anytime I share, I share the yuck and the muck of my life that God has had to cleanse." —Jayme, small groups pastor

Third, look at the total amount of time you spend in each area and compare that to how your time would ideally be allocated. Perhaps pay special attention to time spent in administrative activities as well as investing in people.

What changes could you make in your time allocation to become more of a keychain leader?

When It Comes to Vulnerability, Go First

Our observation of keychain leaders is that it's often not what they *say* that matters most but what they *do*. In your next staff or volunteer meeting, consider how you might be able to set the pace in a crucial aspect of keychain leadership: vulnerability. Given young people's desire for authentic leadership, steps toward vulnerability will likely render you an even more attractive leader. Here are a few discussion questions to help you and your team members swim into deeper relational waters:

- What's the biggest answer to prayer you've seen in the last year? What prayer have you been praying this last year that God hasn't answered quite as you had hoped?

- What's been one of your biggest failures? How has God used that failure to shape you?

- When have you been disappointed with God? What do you usually say or do when you're feeling disappointed with God?

- As you envision the future of your church, what's one aspect that most excites you? What's one area that causes stress or triggers fear?

Don't Surprise Your Supervisor

As we explored the relationship between the pastor and the youth and young adult leaders in churches that grow young, trust emerged as a key theme. The youth pastor trusted the pastor's heart and intentions, and the pastor trusted the youth pastor's judgment. This trust made it easier to share keys.

When leaders were asked for the biggest piece of advice they would offer a youth or young adult pastor, they consistently highlighted, "Don't surprise your pastor."

Obviously, we're not talking about secret birthday parties. When youth and young adult leaders anticipate problems, have already experienced problems, or are trying to make a major judgment call or ministry decision, it's wise to involve their supervisor as soon as possible. While this seems like common sense, we were disheartened by how many leaders, even in churches growing young, shared negative surprises that had come their way because their staff chose not to involve them early enough. It made these leaders want to take back any keys they had ever entrusted.

Whether you are a church staff member or volunteer, we recommend you talk to your supervisor to better understand their preferences. Ask if they've been negatively surprised in the past or if they have any advice about how you might be able to make their job easier or improve communication in the future.

Go Beyond Self-Help

The lead pastor of an Evangelical Covenant church confessed that a turning point in his keychain leadership was when he realized that he couldn't gain the emotional health he wanted on his own.[7] He needed professional help. So he started regularly meeting with a professional therapist.

Given how therapy helped him, this senior pastor now encourages the rest of the church staff to pursue short-term counseling. As one of the other leaders at this church shared, "This is the healthiest church staff I've ever worked with!"

Several leaders from the church mentioned that they had in fact never set out to reach young people exclusively but just wanted to build a healthy church. However, as a result of this newfound health, hundreds of young people began flocking to this congregation.

Consider Your Relational Capacity

How many close friends do you have in your church?

When participants in our study were asked this question, several asked for clarification of the word *friend*. They pointed out that if we were talking about *Facebook friends*, they would give one answer, but *close friends* would yield a different answer.

Church leaders are often expected (and often feel pressured) to maintain a high number of relationships. One recent Fuller Seminary study sought to understand the relational capacity of ministry leaders and how that relates to burnout, trauma, and ministry effectiveness.[8] According to the research, ministry leaders have some unique friend dynamics—including a smaller total friend network than the average person, which results in less overall support.

The best data suggests the ideal relational network is four to five close and supportive friendships and at least 12 (but not more than 15) relationships with people we consider good friends. Given that pastors are often spread relationally thin, it's challenging for them to maintain these deeper relationships so essential for holistic health.

Evaluate the breadth and depth of your relational network by making a list of close and supportive relationships and of good friends you have currently. If those numbers are lower than the data recommends, set a meeting with one person in your "close and supportive" list. Ask for help working on a plan to strengthen your relational ties.

Close the Gap on Social Distance

A primary focus on close, personal relationships does not mean you need to distance yourself from the members in your congregation you don't know as well. The keychain leaders we observed do whatever they can to eradicate social distance. For example, the pastor of First Baptist Church of Chicago makes himself available to his congregation by playing basketball and spending time in church members' homes. Other church leaders are intentional about being near the exit doors of the church after the worship services conclude so they can greet people personally. Another church leader hosts regular dinners in her home and invites church members.

Please hear us clearly. We are *not* saying that you need to be "all access, all the time" and eliminate your personal boundaries. We're also not saying that all of your close relationships should be formed within your church.

What we *are* saying is that Jesus, our example in life and leadership, made time to be with people. We're invited to lead the same way.

Take a hard look at your schedule over the next two weeks. How much of your time will be spent in your office, and how much of your time will be spent with people? What are one or two activities you could add (or more likely, substitute for administrative tasks) so you could be with people? Perhaps it's spending time with a neighbor, gardening with a church member, setting a regular lunch meeting, volunteering at your kids' school, or signing up for a sports league. Whatever fits your lifestyle and context, put it on the calendar today.

Stay Connected as a Staff

Keychain leaders recognize that people share keys best when they know and trust one another. In one church growing young, the pastoral team facilitates this through a standing monthly meeting in which the only agenda item is to have lunch together. No business. Just sharing life over sandwiches and salads.

At another larger church, every staff member has a regular 15-minute meeting with the senior pastor. While the pastor doesn't supervise every person, and 15 minutes is not enough time to accomplish significant agenda items, every staff member knows they have the attention of the senior pastor on a regular basis. The keys at this church are not wasted or kept but shared freely.

Recognize That Keys Aren't What They Used to Be

It used to be that a key was a key. If you went to a hotel, you would put the key in the lock and enter your room. Today you might enter your room via a traditional key, a keypad, a keycard, or even an app on your smartphone! We've found a similar trend in the staffing strategies of some churches that grow young.

There used to be more of a formula for staffing a church—hire a pastor, then a worship leader, and then a youth pastor. While many churches that grow young followed these more traditional staffing patterns, others developed creative staff and volunteer structures. One of the most effective and well-loved youth workers we interacted with was a 75-year-old retired grandfather at an inner-city church. In fact, several congregations utilize retired senior adults as leaders in their church. Others awakened the passion of those in their twenties, many of whom spend significant hours volunteering with their church.

Another difference in churches growing young is that youth and young adult pastors tend not to focus *exclusively* on youth or young adult ministry. They are given a voice (not just more work) in other areas of the church, such as in the children's ministry, men's or women's ministry, senior adult ministry, and church board meetings. This multifaceted involvement naturally erodes the walls between the age-based silos that can so easily divide ministries and congregation members.

Rather than simply following traditional practices or assuming a separate staff person is necessary for every role, churches that grow young show significant creativity and contextual sensitivity when it comes to sustainable staffing. Most important is that each model or division of responsibility works well because it matches and respects the church's unique culture. Next time you're looking to fill a position, pause and ask yourself (and your team) if there are any options to divide up the keys that you haven't yet considered.

Say Thank You

In chapter 1, we referred to the admonition of leadership guru Max De Pree that the first job of a leader is to define reality. According to De Pree, the last job of a leader is to say "Thank you."[9] Gratitude recognizes and affirms the contributions of others as well as shapes the character of the leader.

Whom do you need to thank for entrusting you with the keys of leadership at some point in your journey? Spend some time writing, calling, or texting those keychain leaders God used to position you for the leadership role you have today.

I (Jake) likely wouldn't be writing this book if it weren't for several leaders who saw potential in me as a teenager and emerging adult and began sharing keys with me the moment I was ready to take them on my own. Without those keys, I would likely be working in a business finance office rather than studying and serving churches today. Come to think of it, I can already identify at least a half dozen people who probably don't know about the impact they've had on my life and leadership. Whatever your age or life stage, we bet you can do the same.

Go ahead, put down this book and take some time to thank them now.

Chapter Highlights

- Churches that grow young are brimming with staff, volunteers, and parents who demonstrate *keychain leadership*. By *keys*, we mean the capabilities, power, and access of leaders that can be used to empower young people. By *keychain leaders*, we mean pastoral and congregational leaders who are acutely aware of the keys on their keychain and intentional about entrusting and empowering young people with their own set of keys.

- Keychain leaders can be volunteers, senior pastors, parents, youth pastors, associate pastors, Sunday school teachers, and more. Beyond any particular role, keychain leadership is a spirit and commitment demonstrated by both paid and volunteer leaders that permeates every area of the church.

- Four types of key leadership we've discovered include:
    Key-less leaders: Often young and inexperienced, without much authority or access, they spend their time proving they're worthy to possess keys.
    Key-hoarding leaders: Always holding the keys and refusing to give others access, they run the show.

Key-loaning leaders: Often taking keys off the keychain and letting others borrow them temporarily, they make sure the keys are returned quickly.

Keychain leaders: Very aware of the keys they hold, they're constantly opening doors for some while training and entrusting others who are ready for their own set of keys.

* The research revealed six essentials of keychain leadership. Keychain leaders

are mature, not always young;

are real, not "relevant";

are warm, not distant;

know what matters to people, not just other pastors;

entrust and empower others; they don't try to be a "Superpastor"; and

take the long view, not shortsighted steps.

Strategic Questions to Help Your Church Unlock Keychain Leadership

Research Findings

On a scale of 1 to 5 (with 1 being "we're struggling here" and 5 being "we're nailing this"), rate your congregation on the research findings presented in this chapter:

1. My approach to leadership and the overall culture of our congregation reflect *keychain leadership*, marked by an awareness of the keys we hold and a willingness to entrust and empower young people.

1 · · · · · · 2 · · · · · · 3 · · · · · · 4 · · · · · · 5

2. Our church appropriately balances a focus on mature leadership with a focus on young leadership.

$$1 \quad 2 \quad 3 \quad 4 \quad 5$$

3. The leadership culture at our church focuses on being real rather than "relevant."

$$1 \quad 2 \quad 3 \quad 4 \quad 5$$

4. The leadership culture at our church is warm rather than distant.

$$1 \quad 2 \quad 3 \quad 4 \quad 5$$

5. The leadership culture at our church regularly and carefully listens to and knows what matters to people in our congregation, not just other pastors.

$$1 \quad 2 \quad 3 \quad 4 \quad 5$$

6. The leadership culture in our congregation takes the long view rather than shortsighted steps.

$$1 \quad 2 \quad 3 \quad 4 \quad 5$$

Ideas for Action

1. What are you personally already doing to understand which keys are on your keychain and how those keys might best be used?

2. What are some keys (capabilities, power, and access) that you have already shared or given away to others, especially to young people?

3. Looking back at the four types of key leadership we discussed on pages 57–58, which one best describes you and the leadership culture of your church? In order to move to the next level or improve at your current level, what are one or two steps you or your church need to take?

4. Who else needs to be part of this conversation?

5. What can you do in the next few weeks or months to move toward these changes?

3. Empathize with Today's Young People

Why 25 Is the New 15, and 15 Is the New 25

> The number one adult who's influenced me is Brent. There was a time in the fall when I was suicidal again and he was, like, visibly upset. He said some things like, "Don't do that . . . we need you." And he hugged me and teared up. I think he believes in me more than anyone else. He gets me. —Allen, age 21

"Pastor, if I raise my finger, will God know which one I'm going to raise even before I raise it?"

Thirteen-year-old Steve attended church every week with his parents. This particular Sunday, he had stayed after the worship service to ask his pastor this pressing question. The pastor replied, "Yes, God knows everything."

Haunted by the plight of African children suffering from dire famine, Steve then pulled out a *Life* magazine cover depicting two children tormented by starvation. He asked the logical follow-up, "Well, does God know about this and what's going to happen to those kids?" The pastor gave a similar response: "Steve, I know you don't understand, but yes, God knows about that."[1]

If you were Steve, would you be satisfied with the pastor's answer to your question?

Steve wasn't.

He walked out of his congregation that day and never again worshiped at a Christian church.

The good—even remarkable—news is that Steve was drawn like a magnet to the faith community, and his pastor specifically, for answers to the dilemmas that most troubled him.

The bad—even tragic—news is that his pastor's shortsighted response repelled him from the faith community. Permanently.

Even more disheartening is that the pastor failed to grasp the question behind Steve's question. Similar to the young people in your congregation, Steve wasn't merely asking an existential question about the nature of suffering. Likely behind Steve's rather esoteric inquiry about children in Africa were more personal questions about life and faith. Perhaps Steve wondered why God would allow the suffering he himself had experienced in his 13 years, which included bullying at school, financial struggles at home, and most painfully, being relinquished for adoption by his birth parents. As Steve was trying to make sense of the pain in our world, he wanted his pastor to understand and help him make sense of *his own* pain.

Maybe you have heard of Steve. His last name is Jobs. Steve Jobs, founder and CEO of Apple, Inc., was a churchgoing teenager who wrestled with big questions. He sought out his church to help him pin down answers, but his congregation failed to understand what he was really asking.

Imagine if Steve had been greeted by a different answer from his pastor. One that was an on-ramp to a deeper discussion about faith rather than a conversational dead end. One that acknowledged Steve's curiosity about suffering in Africa, as well as Steve's deeper questions about life goals, divine love, and his own place in the world.

Imagine if the pastor had replied to 13-year-old Steve, "That's a great question. How about if you and I and your dad meet for breakfast this week and talk about it?" Or imagine if Steve's parents had been attentive enough to initiate a discussion with Steve themselves. Or that *any* adult had hit the conversational ball over the net to Steve instead of letting it slowly dribble off the court.

Imagine if Steve Jobs had his questions taken seriously by his faith community and he had later poured his entrepreneurial brilliance not only into furthering high-tech interfaces but also into furthering the gospel and mobilizing others to respond to needs globally. Our world would be different today.

Unfortunately, no adult answered Steve's questions convincingly. No adult peered under the hood of his words to understand the inner cries that sparked his deep dilemmas. As a result, Steve, like so many young people today, walked away from both faith and the faith community.

Young people like Steve who swim in the deep end of challenging cultural and developmental questions often view the church as merely splashing around in the shallow end. Or worse yet, they perceive us standing on the pool deck, wagging our finger and blowing a whistle at them in condemnation of who they are and what they do.

Instead of staying on the deck, churches and parishes that grow young dive into the deep waters of teenagers' and young adults' lives. Both in young people's descriptions of their churches

CORE COMMITMENT:
EMPATHIZE WITH TODAY'S YOUNG PEOPLE

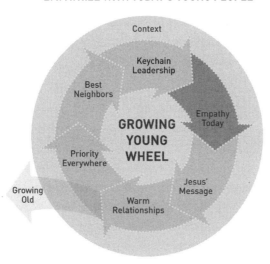

and in our observations during site visits, *empathizing with today's young people* bubbled to the surface as a core commitment of growing young.

By *empathy*, we don't mean patronizing young people. Nor do we mean a superficial or false sympathy. We certainly don't mean judgmentalism, even if it's cloaked in helpful suggestions (e.g., "Instead of playing video games all day, have you thought about looking online for a job?").

When we talk about empathy, we mean *feeling with* young people. As defined by Stanford University's "D" (Design) School, empathizing is "the work you do to understand people. . . . It is

> "Empathy is the essence of what it means to be a pastor. It's the willingness to go to hard places with people. Even if people in my church disagree with me, I hope they know I care about them."
> —Eugene Cho, senior pastor at Quest Church

your effort to understand the way they do things and why, their physical and emotional needs, how they think about the world, and what is meaningful to them."[2] In other words, it's sitting on the curb of a young person's life, celebrating their dreams and grieving over their despair.

Research Findings

Empathy Seeks to Understand Today's Young People

The crux of this core commitment isn't just empathizing with young people in general; growing young begins by understanding *today's* young people. While you may already know many young people from your church or community (or you're still one yourself!), you need to understand more of what's going on internally, beneath the surface, as well as the external cultural forces that influence their lives and direction. We want to help you do that. Instead of asking you to immerse yourself in the last two decades of world-class research, we've done it for you. We've combed through the best recent social science, behavioral science, and practical theology research to help you hit the ground running in your journey with teenagers and emerging adults.

We need to offer you two warnings about what it takes to understand today's teenagers and emerging adults. First, it's an intense journey. That's because the issues that today's young people navigate are intense. Comprehending this generation means slogging through some pretty tough terrain. As a result, the bulk of this chapter's research findings is more disconcerting than in other chapters. We love that you care enough about young people to try to understand not just the good but also the bad and ugly of their lives. Nonetheless, we've tried to balance that unsettling data with a handful of inspiring stories and sidebar quotes from young people grateful for their church's willingness to jog alongside them.

Second, while this chapter is crammed with data and statistics, we are not expecting you to memorize all of them—or really any of them. We offer them to help you understand and build better relationships with the young people in your community (and for many, your family) who have undoubtedly been impacted by these nationwide trends.

Empathy Is Contagious

Pay It Forward. This title of a highly acclaimed film (ironically released in 2000, right around the time the high school students we studied were born) echoes a well-known phrase that has become part of our nation's lexicon. The essence of both the slogan and the film is that when you are the recipient of a good deed, you then "pay it forward" by showing commensurate (or even greater) kindness to others.

We couldn't help but notice that young people who are surrounded by empathetic adults often become more empathetic themselves. When teenagers and emerging adults are appreciated, understood, and valued, they become conduits through which empathy flows.

Perhaps the most vivid example of how young people mirror the empathy they experience is Bennett. As nine-year-old Bennett and his single mom, Vera, were looking for a church home six years ago, Vera had one major criterion: that the congregation be a safe place for her son with special needs. When she asked the children's ministry leaders at one large church in the Southwest, "Will you take care of my unusual child?" their response was, "Absolutely. You tell us what we need to know and do. Please give us feedback on how we're doing." Vera and Bennett were hooked and have been active members of the congregation ever since.

"You know, this woman at church has just continuously reached out to me. She sent me a note the other day—like a handwritten note—that said, 'Hey, I am glad that we are getting to know each other. I am happy you are in my life, and I can't wait to get to know you more in ministry and just as friends.' It was very unnecessary; it was outrageous. Yet welcome." —Aimee, age 24

Vera recounted a memory of picking up nine-year-old Bennett from the children's ministry at the end of a worship service six years ago: "Here's what this church means to me and Bennett. I have a scene playing in my mind. I am picking up my son, and I see an adult bent down on his level, focused on what my son is saying. He puts his hand on my son's shoulder, nods his head, and says something that I can't hear. Both smile, and my son nods his head back. At school, Bennett never feels that understood and secure."

In a world that often doesn't take the time to talk to Bennett, such empathy was a magnet for both Bennett and his mom. But Vera continued, "Now my son is 15. This church is his home, and he's been invited to help serve in the kindergarten class—something I never thought possible. A few months ago, as I again picked him up after worship, he was bent over, listening to a seven-year-old boy. Bennett was nodding his head. I moved close enough to hear what Bennett said as he put his hand on this boy's shoulder: 'I understand. I've felt that way before too.' Bennett never could have said that if he hadn't felt like this church had understood him. He is modeling the empathy that he had experienced."

The Three Ultimate Questions of Every Young Person

Based on the time we spent with Bennett and hundreds of other young people, as well as our theological reflection, we believe that at the core of what it means to be human lie three ultimate questions. If we are going to empathize with today's young people, we have to explore these questions. They are often what keep today's teenagers and emerging adults awake at night.

Who am I?

Where do I fit?

What difference do I make?

The first is a question about *identity*, meaning a young person's conception and expression of who they are. This question holds up the mirror and scrutinizes *me*.

The second is a question of *belonging*, or a young person's quantity and quality of life-giving relationships. This question looks around the room, eager to explore *us*.

The third is a question about *purpose*, or a young person's commitment to and ability to engage in meaningful activities that impact others. This question peers out the window and wonders about *our world*.

THE THREE ULTIMATE QUESTIONS

I'm wondering . . .	My ultimate question is about my . . .	The focus is on . . .
Who am I?	Identity	Me
Where do I fit?	Belonging	Us
What difference do I make?	Purpose	Our world

These Three Questions Are Not Unique to This Generation

When the Fuller Youth Institute gathered the experienced academicians and leaders who serve as our research advisors, we asked them to identify the lies that adults believe about young people. Surfacing at the top of their list was the lie that young people are completely "other." The typical senior leader or congregation member has bought into the myth that young people are not only a problem but also a problem they can't relate to. Or empathize with. If it wasn't for these three questions, that might be true.

But as we've spoken to parents, congregational leaders, and other researchers, it's become clear that these questions of identity, belonging, and purpose traverse across all life stages. During the last 24 hours, I (Kara) have vacillated between pride and insecurity as I've assessed who I am and what motivates me as a wife, parent, and leader. Last night, I wondered if I had the energy and courage required to deepen a friendship with a neighbor. This morning, I prayed a big prayer for the young people of our country—one that now causes me to tear up as I remember how it felt to ask God to do a God-sized work in the hearts and minds of young people.

These questions are not corralled by any one generation; they roam the canyons that separate the generations today. In those moments when the gap seems to be growing between those under and those over 30, these common questions enable us to transcend the particular year in which any of us was born and empathize with the young people in our midst.

The Young People You Know Experience These Questions Acutely

Every one of us, regardless of age, contends with a common angst about our identity, belonging, and purpose. Why then is it that those of us over 30 often feel so different from 15- to 29-year-olds? The first of two reasons that we sense a generation gap is that once we pass through the life stages of adolescence and emerging adulthood, we encounter these questions with less fervor. After age 30, we periodically feel the tension of resolving these three ultimate questions, but young people feel that pressure acutely and constantly. Those over 30 sense these big questions as a back-burner presence, with intervals when the heat is turned up. For people under 30, their relational and self-image struggles keep their identity, belonging, and purpose dilemmas at a constant, churning boil.

A Later Finish Line

In addition to this distinction between young and old, we often sense a generation gap because this current generation also develops at a different pace. The time it takes today's teenagers and emerging adults to mature has changed. On the one hand, their journey toward adulthood has sped up. On the other hand, it has slowed down. Way down.

In comparison with previous generations, today's journey toward maturity often seems to move in slow motion. Young people are older when they turn the corners of identity, belonging, and purpose typically equated with full adulthood.

The median age for first marriage is now 26.5 for women and 28.7 for men, both of which are more than five years later than 50 years ago.[3]

The average age for women bearing their first child is 26 years, which is almost five years later than women in 1970.[4]

Given the uncertainties of today's economic climate and the increased assumption that a college degree is a universal necessity, more young people are pursuing more higher education. Two-thirds of high school graduates now enter college, a higher proportion than ever before in American history. Among those who graduate from college, approximately one-third head to graduate school the following year.[5] While previous generations of young adults plunged into the workforce right after high school or in their early twenties, many of today's young adults often wait until their late twenties or early thirties to take on a long-term career.

When they eventually dive into the workforce, the average American holds six different jobs between the ages of 18 and 26, and two-thirds of these jobs occur between ages 18 and 22.[6]

Partly because of young adults' career and educational odysseys, it takes them longer to become financially independent. In comparison with 1970, parents today provide 11 percent more financial help to young adult children.[7] Forty percent of young adults in their twenties move back home with their parents at least once.[8]

The data paints a clear and compelling picture of what has become labeled an "extended adolescence."[9] The traditional signs that a young person has entered adulthood—a spouse, a family, completed education, a steady job, and financial independence—now occur five or more years later. In no hurry to put down permanent roots and often rejecting one or more of these traditional markers of adulthood altogether, today's emerging adults are explorers.

This role of explorer is not necessarily a conscious desire or intentional choice. The world young people have been handed is more complex, competitive, and diverse. The conventional array of paths available to young adults has been exponentially multiplied. As a result, there is so much more to explore and navigate—whether they want to or not.

That's why 25-year-olds sometimes seem like 15-year-olds.

A LATER FINISH LINE

An Earlier Starting Line

Yet the inverse is also true. Sometimes 15-year-olds blow us away with their maturity, acting like 25-year-olds. Just as the finish line of young people's passage into adulthood is now later, their journey toward identity, belonging, and purpose starts earlier.

Biologically, the onset of puberty, marked by the average age of menarche in girls, has plummeted from age 16 to somewhere between age 12 and 13.[10]

Culturally, young people have been hit with a tidal wave of pressures that immerses them in what had previously been adult-only currents. From highly competitive sports and extra-curricular activities for kindergartners to college preparatory courses for eighth graders, children have arguably seen more, heard more, and done more than almost any previous generation.

AN EARLIER STARTING LINE

At 15, young people carry more access to the world via the mobile devices in their pockets than their parents could ever fathom as teenagers. And yet at 25, they still rely on those same parents to fund the mobile plan that gives them that constant access to the world.

Fifteen is the new 25. Twenty-five is the new 15. Yes, it is that complicated.

Young People's Erratic Search for Identity

Earlier start + Later finish = Longer race

A longer race full of hazardous holes, confusing alternative paths, and stiff headwinds. Many of these obstacles are timeless challenges that were also navigated by young adults in earlier eras. The rest are new, often the result of the pace and paths chosen by previous generations. Regardless of their origin, these obstacles complicate young people's exploration of their identity, belonging, and purpose.

As we seek to keep step with young people in their three quests, we need first to examine how the obstacles of *pervasive stress* and *peripheral faith* hijack their ability to define themselves.

PERVASIVE STRESS

As today's young people seek a more coherent sense of identity, the stress that formerly hit them in college, or even after college, now begins in middle school (or younger). By high school, many middle- and upper-class teenagers juggle digital calendars jammed with extracurricular activities that begin as early as 6:00 a.m., after-school study sessions, college entrance exam tutoring, and sports team practices that leave them trailing home after 10:00 p.m.[11] Followed by two to three hours of homework.[12]

Athletes used to specialize in a single sport in high school; now that starts in elementary school. Previously, musicians and artists could freely dabble in various media and instruments throughout high school; present-day teenagers have to claim their craft in middle school. No longer can a kid flirt with a handful of hobbies, discovering various facets of their personality and passions, before choosing what they love. There's so little time for thoughtful and measured exploration in high school that young adults end up exploring their skills and passions well into their twenties.

A recent study showed that 13- to 17-year-olds are more likely to feel "extreme stress" than adults.[13] Even more alarming is that the adults closest to young people are often blind to their heightened stress levels. Approximately 20 percent of teenagers confess that they worry "a great deal" about current and future life events. But only 8 percent of the parents of these same teenagers report that their child is experiencing a great deal of stress.[14] Parents often don't realize the constant heat felt by adolescents, increasing the pressure for them to figure out who they are and what's important to them.

After adolescence, emerging adults race from the proverbial stress-filled pot into the stress-fueled fire.[15] Fewer college students are reporting "above-average" health since this question was first asked in 1985.[16]

According to sociologist Tim Clydesdale, much of that pressure stems from the hassles of "daily life management." The ongoing tumult of academic, vocational, and relational dilemmas causes young people to put critical parts of themselves, including their religious, political, racial, gender, and class identities, into an "identity lockbox."[17] This lockbox allows young people to keep their religion and foundational values "safe," protected from the stress that buffets them daily. But that upside is dwarfed by the downside—while young people are deciding and expressing who they are, their faith and core values are locked up. As they have life-defining conversations, their underlying beliefs remain muted.

"I spend hours out of my week going to my church's worship services, small group meetings, and activities, but that is my favorite part of my week. And it really deepens my faith." —Carlos, age 19

Although the typical young person is steeped in stress, there is some good news for churches. Thankfully, the hazards caused by stress seem less troublesome for churches and parishes that grow young. Over 80 percent of the young people in the congregations we surveyed agree that their church involvement decreases their stress. Even though church activities and leadership often make young people busier, there's a significant upside. Congregational involvement seems to lessen anxiety by reminding young people of what's important and inviting them to step away from the chaos of their lives to refocus on loving God and others.[18]

PERIPHERAL FAITH

While we applaud that the young people in churches growing young feel less stress, the identity of young people in general is not rooted in their faith as we might hope. The National Study of Youth and Religion (NSYR), a comprehensive sociological study of the faith of over 2,000 13- to 17-year-olds nationwide, uncovered some good news: American teenagers are not hostile toward religion.

But before we celebrate any supposed shift in US religiosity, we must quickly pivot to the bad news. *US teens aren't hostile toward religion because they don't care about it very much.* More specifically, while 3 out of 4 American teenagers claim to be Christians, only about half of those professing Christians view their faith as "very important." Fewer than half regularly integrate faith practices into their daily lives.[19]

The NSYR then conducted a second round of research, following the same cohort of teenagers as they became 18- to 23-year-olds. If anything, the influence of religion diminished. Only 45 percent of emerging adults maintain any semblance of faith practices.

While faith is ideally a central force in identity development, the bland faith offered by the typical church is missing a hefty enough gravitational pull. Rather than define themselves by faith, teenagers and emerging adults wander aimlessly, searching down other paths of meaning.

Case Study: A Church Growing Young Empathizes with a Teenager's Search for Identity

During one of our site visits at an urban Baptist church, we heard the story of Sarah, a high school sophomore who struggled through the identity challenges we've just named. Her family was burdened financially, her grades were declining, and her failure to measure up to her talented older brother's long list of achievements caused perpetual stress. Sarah's personal turmoil cast a long and suffocating shadow on her relationship with God. Overwhelmed by her heavy load and desperate for relief, she overdosed on drugs.

Thankfully, her suicide attempt wasn't successful. When members of the congregation found out that Sarah was in the hospital and why, they didn't judge her or try to minimize her pain. To the contrary, they immediately surrounded her in her hospital room—with prayer and compassion.

And while their support was immediate, it wasn't only short term. As Sarah returned to home, school, and church, her congregation made space for her to share her ongoing stress and sadness. They let Sarah know it was okay to take baby steps, and sometimes even slide backward, in her journey to explore her identity. Sarah's faith, which had previously been feeble, has grown stronger because her congregation has rallied and walked with her through the "valley of the shadow of death."[20]

Churches that grow young aren't perfect. The young people who are part of them aren't perfect either. We wish that Sarah's search for identity had been smoother and more even. But stumbles are inevitable. What sets churches that grow young apart is not the absence of struggling young people. It's that *when* their young people fall, the faith community is there to help them find their footing and then walk with them on the quest to know and express who they are.

Young People's Uncertain Quest for Belonging

As Sarah's life demonstrates, young people's search for identity is closely linked with their quest for belonging. Unfortunately, teenagers' and emerging adults' erratic identity development makes forming community more challenging. After all, it's difficult to develop a tribe when who you are keeps changing. So the teenagers and emerging adults in your church and community often end up socially overstimulated and relationally undersupported. Young people need periodic bursts of energy to continue to pursue social relationships, and technology and sexual experimentation are two such bursts. Yet the relational breadth and quick momentum these bursts offer are ultimately stalled by the absence of adult support.

DIGITAL TECHNOLOGY

Today's digital technology helps young people connect globally—with their closest friend across town, their favorite musician across the country, and fans of an obscure hobby across an

---

Here are some quick facts to help you understand how teenagers use digital technology to stay in touch with others:[21]

Ninety-two percent of teenagers report going online at least once per day. Twenty-four percent of teens confess going online "almost constantly."

A majority of teenagers—approximately 71 percent—use more than one social media platform to keep in touch with friends.

The median number of texts a teenager sends and receives per day is 30, but that number increases to 50 for 15- to 17-year-old girls.

As parents, we navigate questions about our kids' use of technology every day. For more about how families can chart new, positive paths in their use of technology, visit StickyFaith.org/family.

ocean. Teenagers and emerging adults can—and do—connect with everyone and learn about everything online.

It's tempting for older generations to greet young people riveted to their devices with four words: "Put that thing down." But a better—and growing young—response is to understand *why* they hunger for that digital connection. As technology scholar and researcher danah boyd suggests, "Fear is not the solution; empathy is."[22]

Young people use social media for one major reason: *connection*. Digital media offers young people desperate for community unprecedented access to their friends, family, and the rest of the world.

But churches growing young appreciate and empathize with how technology is a double-edged sword for young people eager to belong. Digital media magnifies any cracks or holes that exist in young people's social support structure. Pictures and social media posts about Tuesday afternoon study sessions and Friday night parties can make young people feel like "everyone else" has more friends.[23] For teenagers and young adults desperate for a sense of belonging, technology provides quick bursts of momentum that can end up unfortunately petering out.

SEXUAL EXPERIMENTATION

Hoping to connect with others through more than just a screen, the majority of teenagers—including those who view their religion as very important to them—turn to sex. As mentioned earlier, the average age of marriage is now in the late twenties, while the average age of biological puberty is approximately age 13. That 12- to 14-year gap between biological puberty and marriage is a long time for sexually maturing young men and women to wait for sex.[24]

So they're not. By age 18, over 75 percent of those who never attend church, and almost 53 percent of those who attend church weekly, are no longer virgins.[25] In our (mostly) "anything goes" sexual culture, young people are also exploring sexting, oral sex, and anal sex.

In addition to heterosexual encounters, a common topic in both the media and controversial church discussions is same-sex attraction and identity. When it comes to LGBTQ behaviors of college-aged young adults, 5.2 percent of young men and 14 percent of young women have had sexual contact with a same-sex partner.[26]

Beyond their quest to belong, a host of reasons motivates teenagers and emerging adults to engage in sexual relationships—pleasure, peer pressure, and inquisitiveness to name a few. Whether young people look to sexual exploration as a fast track to gratification or a shortcut to community, their sexual choices often detour them from the sense of belonging they ultimately seek. More than 55 percent of sexually experienced 15- to 19-year-olds wish they had waited longer to have sex. For 12- to 14-year-olds, that number climbs to 81 percent.[27] What initially felt like a speedy path to connection often degrades into a dead end of pain and regret.

ADULT ABANDONMENT

Empathizing with young people today means admitting that perhaps the allure of technology and sexual exploration stems in part from the lack of support offered by adults. According to our friend and colleague Chap Clark, a defining experience

"A man in our church became my mentor right around the time my parents ended up separating. He basically became another father figure that I could talk to and ask for advice and hang out with. He has definitely been the most important person in my life from the church. I still talk to him on a regular basis for support and advice eight years later." —Marcus, age 26

for this generation of teenagers is systemic abandonment. In his ethnographic research, Clark commonly encountered teenagers who viewed neighbors, relatives, teachers, coaches, pastors, priests, and parents as too busy or too self-absorbed to invest in them without an agenda. The family, once a hub of belonging for young people, now increases pressure and a sense of loneliness. Clark contends, "We have evolved to the point where we believe that driving is support, being active is love, and providing any and every opportunity is selfless nurture."[28]

Young people's hunger for caring adults doesn't end at the conclusion of adolescence. In a season when emerging adults need the loving presence of others to help them navigate a host of new decisions, that safety net is often ripped away. Wuthnow argues:

> We provide day care centers, schools, welfare programs, family counseling, colleges, job training programs, and even detention centers as a kind of institutional surround-sound until young adults reach age 21, and then we provide nothing. . . . Yet nearly all the major decisions a person has to make about marriage, child rearing, and work happen after these support systems have ceased to function. This is not a good way to run a society.[29]

Churches that grow young recognize that the absence of caring adults and healthy families is the Achilles' heel that thwarts young people's ultimate quest for a tribe.

I'm all for empathy, but what do I do when young people I know make choices that are clearly unwise? Does being supportive mean I have to stay silent?

While sometimes our best move is to stay quiet and pray, at other times, the most compassionate and supportive step we can take is to speak up. Based on the empathy we have seen in churches growing young, if you feel called to share your concerns, we recommend you follow this principle: *first connect, and then correct.* Embracing this approach with young people might mean you:

- Pay attention to how you are feeling before you talk with them. Are you nervous or scared? Do this young person's choices surface old memories or wounds in your own life?

- Start your conversation by affirming what you appreciate about them.

- Gently probe how they are feeling about the particular issue that concerns you, instead of diving into a lecture or tirade.

- Ask if they can think of any other ways they could respond to that issue.

- Help them explore the pros and cons of those potential responses.

- Share your concerns, and then ask what they think is wrong about any observations you share, as well as what may be right.

- Ask how you can help them make any shifts they desire to make.

- Shower them with the same response whether they don't want to change, or try to change and fail, or try to change and succeed: unconditional love. Even—or maybe especially—when they disappoint you, please don't be one more adult who makes them feel abandoned.

- Pray for them. And with them.

Case Study: A Church Growing Young Satisfies a Young Person's Hunger for Belonging

Seventeen-year-old Ariana had given up hope that her family could provide her with the sense of belonging she craved. The ongoing conflict between her divorced mom and dad consumed so much of their emotional energy that they had little left over for Ariana. Texting friends and dating boys filled some of that hole but not nearly enough.

Ariana's emotional abandonment soon became physical. Due to her immigration status, her mom was deported to Costa Rica. Now instead of bouncing back and forth between her two parents' homes, Ariana moved in full-time with her dad. All the anger her dad had showered on her mom was soon aimed toward Ariana. Ariana's sassy teenage attitude made him all the more furious.

Through her church, Ariana came face-to-face with empathy in a human form. Denise was a single mom who felt like she could relate to Ariana's pain and isolation because her own parents had divorced when she was in elementary school. When Denise heard that Ariana had a weekend cheerleading competition, she went and sat in the stands. Ariana was so touched that she began texting prayer requests to Denise. The two started sharing meals together, and Denise did her best to attend all of Ariana's cheer contests.

For most high school seniors, prom is something to look forward to. But for Ariana, it was a night to dread. Since her mom was now absent, Ariana had no one to go shopping with her for just the right dress or help her that evening with her hair and makeup. If you've never been a 17-year-old girl, that might not sound like that big of a deal. Trust us. It's major.

Denise had taken enough steps toward Ariana that Ariana decided it was time to throw the door wide open. Ariana asked Denise to take her shopping and come over on prom night to help her get ready. Knowing how much prom meant to Ariana, Denise cleared her schedule and found a babysitter for her own daughter so the two could shop at local secondhand stores until they found just the perfect dress.

What could have been a time of despair for Ariana was transformed into a time of delight. On the big night, Denise went over to Ariana's apartment to finesse her hair and makeup. Joining them by video conference was Ariana's mom in Costa Rica. It was the first time that Denise had "met" Ariana's mom. Through tears, her mom thanked Denise for being like a "mom" for prom. As Denise described afterward, "When I see kids like Ariana who lack support systems, I try to figure out at least one thing I can do so they know I care. Showing up for Ariana's cheerleading competition opened a relationship door that not only changed Ariana, it shaped me too."

Young People's Meandering Journey toward Purpose

For Ariana and the teenagers you know who crave meaningful community, the path to feeling significant is equally daunting. Young people's search for purpose is fueled by their deep desire to make a difference, but the robust forces of jaded realism and cultural pluralism often stall their progress.

JADED REALISM

An early 1990s cartoon captured the mixed messages barraging young people in that decade. A young adult in his twenties stands in his bedroom, staring at his bed. Covering his bed are two T-shirts, implying that the young man is trying to choose which to wear. One T-shirt proclaims, "Just Do It" (à la Nike). The other counters, "Just Say No" (an anti-drug slogan from the 1980s). The young man scratches his head, paralyzed by ambivalence about which message he should declare that day.

We hear similarly contradictory messages about young people's level of passion. On the one hand, today's young people are touted as justice crusaders devoted to helping those who are poor or marginalized. They are portrayed as selfless revolutionaries ready to change the world one dollar and social media post at a time. On the other hand, the very same cohort of young people is depicted as egotistical and entitled, motivated primarily by whatever best serves their pursuit of their own happiness.

Which is it? Are today's young people selfish or selfless?

Yes.

They are both. (Just like all of us.)

In previous FYI research, we asked 500 youth group seniors what they wished they had more of in youth group. Of the 13 options we provided, students' top answer was "time for deep conversation."

Second was mission trips.

Third was service projects.

Last was games.

Granted, these were high school seniors. A survey of seventh graders probably would have yielded a different hierarchy. Nonetheless, churchgoing teenagers seem inclined to be changed by Christ to change the world around them.

And yet all too often, this march to "save" the planet and its inhabitants gets tripped up. Outside of the faith community, by the time teenagers enter emerging adulthood, those still interested in changing the world appear to be in the minority. While many church leaders boast about how their young people are involved in service and justice, the best studies of young people in general leave less to shout about.

All too often, young people can't get their "dream job," or they find their dream job and get burned out. Or the job they thought was a dream job turns out to be a dead end. While almost 1 in 5 young people attempts to start or run a new business themselves,[30] the challenging vocational path that today's young people explore can easily lead to broad disillusionment and lethargy. Although the young people at churches that grow young are often less jaded, the majority of emerging adults in the US are either consumed by or disappointed with their own haphazard

"I had just recently moved to the city, and one of the pastors at our church went out of her way to get to know me. She connected with me every time I was at church. It meant a lot that someone who was in leadership cared about me as a post-college adult. It was so organic and informal that it took me a while to realize that it was happening." —Soo Yeon, age 23

journey. Consequently, they become jaded realists who don't believe their efforts can move the needle to help others.[31]

CULTURAL PLURALISM

As a result of immigration, the average US resident is more exposed to diverse cultures than ever before. By 2020, more than half of our country's children are expected to be part of a minority race or ethnic group.[32]

Like the US population in general, American Christians are becoming more diverse. Non-Hispanic whites now represent smaller shares of evangelical Protestants, mainline Protestants, and Roman Catholics than 10 years ago. Racial and ethnic minorities now comprise 41 percent of Roman Catholics (up from 35 percent in 2007), 24 percent of evangelical Protestants (up from 19 percent), and 14 percent of mainline Protestants (up from 9 percent).[33] This increase in racial and ethnic diversity in the US church is something to celebrate.

Because the influx of recent immigrants has skewed younger, the teenagers and emerging adults in your community are even more likely to have cross-cultural friendships.[34] Perhaps not coincidentally, virtually since birth, the value of cultural diversity is the air this generation has breathed.[35]

But this appreciation for diversity—meaning an appreciation of others who are different—can also devolve into pluralism, meaning an acceptance of different religious and value systems as equally valid.[36] It takes intellectual, social, and worldview maturity to be committed to one belief system while simultaneously recognizing the value of other belief systems. Not all young people (or adults) have this maturity.

Thus the initial burst toward purpose that comes from cross-cultural relationships degenerates into a social and religious inclusivity that thwarts young people's progress. Struggling in their exploration of a pluralistic culture that either implies or states explicitly that all belief systems are equally valid, many teenagers and emerging adults lack the motivation to share their faith with others. They lack a worldview or faith grand enough to encompass the nuanced and sometimes contradictory beliefs held by themselves and those they care about. Pluralism can become a slow drain on a young person's energy, emptying them of their passion to impact the world.

On the upside, in churches that grow young, the energy that teenagers and emerging adults pour into civil rights activism—one of the primary justice passions for young people today—often flows directly from their diverse friendships. It is typically a growing relationship with someone who is different—through their race, ethnicity, gender, or sexual preference—that motivates teenagers and emerging adults to march, give, and stand up for those they believe have been marginalized. Sometimes this activism is also grounded in a deep and biblically rooted conviction that reconciliation and social activism on behalf of marginalized groups advances Christ's kingdom on earth.

Case Study: A Church Growing Young Channels Young People's Need for Real Purpose in a Pluralistic World

For City Church in downtown Baltimore, ethnic diversity isn't a drain on the congregation's energy; it's one of their primary sparks.

Three years ago, Chapelgate Presbyterian Church, located in the city's suburbs, birthed the church plant. When confronted with a key question—*Is our primary goal as a congregation to grow as large as we can?*—Chapelgate resolved that while they wanted to grow, they would best grow young by launching a new congregation in an ethnically diverse downtown district.

The thriving church plant of 75 is now full of college students and young professionals from the neighborhood, as well as older adults drawn to the church's youthful spirit. At the heart of City Church beats a shared commitment to engage all of its members—whether entrepreneurs in their twenties and thirties or middle-aged parents in their forties and fifties—in purposeful ministry.

That purposeful ministry is grounded in the congregation's willingness to enter into and empathize with the pain of the city. By launching a community counseling center, the church is helping its neighbors navigate their social and emotional struggles. By serving in community outreach as well as in church programs and worship, young people move past the jaded realism and entitlement that can otherwise thwart their search for purpose. The appeal of City Church is so strong that young people are actually moving into the downtown neighborhood or finding jobs nearby just so they can call the congregation home.

Keyanna, a full-time licensed professional counselor, uses her vocational skills to lead City Church's benevolence team and provide relief and support for neighbors in trouble. Under her leadership, the church empathetically offers those in dire circumstances both financial and emotional support.

As a major in family studies, Candice finds coordinating the church's children's ministry a logical outlet for her career passions.

Frank has an administrative job at the local college, so he values leading worship as his best chance to exercise his guitar and music muscles.

As Patrick, City Church's minister, explains, "All of these young people dabbled in ministry before, but they are now diving in fully. They have learned what it means to be part of a community and contribute to what God is doing in a grassroots way. Serving in our church has put their spiritual development on overdrive."

Ideas for Action

As you review the following ideas, perhaps make notes in the margin. Mark if the idea is a fit for your church, who should implement the idea (you or another leader), and whether it can happen now or later. Please don't try to do everything—instead, aim for two or three ideas that *you* can act on now. Then at the end of the chapter, use the strategic questions to guide your church toward a specific plan to empathize with today's young people.

Respond with Grace, Love, and Mission

As academics, we try to lay aside our biases while conducting research, but we are going to let you in on a few biases we hold related to young people's search for identity, belonging, and purpose. They're strong ones. We believe the gospel, the Good News of Scripture, matters and offers the most profound answers to young people's three ultimate questions.

We think that young people's deepest questions about identity are best answered by God's *grace*.

We are convinced that teenagers' and emerging adults' need to belong is ultimately met through the unconditional *love* of community.

We believe their hunger for purpose is satisfied by being involved in God's *mission* in the world.

Thus the table we initially presented on page 95 needs a new column.

Grace. Love. Mission. In many ways, these represent the crux of what we—and more importantly, Jesus—offer young people. Since the rest of this book often touches on these three themes, the tangible action steps in this chapter specifically focus on helping you empathize with this generation's trek toward—or sadly, often away from—good answers. But in the midst of your patient journey with teenagers and emerging adults, don't be afraid to point them to grace, love, and mission as God's best resolution to their often painful dilemmas. As you now consider how to best walk alongside young people, we urge you to keep these three generative themes in mind.

THE THREE ULTIMATE QUESTIONS

I'm wondering . . .	My ultimate question is about my . . .	The focus is on . . .	My question is best answered by God's . . .
Who am I?	Identity	Me	Grace
Where do I fit?	Belonging	Us	Love
What difference do I make?	Purpose	Our world	Mission

Rewind to Your Own Journey

It's hard for many of us to turn back the years in our memories, but each of us once lived through the teen and young adult stages. If you have access to your old yearbooks, pictures, videos, or journals from those seasons, take a few moments to peruse them.

What was your own quest for identity, belonging, and purpose like? What helped you surge ahead? What roadblocks slowed your progress? How can these memories increase your empathy for today's teenagers and young adults?

One leader who wants to help his church grow young keeps a picture of himself as a teenager displayed prominently in his

"I think about what I would have wanted in high school. Someone knowing my name and checking in with me would have been amazing." —Donya, youth ministry volunteer

office as a continual reminder of that awkward phase. As much as the three of us love young people, that's a bridge too far for us. But we hope his commitment and creativity inspire you to rewind to your own bumpy journey as a young person.

Stereotype No More

You or others in your congregation likely have stereotypes about young people. Perhaps . . .

An unemployed 24-year-old = lazy

A 19-year-old taking a "gap year" before starting college = noncommittal

An unmarried 26-year-old = loser

A 28-year-old living at home = codependent parents

Any teenager = rebel

As you hold up these stereotypes against the lengthened explorations of this generation of young people, they start to fade away. When you hear others in your church judging, try gently nudging them toward your growing understanding of identity, belonging, and purpose. If you realize you're the one doing the judging, put down your gavel and pick up an appreciation for the unique hurdles that teenagers and emerging adults face today. Consider having a conversation with a young person to better understand their choices and behaviors that feel foreign to you.

When You See Something New, Confusing, and Maybe Even Offensive in Culture, Ask Why

Hashtags. Selfies. Apps.
Metrosexual clothing.

Music so loud that you can't understand the lyrics. (That's okay, though, because you're pretty sure if you could, you'd be offended.)

At best, these pieces of youth culture are confusing to many of us over 30. At worst, they are downright annoying. But when you place any one of these pieces in the jigsaw puzzle of a young person's search for identity, belonging, and purpose, a different picture takes shape. Clothing choices are part of a young person's quest to explore and define themselves. Constant texting helps them stay connected to their community. Music captures the joys and laments of being young.

Immediately adjacent to almost every confusing cultural trend is a young person's quest for a meaningful relationship with themselves, their community, and the world. If you can't decipher the connection between their choices and the three ultimate questions, feel free to ask a young person to help you. Ask them why that trend is popular. Imagine with them how that fad is connected with identity, belonging, or purpose. That conversation alone could help your relationship with one young person, as well as your empathy for young people in general, leap forward.

Walk through Your Facility and Worship Service with the Eyes of a Young Person

"Time in erodes awareness of."[37]

This aphorism by pastor Andy Stanley captures how some of us have been part of our congregation for so long that we are blind to how it feels to guests. Especially if those guests are from a generation other than our own.

Your worship center may be the only place emerging adults visit where they are not allowed to bring coffee.

Your worship service may be the only time in the week of high school students when they are sung *at*. By adults. In robes.

We are *not* saying you should welcome clumsy coffee drinkers into your worship space. Nor are we implying that you should eliminate your choir.

We *are* saying we want you to empathize with how the church culture you've come to love feels to a first-time visitor, especially a young person. In the spirit of growing young, we hope you take a few steps to make your worship facility and service even more welcoming to young people.

Maybe you take a cue from a Colorado church that offers a cereal bar to middle schoolers and breakfast burritos to high school students.

Perhaps you swap out your uncomfortable Sunday school chairs for cozy couches and beanbags.

Even upgrading your coffee sends the message that you care about weary, caffeine-craving young people.

To figure out which changes make the most sense in your context, start in the parking lot and approach your church campus with the fresh eyes of a first-time young person. Walk your campus, imagining where young people feel accepted and where they feel misunderstood.

Since your church's online presence will often be a young person's first impression of your church, invite a teenager or emerging adult to sit next to you as you visit your church's website. Ask them to show you which portions of your website draw them in, as well as which create distance.

Odds are good that the insights you glean that would make your church culture more hospitable for young people will make all generations feel more at home.

Learn the Name of One Young Person . . . or Two . . . or Even Three

Teenagers and emerging adults want to be known. As we seek to become more empathetic, knowing their name is low-hanging fruit. Every time you show up to church for the next month, make an effort to learn the name of one new young person, with a goal of saying it to them the following week. Bonus points if you remember their name two or three months from now.

Dive Deeper with One Young Person

Understanding identity, belonging, and purpose helps you empathize with the currents and waves navigated by teenagers and emerging adults as a whole. But you will likely stay in the shallow end until you build a quality relationship with *one specific young person.*

Your niece. Your neighbor. Your neighborhood barista.

If you are stuck and can't think of anyone, ask a leader at your church if there's someone they recommend based on a shared hobby (computers, gardening, cooking Thai food) or overlapping vocational interests.

When you meet with that teenager or emerging adult, let them know that you want to understand their world. If you feel out of touch with youth culture, or even culture overall, admit it. Ask them to help you. And thank them repeatedly.

"I grew up in a fatherless home and so I never saw what a biblical dad looked like. But a man in my church invited me to spend time with him. I was able to go over to his house and watch how he would love on his wife and his children. I feel like I can go to him and share my struggles with him. The way he loves me for who I am gives me a picture of what God is." —Keith, age 24

Huddle Regularly with a Few Young People

One of the members of our Pastor Advisory Council meets every four weeks with the same group of high school students. It's his monthly opportunity to ask questions about trends in youth culture, as well as hear how they feel about what's happening in the congregation and even his own preaching. This astute leader is quick to admit that he learns far more from them than they from him.

Don't Leave Singles Feeling Singled Out

In the past, churches and parishes could offer programs for high school students, college students, and young married couples to cover the developmental stages of 15- to 29-year-olds. But thinking in terms of only these three demographic categories leaves holes in our ministry offerings today. Extended adolescence means there's a new gap between college and marriage that most congregations ignore. We often blame folks in their twenties for not being involved in our churches, but the reality is that we aren't offering much (or anything) for single adults that age. Rather than feeling noticed and welcomed, they feel overlooked or somehow inferior.

Empathizing with extended adolescence doesn't mean you have to launch a full-blown emerging adults or singles program. Instead, invite some emerging adults (perhaps both single and married) into your living room for a meal or to a nearby restaurant to watch the upcoming big game. Ask them what it feels like to be single in your church. Creatively connect them with people from other demographics. See what unfolds naturally as single and married young people get to know you and each other. When it comes to ministry with single emerging adults, slow and organic is usually best.

Support Marriages . . . Tangibly

Most churches' marriage support can best be described as a few premarital classes, an annual seminar (typically attended by couples who need it the least), and a fairly competent wedding coordinator. Churches growing young in our study took a few small steps—and sometimes a few large leaps—beyond that norm.

They paired up engaged and married couples with older mentor couples.

They offered premarital groups, not just classes, to provide both training and supportive long-term community.

They even offered scholarships for couples to attend therapy together at local professional counseling centers.

The average age at which young people wed is certainly getting later, but empathetic congregations are primed and ready to provide effective support—if and when those wedding bells ring.

Chapter Highlights

- Churches grow young by empathizing, or *feeling with*, this generation of young people.

- Young people wrestle with three ultimate questions: Who am I? (a question of *identity*), Where do I fit? (a question of *belonging*), and What difference do I make? (a question of *purpose*).

- While these questions are not unique to young people, teenagers and emerging adults generally feel them more intensely than older generations.

- Now that adolescence has been extended and young people are in a longer season of exploration, 25 feels like the new

15, and 15 often seems like the new 25. Their journey has both an earlier starting line and a later finish line.

- Young people's search for identity is made erratic by their pervasive stress and their peripheral faith.

- Teenagers' and emerging adults' quest for belonging is thwarted by omnipresent technology, sexual experimentation, and adult abandonment.

- This generation's hunger for purpose remains unsatisfied because of their jaded realism and cultural pluralism.

Strategic Questions to Help You Empathize with Today's Young People

Research Findings

On a scale of 1 to 5 (with 1 being "we're struggling here" and 5 being "we're nailing this"), rate your congregation on the research findings presented in this chapter:

1. Our congregation is patient with young people in the midst of their extended adolescence.

1   2   3   4   5

2. Our congregation understands the pervasive stress and peripheral religion that stall young people's search for identity.

1   2   3   4   5

3. Our congregation recognizes the digital technology, sexual experimentation, and adult abandonment that handicap this generation's quest for belonging.

1   2   3   4   5

4. Our congregation grasps the jaded realism and cultural pluralism that obstruct young people's path toward purpose.

1 .... 2 .... 3 .... 4 5

5. Our congregation knows how to empathize with today's teenagers and emerging adults.

1 .... 2 .... 3 .... 4 5

Ideas for Action

1. What are you personally already doing to empathize with present-day teenagers and emerging adults?

2. In what practical ways is your congregation already empathizing with this generation of young people? What gets in the way of your empathizing with this generation?

3. Given your ranking of the findings in the previous section, as well as the ideas you've read in this chapter, what one or two shifts might you or your church want to make?

4. Who else needs to be part of this conversation?

5. What can you do in the next few weeks or months to move toward these changes?

4. Take Jesus' Message Seriously

What's Young about the Good News

Yeah, I think the goal for our church is not really effectiveness with young people but serving and following Jesus. And young people like me are attracted to churches that want to do that.

—Adam, age 26

Darren wasn't sure why the Jacobsen family wanted to meet with him. But when both parents, their daughter Janeen, and her boyfriend, Edgar, filed silently and grimly into his office, the pastor had a pretty good guess.

Janeen was pregnant.

Janeen's parents had been pillars of the church for ages, so she was well known in the congregation. Her parents pressed marriage. At 18 and 19 years old, neither Janeen nor Edgar wanted to marry right away, but they also didn't consider abortion an option. They talked about placing the child for adoption.

After an intense hour, Darren scheduled a follow-up meeting with just Janeen and Edgar, suggesting they continue their dialogue. The three met regularly to explore Scripture and discuss its teachings about both marriage and parenting, "just in case."

During one conversation, Janeen asked, "What do we do when I start showing?" Their pastor responded, "Why don't you tell the church?" At first both young people shut down this idea. Darren wisely let them sit with the question on their own.

A few weeks later, the couple sat facing him again. Edgar spoke first. "We want to tell you two things. First, we're getting married. Second, we want to tell the church everything." *The whole congregation.* Darren was surprised but grateful. He was already on board with their plan.

After an initial meeting with the church elders—who were incredibly gracious and encouraging—Janeen and Edgar found themselves standing before the congregation. That Sunday morning they were nervous, but they were not alone. Darren stood between them, his arms around their shoulders as the couple shared the news of the baby, as well as their upcoming marriage. The congregation surrounded them with support not only in that moment but also in the weeks and months to come.

A surprise baby shower from their small group.

A surprise wedding reception from her parents' small group.

Reflecting back on that season, the pastor commented, "No one wondered if supporting the couple would encourage other girls to get pregnant. People were just filled with gratitude to be part of such a community of grace."

That gracious support extended to the baby boy who arrived a few months later. It also extended to others who felt safe enough to share their own secret pain and brokenness because of the way ministry leaders had loved Janeen and Edgar.

Two years later, Janeen, Edgar, and their son are a vibrant part of this congregation growing young. When we visited, people shared the family's story as a marker of how the church embodies Jesus' message—not a story of shame but of redemption. Not a narrative of being cast out based on sin but one of being embraced and restored. One parent of teenagers in the congregation reflected, "Here it is not all about being perfect. That is what we loved when we were looking for a church. We said, 'Our kids are going to screw up. How are we going to be treated when they do?' We want our kids to be in a place where God's people say, 'Okay, you messed up. What now?' Not a place that says, 'You messed up and we don't know what to do with you. You might be better off someplace else.'"

This is a congregation following Jesus earnestly today.

The Jesus who did not condemn but set free.

The Jesus who took what seemed broken and restored wholeness.

The Jesus who invited followers into a life of discipleship that required sacrifice.

CORE COMMITMENT:
TAKE JESUS' MESSAGE SERIOUSLY

The Jesus who embodied the fullness of God's unconditional love and unending faithfulness.

The teenagers and emerging adults you know face a long list of obstacles that threaten to hinder their pursuit of Jesus, including not only our pluralistic culture and their own extended adolescent journey but also churches drained by a thin gospel.

But in churches growing young, Jesus reigns over poor theology, and his words ring true for young sojourners hungry for life-giving direction. Proclaiming Jesus as the centerpiece of the story of God and seeking to live out his message in everyday relationships, these churches are reclaiming the very heart of the Good News. One church growing young captures this proclamation through a mantra. Nearly everyone we interviewed—young and old—repeated, "People are our heart; Jesus is our message." This is the foundation of their ministry.

Our team was struck by how the commitment to take Jesus' message seriously is both a demonstrated action and an overall spirit or ethos in churches growing young. Of course, Jesus' message is not contained in just one core commitment; rather,

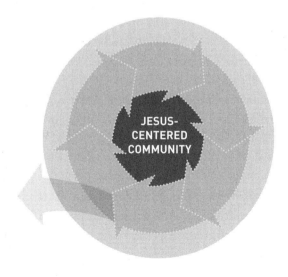

the Good News of Jesus permeates and indeed *animates* all other commitments. Just as Jesus is "before all things, and in him all things hold together" (Col. 1:17), pursuing *Jesus*—not just pursuing young people—is the heart of churches growing young. As we mentioned in chapter 1, we could imagine the entire set of core commitments orbiting around the basic commitment to a Jesus-centered community.

Research Findings

Moralistic Therapeutic Deism Still Threatens to Distract Young People from Jesus

You might have heard less-than-inspiring news about the faith of today's young people.

"American young people are, theoretically, fine with religious faith—but it does not concern them very much, and it is not durable enough to survive long after they graduate from high school."[1]

These stinging words from practical theologian (and project advisor) Kenda Creasy Dean sum up one of the central findings of the National Study of Youth and Religion (NSYR). Sifting through hundreds of discussions with American teenagers, researchers identified the dominant, de facto religious belief system of teenagers today as *moralistic therapeutic deism*.

It is *moralistic*, meaning that religious young people equate faith with being a good, moral person (generally, being *nice*).

It is *therapeutic*, so faith becomes a means of feeling better about themselves.

And it is *deistic*, meaning God exists, but this God is not involved in human affairs with any regularity.[2]

Thanks to moralistic therapeutic deism, or MTD for short, God has essentially become a heavenly butler for teenagers,

Is MTD a result of poor understanding, or do we just do a good job teaching a poor version of the gospel?

Research suggests it's likely *both*. Developmentally, adolescents are perfect candidates for MTD. Their concrete (though becoming increasingly abstract) thinking leads them to focus on behaviors, and their self-focus causes them to think both that others exist to make their lives more pleasant and that God doesn't need to be actively involved in their world. But on the other hand, parents and significant adults are the greatest influence on young people's faith, including the language they use to talk about faith. Teenagers are much more likely to mirror back flawed teaching than to mutate sound theology into something with an altogether different meaning.

inspiring them at best to become cordial to others. While a more passionate faith would provide young people with the anchor they need to ground their identity in Christ, this halfhearted religious worldview leaves teenagers and emerging adults adrift in a ho-hum sea of bland religious niceness.

When we asked all 535 interview participants from churches growing young to describe their faith, we found a much more robust gospel. Among 19- to 23-year-olds in particular (as we will see shortly), the message of Jesus trumps the MTD gospel. However, it *is* true that high schoolers in our study are more likely to talk about the gospel in terms akin to MTD than other groups. High school–aged respondents refer more to the general idea of "doing good," and they describe God in deistic terms more often than other age groups. Further, only 1 out of 5 of the teenagers we surveyed used relational language when describing the message of Jesus. The following cringe-worthy interview excerpt illustrates this mixture of behavior-based faith well:

> The central message of the gospel is that someone is always there for you and that there are many different paths you can take but ultimately they lead to the same thing, which is heaven. I feel like there are many good things you can do and many bad things you can do, but no matter what, you are always going to be forgiven. Even if you think something is unforgivable, God is like this magic person that can always cure it and can make it okay. And there is always going to be a happy place even when you are in your darkest of darks. There is always going to be a light that is there for you. (Alyssa, age 18)

Notice a few features of Alyssa's description of the gospel: it is fairly universalist, focused on an abstract notion of "heaven" (or "a happy place," or "light") off in the distance; it describes grace like some kind of vague magic performed by a mystic fairy godmother figure (another high schooler similarly described God as someone "like the ice cream man"); and it fails to mention Jesus and his life, suffering, death, and resurrection.

How do theological differences affect our understanding of the gospel of Jesus?

We studied a breadth of Christian traditions, from Roman Catholics to Southern Baptists, in our search to find churches growing young. We would be naïve to think everyone will read or interpret the findings in this chapter the same. By writing to a broad audience, we hope you can locate your tradition within the frameworks and stories shared here while realizing that we tried to represent accurately the particular nuances of faith represented in particular congregations.

But before we blame teenagers like Alyssa for this weak gospel, let's look in the mirror. The NSYR and our own research suggest that Alyssa didn't make this gospel up out of thin air. She has likely been breathing the tainted fumes of an ambiguous behavior-based gospel all her life. Dean refuses to let us off the hook by reminding leaders, parents, grandparents, and congregation members, "And one more thing: We're responsible."[3]

Teenagers and emerging adults in America are not devising this tepid faith on their own. They are not substituting moralistic therapeutic deism for the messages they hear and the modeling they see in churches today. Instead, they are mimicking a tame version of faith that permeates both their churches and their homes. In a fascinating twist, missiologist George Hunter used the exact same phrase, moralistic therapeutic deism (with an added prefix: *consumerist*), to describe the general milieu of *adult* Christianity in America *half a decade before the first NSYR results emerged*.[4] So rather than shake our heads in disapproval at faith like Alyssa's, we need to let these repeated descriptions invite us to place our own understanding of the Good News under a magnifying glass.

The Golden Rule Gospel Is Also Toxic to Faith

A corollary to MTD is the Golden Rule gospel, generally relayed as some version of "Do to others as you would have them do to you" (Luke 6:31). In looking at young people's tendencies to reflect Golden Rule language or themes, we found that those who profess this gospel show less faith maturity in general. More specifically, they tend to read the Bible less, attend worship less, talk less with others about their faith questions and struggles, and respond less to social issues in light of faith. The passion generated by Golden Rule faith is lukewarm at best.

How do Scripture's commands to obey God and live holy lives fit with all this concern about avoiding a behavior-focused gospel?

Both moralistic therapeutic deism and Golden Rule Christianity are flawed because of their overemphasis on behaviors. But by suggesting these two belief systems are inadequate versions of Christian faith, we are not promoting the divorce of morality or faithful obedience from spirituality. Following Jesus certainly affects our behavior. What separates *biblically* rooted obedience from *behaviorally* rooted obedience is our motivation and the work of the Spirit. We can be driven by the defective notion that it's possible to work to please God or earn salvation, or we can act morally as a response to grace and the transformation of God. We will explore alternatives for inviting young people toward obedience later in the "Ideas for Action" section, and chapter 7 profiles how churches like yours can energize teenagers and emerging adults through the related roles of service, social justice, and vocation.

Congregational studies expert Nancy Ammerman helps give more context to these findings by describing Golden Rule Christianity as emphasizing "right living" rather than "right believing." Ammerman has found this focus on good deeds most prevalent in mainline Protestant and Roman Catholic congregations, as well as in predominantly middle-class, suburban, and White communities. Ammerman sums up the practice of Golden Rule religion in this way:

> Most important to Golden Rule Christians is care for relationships, doing good deeds, and looking for opportunities to provide care and comfort for people in need. Their goal is neither changing another's beliefs nor changing the whole political system. They would like the world to be a bit better for their having inhabited it, but they harbor no dreams of grand revolutions.[5]

At a surface level, this faith doesn't seem too alarming. These believers want to help others, and in many cases they practice hospitality and care for those around them in ways that put some more spiritually vibrant congregations to shame. After all, right believing without right living is no good news either. But the root of this version of Golden Rule faith isn't really faith at all: it's behavioralism. God is found through good behaviors, and along the way we learn to tolerate and embrace those who are different, at least in theory. It takes "nice" a step closer toward kindness and even solidarity but stops short of the transformative neighbor love that is undergirded by grace.

Most disturbingly, Jesus is largely absent from the picture.

A More Robust Gospel Is Emerging in Churches That Grow Young

Encouragingly, while there are traces of a behavior-based gospel even in churches growing young, they are fainter than we feared. Only about 11 percent of high school–age students, and less than 5 percent of either college-age or 24- to 29-year-olds gave a Golden Rule–themed response. Further, behavior-based descriptions of the gospel overall account for just over 10 percent of total interview responses among leaders, parents, and young people combined.

As a research team, we were especially impressed with the responses of emerging adults, who proved as articulate as older adults in their descriptions of faith. Here's a sampling of what they had to say about Jesus' message:

> The surprise ending is that the gospel ends with Jesus losing, but in reality losing is winning. I think that is the most fundamental—the most basic—telling of the gospel, that our hero essentially lost. But in losing, he won. (Tamara, age 25)

There is nothing that you have done that makes you unlovable or unforgivable in God's eyes. This man Jesus—he came to tell us that it is not about being the cleanest, shiniest-looking person on the outside. He cares about the hurt in your heart and is able to hold that and walk with you through it. Ultimately, he died for everyone's sin, so the weight of this world is not so heavy on our shoulders. (Armen, age 21)

Across all age groups, one corollary of both vibrancy and faith maturity in our study was the characteristic "Understanding that faith is about more than behaviors or following rules." As congregation members rated their church higher on this characteristic, faith maturity and vibrancy rose too. The more entire congregations move past the superficial teaching of the Golden Rule gospel and MTD, the more everybody flourishes.

Churches growing young are eschewing behavior-based gospels like MTD and the Golden Rule by making three key shifts in how they describe the message of Jesus:

Shift 1: Less talk about abstract beliefs and more talk about Jesus. Instead of simply agreeing with abstract theological truths, young people are drawn to the person and work of Jesus Christ.

Shift 2: Less tied to formulas and more focused on a redemptive narrative. Rather than insist the Good News is about specific words or linear steps to obtain salvation, young people use story language to describe God's work in the world.

Shift 3: Less about heaven later and more about life here and now. Salvation means more to young people than the assurance of heaven later; it also invites us into a new way of life in the present.

This emphasis on Jesus, a bigger story, and life today means that the central message in churches growing young isn't your grandmother's gospel.

We love grandmas. We have loved our own grandmas, and if we met yours, we'd probably love her too. When we say "grandmother's gospel," we're not suggesting that Grandma had it all wrong. She just might not completely resonate with the faith we discovered among young people in our study.

Let's now flesh out these three important shifts in how young people are talking about Jesus and how taking his message seriously improves how we engage teenagers and emerging adults.

SHIFT 1: LESS TALK ABOUT ABSTRACT BELIEFS AND MORE TALK ABOUT JESUS

Interviewer: On a scale of 1 to 5, how true is it that your church helps people know and understand the gospel, or Good News, of Christianity?

Participant: Of Christianity or Jesus?

Interviewer: Of Christianity.

Participant: Well, Christianity is the name that we gave to the gospel of Jesus. So I don't like the question. Sorry! I get what you mean by the "Good News of the gospel." But it is not *of* Christianity. It is of Jesus Christ who is the Son of God. And it is not Christianity that brings the Good News. It is Jesus. So as followers of Jesus, we bring the Good News. But "Christianity" itself is a convoluted term, and it can be really harmful in the world. So I don't want to say that our church is trying to preach a gospel of Christianity.

Is this twenty-something parsing terms more critically than necessary? Perhaps. But clarity of language is important to many young people. They want to know the meaning of tradition-laden religious terms and to dig up the soil around them to rediscover the roots of what Jesus said and did. The Good News *of Jesus Christ*, nothing less, is what young people want to take seriously.

When young people and adults in churches growing young talk about the gospel, nearly 7 out of 10 specifically mention Jesus.[6] Most of those who talk about Jesus mention Jesus' role in salvation or Jesus as God's Son. We also heard descriptions of Jesus' work as *restoring*, *liberating*, *freeing*, and *making new*.

Also quite telling, when we coded responses that did *not* mention Jesus, the three most common themes were *moralistic*, *therapeutic*, and *deistic*. So it seems that the Jesus-focused gospel not only is more prevalent than MTD in churches growing young but also clearly stands in contrast to it. This is news we can cheer.

But that doesn't mean talking about Jesus is easy. Or universal. If 7 out of 10 mentioned Jesus, it also means 3 out of 10 didn't. Further, simply *mentioning* Jesus does not equate with understanding Scripture's portrayal of who Jesus was and what he did.[7] Nor is it the same as following him today.

So whether you're encouraged or discouraged by our findings, we propose that the centrality of Jesus in nearly 70 percent of respondents' descriptions of the gospel offers congregational leaders both clarity and hope.[8] Jesus is compelling, and the vast majority of young people in churches growing young want to talk about him. While the language and accessories of Christian religion in America might be waning, Jesus is no less of a beckoning figure on the horizon.

SHIFT 2: LESS TIED TO FORMULAS AND MORE FOCUSED ON A REDEMPTIVE NARRATIVE

With all this talk about the importance of Jesus, you might wonder about the role of God the Father and God the Holy Spirit. By suggesting we focus more on Jesus, we're not suggesting omitting the other two members of the Trinity. Every distinctively Christian denomination holds the doctrine of the Trinity as an orthodox essential, though our language may skew toward God the Father, Son, or Holy Spirit based on our tradition.

Nor should we ignore the entirety of the Old Testament. By placing Jesus at the center of the story of God, we open an entryway through which young people can discover an enormous house of faith. Within its walls they find a massive and complex floor plan, its corridors and chambers containing storied histories that, when combined, tell a surprisingly coherent family account of an unlikely clan and the God who refuses to abandon them to their own ruin.

That clan is our clan. But for many young people like Janeen and Edgar, this story is disjointed. The Bible and its numerous books feel more like a random puzzle fit for Ancient Lit 401 than a family scrapbook that both unveils our roots and foreshadows our future hope.

One 16-year-old Asian American boy grasped this family story deeply. Speaking vulnerably while sitting among a circle of peers, he choked up as he shared, "God is the Creator of the universe; he made everything. And he not only wants to be your friend . . . *he wants to be your Father.*"

Because Jesus' message best makes sense when it's understood as part of a larger story, the role of narrative theology and narrative teaching has been reemerging of late, and this trend is a hopeful one for churches like yours. By *narrative theology*, we mean interpreting each part of the Bible within the whole unfolding story of God and God's people. *Narrative teaching* is closely related in that leaders locate particular texts in the context of the whole story.[9] Everywhere from the pulpit to children's ministry, leaders we studied are tapping into the power of narrative to shape congregational imaginations.

"In the past God spoke to our ancestors through the prophets at many times and in various ways, but in these last days he has spoken to us by his Son, whom he appointed heir of all things, and through whom also he made the universe. The Son is the radiance of God's glory and the exact representation of his being, sustaining all things by his powerful word." —Hebrews 1:1–3

When a people can see their story located within God's story, the work of the church gains greater meaning.[10]

According to our research, churches that communicate the gospel of Jesus as the centerpiece of God's story are more likely to have young people with greater faith vibrancy and maturity. What's more, those who talk about the gospel in narrative terms also tend to rate their churches higher on teaching people how to interact with culture, and they rate themselves personally higher on responding to current social issues in light of faith. It may be that interacting with the story of Scripture increases a young person's ability and commitment to interact with the story of their culture.

Linked with this shift toward narrative is a step away from myopic spirituality. When interview participants were asked about the practices that most help build their faith, their responses split evenly between practices that take place in a group (47 percent) and those done individually (53 percent). A closer look reveals that when young people talk about their faith, they focus *less* on "me and my Bible" or "me and Jesus" in a manner that ignores the world around them.

Instead, young people focus *more* on worship with others, communal small groups and Bible studies, and service in the neighborhood or around the world. Churches that take Jesus' message seriously emphasize an integrated, holistic spirituality.

SHIFT 3: LESS ABOUT HEAVEN LATER AND MORE ABOUT LIFE HERE AND NOW

A majority of people in churches growing young talked about here-and-now faith. There was very little focus on going to heaven and hardly any talk of hell. Salvation was a major theme, but a kind of salvation that is more focused on life in the present than something way off in the future. In other words, young people, leaders, and parents seem compelled by a faith that promises not only reward at the end but also transformation now, in everyday life.[11] One pastor of a multisite congregation summed this up well:

> The gospel reorients the way we look at all of life. That's our preaching paradigm, our language, and how we explain the heart issues behind why we do what we do. The gospel works itself into every nook and cranny of our lives; it is constantly messing with how we think about things. The gospel reorients how we view ourselves as neighbors, parents, and children.

These findings are refreshing. They remind us of Dallas Willard's insistence that taking Jesus seriously means that rather than succumbing to the gospel of "sin management" that mostly deals with reward when we die, we pay attention to real life, in this moment, in this place, with these people.[12] This gospel is not simply something from two thousand years ago or for two thousand years from now. It's for *today*. A church leader from the West Coast shared, "The gospel is not a moment or transaction; it is not even simply a message; it is actually a *new way of living*, a new reality that is intended to pervade everything in this life, and it has both present and eternal implications."

It's Not Just about Being Saved from, It's about Being Saved For

As parents, we are often tempted to give only nos and miss the opportunity for yes.

141

For example, rather than simply correct behavior like racing through the crowded church sanctuary with a "No running!" command, we might pair it with, "No running in the sanctuary right now, but you can run out on the playground." Or taking out the no altogether to redirect positively: "Let's walk inside and run outside."

Kids need to hear boundaried nos, of course, but too many restrictions without hopeful yeses create more than boundaries; they create identity, belonging, and purpose dead ends.

Similarly, some young people wonder whether Christianity is offering them anything to *do* or simply a list of things *not* to do. Don't do drugs. Don't have sex. Don't curse. Don't watch R-rated movies. Don't become a social liberal. Don't become a hyperconservative. The nos declare a boundary, but they don't provide a hopeful way toward a new vision for living.

Young people's resistance to a gospel presented as a list of nos is both fair and logical. Young people don't just want to be saved *from* something later; they want to be saved *for* something now. They want to get to work. They want to be significant. They want lives filled with action, not just restriction. Or as one volunteer of a 15-year-old church plant summed up their message to young people, "It's less, 'You're a sinner, change now,' and more, 'This is awesome, come be part of this!'"

The good news is that this is not only the kind of life young people want, *it's what Jesus wants too*. Following Jesus is costly, requires sacrifice, and invites us to actively participate in God's kingdom. In fact, the church by its very nature is participatory, which means everyone shares the work. It's a body (Rom. 12:5–8; 1 Cor. 12:1–31; Eph. 4:1–16), and every part needs to play its role in order to build up the whole. As indicated by Jesus' command to both "follow me" and "take up your cross

"I think many churches have fallen into a consumer mindset as a default mode. Churches have tried to appeal to people's desire to feel good. But the problem is, if you're just trying to make people feel good, church isn't going to measure up to that." —Terry, age 29

daily" (Luke 9:23), pursuing Jesus requires no less than every-thing, every day (Rom. 12:1). There's nothing therapeutic about that call.[13]

Challenge Is Not Something to Avoid

During interviews, 40 percent of young people specifically mentioned "challenge" when they talked about why their church is so effective with their age group. They appreciate challenging teaching in their church, even when it makes them feel uncomfortable and invites them to make changes based on Scripture's teachings. Contrary to popular thinking that young people today want it easy, many told us they love their church *because* their church inspires them to act. As chapter 2 revealed, keychain leaders who model authenticity and humil-ity extend the challenge of following Jesus not from a place of superiority or power but out of an invitation to pursue the way of Jesus together.

In short, teenagers and emerging adults in churches growing young aren't running from a gospel that requires hard things of them. They are running toward it.[14]

Evangelism Isn't Dead among Young People—It's Just Different than We Might Think

This new and pervasive gospel-centered living motivated 16-year-old Ian to take his Bible to school. He intended to use it at a Christian club meeting. Another student spotted

"Since my sophomore year of high school I've been texting my friend a Bible verse every night. I started at a time when her life was going downhill. I had no clue how to help her, so I just texted her a Bible verse every night. It has been 967 days, I think." —Keely, age 19

the book, however, and sensed an opportunity for fun. "I'll burn it!" he yelled, grabbing the Scriptures out of Ian's open backpack. He was kidding. Sort of.

Ian took a chance and pressed his classmate a bit by asking, "What *do* you believe in?" The student responded with anger, and the conversation ended abruptly.

Recalling the moment, Ian reflected, "It's hard. I know the gospel, but it's hard to know how to bring someone to faith." Others in the focus group chimed in. They shared that while sometimes it's discouraging to try to share their faith with others, their youth ministry talks about planting seeds and watering them, then letting God cause faith to grow. That process often takes a long time. Like other young people in our research, they were less concerned about convincing a friend (much less a stranger) to recite a formulaic prayer and more concerned about generating authentic dialogue about faith.

The word *evangelism* and its derivatives were hardly mentioned by young people in our study. Talking about faith with non-Christians was the least common practice among a list of variables related to faith maturity.[15] But that doesn't mean evangelism is dead. While fewer young people in our study are talking about faith with nonbelievers than we might hope, one of the characteristics most significantly related to gospel sharing is increased honesty about questions and struggles.

Perhaps it's not *certainty* that makes young people better evangelists but *honesty*.

Let that finding sink in for just a moment. It's not that teenagers and emerging adults simply want to avoid certainty but that questions—when articulated—open up deep exploration of both doubt *and* faith. What's critical is that the young people you know not walk alone through those canyons.

Not only is honesty correlated with sharing faith in our research, but those who are honest about struggles also tend to read the Bible more. Perhaps they are turning to Scripture to find answers to their tough questions. Or maybe the more they read the rich—and complex—teachings and stories of the Bible, the more questions emerge.

Evangelism among young people today is typically more about seeking understanding than about direct "conversion." In the past, evangelism often was taught to young people almost like a game they were trying to win by scoring salvation goals. Sometimes even in what's called "relational" evangelism, the relationship becomes reduced to the means through which salvation is won, diminishing friends to notches in a young person's evangelism belt. Rejecting this approach, the young people in our study share faith in a posture that communicates, "I get you, and I can walk with you as a witness of Christ without being intrusive or arrogant." This approach to evangelism is more multidimensional and less linear than many of us—young or old—have been taught.

Recently, I (Brad) had the opportunity to meet with a group of high school seniors from a local Christian school. Our conversation centered on processing doubts and struggles as part of Christian formation, and the students shared about an assignment their Bible teacher had given them to listen to the questions of people outside the faith. The students were instructed to have at least three conversations with someone who self-identified as either a non-Christian or a non-churchgoer. Each student had to ask their dialogue partner if they would be open to sharing which Bible passages or Christian beliefs were most troubling to them.

But there was a catch. The students were not allowed to share their faith overtly, to dispute the questions, or even to give answers. They were simply to listen well and then say, "Thanks for sharing." Afterward, each student picked one of the questions or objections, did some research, and wrote a response to help them better understand more of Scripture's teaching in those particular areas.

Overwhelmingly, the students said that their most important discovery was how powerful it was to actually *listen*. Not only did they learn more than if they had tried to give an immediate response, but once people realized that they truly were just going to listen, they were much less defensive and more eager to talk.

Many of yesterday's evangelism tactics sit like awkward lawn decorations in the front yard of American Christianity. While plastic pink flamingoes seemed attractive to our neighbors a few decades back, today we would only put them out on a dare (or to prank a friend). In the same way, suggesting to young people that they confront their friends with propositions about sin and separation from God often feels about as winsome as gaudy yard art.

And yet the Good News of Jesus and his in-breaking kingdom deserves a hearing with today's young people, as with every generation. While effective evangelistic approaches with this generation deserve more research and innovative experimentation, the early indicators seem to point to forming authentic relationships, being honest about our own questions, and listening well before we speak.

Ideas for Action

As you review the following ideas, perhaps make notes in the margin. Mark if the idea is a fit for your church, who should implement the idea (you or another leader), and whether it can happen now or later. Please don't try to do everything—instead, aim for two or three ideas that *you* can act on now. Then at the end of the chapter, use the strategic questions to guide your church toward a specific plan to take Jesus' message seriously.

Elevate Faith Education beyond an "Elementary School for Morals"

Often our youth and emerging adult ministries inherit the good, bad, and ugly theology ingrained in kids during their pre-school and elementary years. Well-meaning children's ministry leaders and volunteers want to make the gospel "practical" for kids. So they end up teaching every Bible story with a moral punch line, resulting in a behavior-based gospel that feels a lot more like a list of dos and don'ts we must follow to please God than an invitation to participate in a beautiful story of God's transformative grace.[16]

Lest we think this is only a children's ministry problem, the moral-behavior gospel lives on in youth and adult teaching as well. As the NSYR research discovered, formation across the congregation ends up being a lot like an elementary school for morals.[17] To help your church take Jesus' message seriously, evaluate the curriculum and teaching messages throughout your congregation—from children's through adult education, as well as the weekly sermon. Ask questions like:

- Do we let Bible narratives speak for themselves, or do we impose moral obligations or rules for people to follow?

- In what ways do we create space for wonder, questioning, and reflection on Scripture to aid self-discovery or group-discovery *processes* rather than teaching predetermined *points*?

- Like Paul, how do we couch specific moral teaching in reminders of God's grace and our identity in Christ? (Reread Paul's epistles for ample evidence of this pattern.)

- How does our teaching emphasize that it is the Holy Spirit's work to produce fruit of transformation in us rather than our own effort (Gal. 5:22–25)?

- How are our invitations to life change centered in a call to follow Jesus instead of a call to follow our own moral or political agendas?

Teach Creeds over Formulas

Moving beyond the formulaic gospel presentations of the past century does not mean we abandon the ancient creeds and prayers of the church. Quite the opposite. While young people want to talk about Jesus, they often have malformed images of who Jesus is and what his life, death, and resurrection mean. The early church faced the same problem and responded by forming creeds.

These creeds are not hip, they don't follow a catchy tune, and yes, they can sound like prescriptive dogma. But their ancient words remind us of the historical church that faithfully held the tension of Jesus as both fully God and fully human. Jesus' bodily life and resurrection testify to the one who "shall come again, with glory, to judge the quick and the dead; whose kingdom shall have no end," as the Nicene Creed declares.

Young people are often interested in exploring the earliest traditions of our faith, those chronologically closest to Jesus and the first-century church. A few examples of creeds to use in worship, discipleship, and other formation environments include:

- the Apostles' Creed
- the Nicene Creed
- the Lord's Prayer (Matt. 6:9–13; Luke 11:1–4)

- Pauline creeds and sayings from the early church, such as Ephesians 5:14; Philippians 2:5–11; 1 Timothy 3:16; and 2 Timothy 2:11–13
- creeds and prayers unique to your tradition

Try including creeds regularly in worship, investigating creeds one phrase at a time, comparing creeds to one another, or inviting young people to rewrite creeds in today's language.

Tie Each Part of Scripture into the Grand Narrative of God

Even as we teach the Bible regularly to teenagers and emerging adults like Edgar and Janeen, they may struggle with identifying how particular stories, teachings, or relationships fit within the whole. After all, the Bible looks like one book but is really a collection of dozens of books by a host of authors written over several centuries. The more we connect the dots for young people when we teach, the more a holistic story emerges.

This drama can be described in just a few movements or many.[18] While some traditions emphasize particular acts more than others, consider this basic narrative arc:

THE NARRATIVE ARC OF SCRIPTURE

Creation Fall Promise Slavery Exodus Law/Kingdom Exile Return Incarnation Church New Creation

One midwestern church in our study intentionally connects the dots from week to week in its youth ministry. Whenever students open the Bible together, the leaders display a simple slide that lists all of the books of the Bible, locates the passage within it, and shows how that book and passage fit within the larger story of Scripture. Here are some other ideas you might try:

- Teach straight through the Bible, through books of the Bible, or through the life of Jesus.

- Utilize the seasons of the church year (called the *liturgical calendar* in some traditions) to ground congregations in an annual cycle of the life, work, death, and resurrection of Jesus, and the coming of the Holy Spirit.[19]

- Develop a scope and sequence for how various ministries or the entire congregation move through the story of Scripture, or alternate among different theological emphases and scriptural stories. For example, we know youth ministries that have formed a one-, three-, or even seven-year teaching sequence to ensure they don't bounce around the Bible and inadvertently omit important parts of God's story.

Ground Moral Obedience in the Invitation of Grace

What's the role of obedience in the Christian life? How can we guide young people toward that obedience without reducing that message to mere moralistic obligation?

My (Kara's) favorite approach to explaining the role of obedience is related to the movements of Scripture, focused specifically on our relationship with God. Taking the basic "guilt—grace—gratitude" model of the Heidelberg Catechism from Reformed theology,[20] we have added a few movements to help articulate how grace and our action work together. We teach this model with adults and young people alike.

- *Good* (Gen. 1:26–27): God created us good, in God's image.

- *Guilt* (Rom. 3:10–12): We then chose to disobey God, leaving us with the guilt of sin. All of us carry this mark and it impacts us every day.

- *Grace* (Rom. 3:23–24; Eph. 2:6–10): Through the life, death, and resurrection of Jesus, God has extended grace to us to make things right and restore us to relationship with God and one another.

- *God's People* (Eph. 2:19–22): As we experience grace, we are adopted into the body of Christ, enacting God's reign in the world. We join the mission of God, participating in the work of God happening in and through God's people today.

- *Gratitude* (Col. 2:6–7): Out of this gift of grace, we respond in gratitude toward God. *This* is the well out of which our obedience—which includes moral behaviors—flows. In other words, the gospel doesn't begin with behaviors nor is it dependent on behaviors. The behaviors are an act of thanksgiving to God in response to grace. As we grow in trust, we naturally grow in obedience.

- *God's Vision* (Rev. 21:1–5): We are living in between Christ's first coming and his second coming, when he will make everything new. Service work and the ways we seek justice on behalf of the poor and oppressed are part of the in-between story of God's kingdom emerging right in front of us. We get to participate in something Jesus started and that ultimately Jesus will finish.

Locating obedience as a response to grace—not a prerequisite or alternative to grace—helps young people stand on more solid theological ground for their actions and decisions.

Ask Young People What They Believe

Think the young people in your church clearly understand the Good News of Jesus? You might be right. But if you haven't asked, it's hard to know.

Meet individually or in small groups with a few high school students, college-age emerging adults, and young adults in their late twenties. Invite them to describe the gospel to you as they understand it. You might use a question similar to one we asked: "What do you believe is the central message of the gospel (or Good News) of Christianity?" Or something like, "How would you describe your faith to others?"

Their responses can help you identify gaps in understanding and may inform how you teach, preach, or select curriculum in your congregation.

Model Sharing the Gospel without Judgment

"If you want a friend to know Jesus, our youth pastor won't take that friend out to pizza to talk to them about Jesus. He'll take *you* out to pizza to talk through how to talk to your friend about Jesus. He wants us to share naturally in our relationships, but he's not leaving us to figure that out on our own."

This high school junior in an urban church growing young articulated an approach to evangelism that has moved away from the attractional "bring friends to church and we'll take care of the rest" model and toward an organic relationship-based approach that trusts young people to share their own experiences and testimonies with their friends. Yet most young people aren't sure how to bear witness to their faith without seeming judgmental. Let's give them handholds by modeling how to engage nonbelievers through winsome and gentle means.

- In our teaching: Explore passages of Scripture that invite young people to follow Jesus' way without needing to know all of the "right" answers or do all of the "right" things.

- In one-on-one conversations: Listen well to young people's questions, invite deeper reflection, and share glimpses into our own faith journeys.

- In group discussions: Preserve the dignity of young people whose responses reveal a gap in their understanding of Scripture or the gospel.

- In our local service work: Invite young people who are not currently part of our church to participate in service and justice work, later explaining how the gospel and Scripture's teachings fuel our relationships with "the least of these" and help us encounter Jesus himself (Matt. 25:31–46).

As the apostle Peter urges, "Always be prepared to give an answer to everyone who asks you to give the reason for the hope that you have. But do this with gentleness and respect" (1 Pet. 3:15). We can practice this with the young people in our churches as much as with those who have never entered the doors.

Allow Salvation to Look More like a Journey

During much of the past few centuries, a great deal of evangelism has emphasized conversions like Paul's: dramatic, instantaneous, and featuring repentance from some "major" sin or sinful lifestyle. Yet in one study of teenagers, over two-thirds described a conversion experience that sounded a lot more like Peter's: slow, incremental, more getting it wrong than getting it right, and in need of ongoing grace.[21] One scholar suggests that throughout Mark, all 12 of Jesus' closest disciples are presented as in-process converts.[22]

> "There is never a time, even in just catching a meal with someone from our church, that the gospel doesn't come into the conversation. The quality of the conversation with people from my church is consistently Christ-centered. The gospel comes up everywhere." —Stacy, age 24

The young people in your church or community may respond less positively to the direct evangelistic approach of, "Will you receive Jesus as your Lord and Savior today?" or "Have you asked Jesus into your heart?" yet be very open to talking about questions like, "Where are you in your spiritual pilgrimage?" and "With what issues are you wrestling when it comes to God?"

Ask a handful of young people in your congregation whether they relate more to Peter's conversion or Paul's. Consider that for many emerging adults, salvation is more like a long, winding road than instant belief or "conversion."

Share Testimonies Frequently

As Immanuel Church of the Nazarene grew over the years, the leaders realized that the regular practice of sharing testimony to God's faithfulness was getting lost. God was no less active in this Philadelphia suburb or in the lives of the people in the congregation, but they needed a way to tell these stories. So nearly 20 years ago, a member built a lighthouse in the sanctuary that was lit whenever someone gave their life to Jesus. Over time the lighthouse was replaced with a lantern, and today the lantern is lit during worship whenever someone has made a decision to follow Christ.

When the current senior pastor began serving nearly a decade ago, a new ritual joined the lantern. A pile of stones sits at the front of the sanctuary on the altar. These stones serve as sym bols of answered prayers and signs of God's faithfulness. On any given Sunday, members can take a stone and add it to the pile on the altar. Some even bring their own rocks from home, carrying a physical reminder that God is on the move outside of the church walls. One member explained, "These traditions have helped all generations grasp our church's belief that we are a lighthouse and that God is faithful!"

Across traditions and denominations, churches growing young frequently integrate testimony as part of their regular worship and spiritual formation. These testimonies include conversion experiences, breakthroughs, the provision of new jobs, and stories of God's ongoing work in and around the people of the church.

Don't stop with congregation members' testimonies. We were struck on one of our parish visits that several of the young people we interviewed knew pieces of their priest's testimony of faith. It was clear that he shares elements of his journey—past and present—during his regular preaching. For those of us who are pastoral leaders, integrating our own stories into our teaching can powerfully connect with young people who look at us across decades and vastly different life experiences and wonder if we can relate to their everyday struggles.

Lean into the Potential of Rituals

We believe words matter. We wouldn't be writing this book otherwise. But we also share a conviction that rituals help us embody something more powerful than words. When it comes to counteracting moralistic therapeutic deism and Golden Rule Christianity, we not only need better teaching. We also need concrete actions that draw young people into a better story.

Rituals have served throughout Christian tradition as channels through which to answer deep questions of identity, belonging, and purpose with God's response of grace, love, and mission. Rituals embody meaning through actions that are often deeper than words alone can convey.

One church growing young determined from its founding that it would center weekly worship in the sharing of the Eucharist, or Lord's Supper. Hailing back to the tradition of the earliest churches (and the ongoing tradition of the Roman Catholic

Church and numerous others), the church suspected that sharing bread and wine together week after week would form them in profound ways that teaching alone could not accomplish.

Upon their 10-year anniversary, this congregation of under 200 asked for written reflections on the church and its impact on people's lives. Nearly 100 stories poured in. A through-line across those reflections was that the Eucharist had become not only a central act of worship but also the organizing narrative for life together. The congregation's stories unveiled the impact of this ritual on how young people viewed relationships, brokenness, their own stories and pain, and Jesus' work of healing and restoration.

Other meaningful rituals to embody faith in action include:

- baptism and subsequent rituals to help remember our baptism
- confirmation or membership rituals
- confession of sin—privately, in small groups, or publicly when appropriate
- seasonal rituals such as hanging greens during Advent or enacting the stations of the cross during Lent
- rituals marking particular developmental milestones or significant life experiences (for example, baby dedication, graduation from high school, engagement, marriage, or pregnancy)
- annual congregation-wide "birthday parties" to celebrate the new birth we collectively share in Christ

What are the rituals that have been especially important in your church or broader tradition? How could you tap into the significance of ritual even more? What new rituals (or old rituals that are new to your community) might add deeper layers to the formation of young people beyond word-based discipleship alone?

Embrace Young People's Doubts about Faith

In her investigation of what it takes to support emerging adult spirituality, Sharon Daloz Parks once asked a pastor, "Why do you think that so many young adults are present in your church?" His thoughtful response is one we might do well to emulate: "I think it is because we are willing to welcome a lot of questions."[23]

According to our Sticky Faith research, 7 out of 10 high school students harbor significant doubts about God and faith. Yet less than half of those students talk with either ministry leaders or peers about their struggles.[24] One of the factors that determines whether young people's doubts positively or negatively impact their faith development is if they have opportunities to express and explore doubts. When they do have those opportunities, doubt is actually correlated with greater faith maturity. As we at the Fuller Youth Institute have come to say, it's not doubt that's toxic to faith. It's silence.[25]

In your teaching, small group environments, or one-on-one mentoring relationships with young people, equip leaders to be sensitive to questions and doubts and to see them as faith-forming opportunities rather than freak-out moments of failure. Sometimes simply knowing that questions are part of the faith identity journey can be enough to quell young people's fears that their faith is falling apart. One pastor shared that their ministry team encourages young people, "'You need to make this your own. Express your doubts, ask questions, have a thinking faith.' That disarms young people's presuppositions about Christians and church leaders. We're pretty patient."

Ministry leaders and parents are occasionally caught off guard by a tough question from a teenager or young adult. When that happens, here are four words we recommend every parent, leader, and mentor keep handy in their back pocket for moments like these: "I don't know, but . . ."

We can complete that sentence with any number of helpful phrases to communicate that questions are not only allowed but even welcomed. *I don't know, but . . .*

> that's an important question.
> let's find out together.
> I wonder that too.
> I bet you're not the first person to ask that.
> who do you think we could ask about that?
> I wonder what stirred up that question just now?
> God is big enough to take that question.
> here's what I have experienced about God . . .
> thanks for sharing this with me.

You might, of course, have an answer to their question. Even if you do, though, it might be wise to step back and probe a bit before unleashing your "right" answer. Being heard can at times be as—or even more—important than the answer itself.

See Faithing and Churching as Work We All Do

Despite all the language about "passing faith down" or "transmitting faith to the next generation," faith isn't really an object we can possess or hand off to anyone. Nor is it a commodity that one generation "owns" more than any other.

Our Fuller colleague Steve Argue asserts that we can't simply hand faith to adolescents or emerging adults—they have to *birth* it through the work of the Holy Spirit. Leaders and

"The people in our church just let you be normal, and let you rage, and let you question, and let you intellectually interact with the space. That is so huge. No one had ever let me do that before! Or at least let me do it in grace, you know?" —Gina, age 26

trusted adults, then, are more like midwives in this process. If faith is a noun, then we might say *faithing* is an appropriate verb to describe this process of formation and meaning-making.[26] It is how we ask, reach, and doubt our way toward a mature faith identity.[27]

If we commit to bear with young people on a journey of faithing, perhaps *churching* is how we can talk about doing this together, following Jesus as a community discovering faith in our particular context day by day. So rather than assuming a young person is "losing" their faith when they doubt, struggle, or push back against our understanding of God and faith community, we welcome their angst as an opportunity for us to "church"—as a verb—together toward even deeper shared experiences of the living Spirit of God.

When we "faith" and "church" together, we teach young people like Janeen and Edgar not just *what* to believe but *how* to believe—and live out—the Good News. And we refuse to leave them alone in the process. Which sounds a lot like taking Jesus' message seriously.

Chapter Highlights

- Moralistic therapeutic deism (MTD) has been identified as a pervasive religious framework of adolescents and much of the US church. However, while high school–aged participants in our study exhibited signs of MTD coupled with Golden Rule Christianity, by and large churches growing young sidestep this pothole in their quest for a more robust faith.

- Taking Jesus' message seriously means churches pay attention to the life and words of Christ. Young people can then articulate a gospel that is less talk about beliefs and more talk about Jesus, less tied to formulas and more focused on redemptive narrative, and less about heaven later and more about life here and now.

- Young people want to know not only what they are saved *from* but also what they are saved *for*. They want to take action, not just hear about what they can't do. *Participation* and *challenge* are two central features of churches growing young.

- Evangelism isn't dead among young people, but it looks different than in the past century. Vital factors to help young people share faith today include building authentic relationships, listening well, and being honest about questions and doubts.

Strategic Questions to Help You Take Jesus' Message Seriously

Research Findings

On a scale of 1 to 5 (with 1 being "we're struggling here" and 5 being "we're nailing this"), rate your congregation on the research findings presented in this chapter:

1. Our congregation moves beyond the behavior-based gospel of moralistic therapeutic deism and the Golden Rule toward a more robust gospel.

   1 .... 2 .... 3 .... 4 5

2. We talk about Jesus more prominently than abstract truths about God, and we frequently tell stories of his life, death, and resurrection.

   1 .... 2 .... 3 .... 4 5

3. Our church allows young people to safely express doubts and struggles about faith.

1 · · · · · · · 2 · · · · · · · 3 · · · · · · · 4 · · · · · · · 5

4. Young people in our church hear invitations to put their faith into action rather than simply focus on what behaviors to avoid.

1 · · · · · · · 2 · · · · · · · 3 · · · · · · · 4 · · · · · · · 5

5. We frame evangelism in the context of authentic relationships and listening well to others.

1 · · · · · · · 2 · · · · · · · 3 · · · · · · · 4 · · · · · · · 5

Ideas for Action

1. What are you already doing to help your congregation take Jesus seriously?

2. What words and phrases does your congregation use to talk about Jesus, the gospel, and evangelism? How do young people respond to that language?

3. Given your ranking of the findings in the previous section, as well as the ideas you've read in this chapter, what one or two shifts might you or your church want to make?

4. Who else needs to be part of this conversation?

5. What can you do in the next few weeks or months to move toward these changes?

5. Fuel a Warm Community

Warm Is the New Cool

> I love my church. I think it is amazing. Everybody knows each other and we all care about each other. It's not, like, compartmentalized between generations or between different types of people. It is just like a big family. —Katie, age 20

Laurence became disillusioned with church somewhere in the middle of his sophomore year of college. Despite squeezing in church (most) every week while at a Christian university, something wasn't clicking. So Sunday by Sunday, he began drifting away.

Until he just quit.

The attraction that had once kept Laurence orbiting around both faith and the faith community dissolved, leaving him floating free.

For the next couple of years, Laurence would occasionally drop in on a worship service, usually sitting in the back, highly critical of every act of worship offered and word spoken. Until his fiancée moved to town, and together they decided it was time to pick up the search again. Since faith had been important in their relationship in the past, they sensed that finding a church community could reignite something they had lost.

A few months later, someone told them about a congregation that almost sounded like a secret. With little online presence or physical allure, this small community seemed to be found by word of mouth. Laurence and his fiancée gathered their courage and stepped cautiously into worship one Sunday, first walking in the wrong door of the ancient pink church building before winding through the halls and stairwell down to the right gathering in the basement. They were readily welcomed, took their seats in two rickety folding chairs, and experienced what Laurence would later describe as being caught up in a gravitational orbit. They felt drawn into this growing young faith community not only that morning but also for weeks and months to come.

It wasn't the preaching or teaching.

It certainly wasn't the building or the worship style.

It was the *life* shared among the congregation that drew them in.

It was the moment at the end of the service when the smiling older lady in the wheelchair mentioned the giving box. It was how a particular redheaded child grabbed an oversized portion of communion bread each week and dunked it to the bottom of the cup. It was the way honest petitions were shared during prayer by tearful twenty-somethings and eager seven-year-olds. It was the steady stream of invitations to meals in homes of caring adults who fed them as poor newlyweds-to-be.

For Laurence and his fiancée, every doxology the church sang, every long decision-making process, and even (or perhaps especially) every little imperfection in the worship service drew them ever closer to what they had been looking for all along: a home.

A place to belong.

CORE COMMITMENT:
FUEL A WARM COMMUNITY

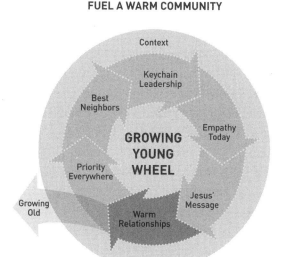

Laurence experienced a core commitment of churches growing young that our research clearly and emphatically identified as *warmth*. It's what you want your home to radiate to your family and friends. It's like sipping hot tea fireside with your spouse or close friend on a brisk winter evening.

We had a hunch at the start of our research that authentic community would be important to young people in your church and neighborhood. But we were surprised by how much of growing young is influenced by whether or not congregations are warm and accepting.

Research Findings

Why Structure Alone Isn't Enough to Grow Young

If you're like us, you have served in ministry settings in which you've wanted to boost relationships. So you created a small group program. You invited people to sign up for these communities, then clustered them together and set them free with a small group starter guide.

And it worked. For a few months.

But for the majority of people, those small groups felt forced and awkward. Either they never gained momentum or they started with a burst of energy that then dissolved. In both cases, the groups ended up dissolving too.

Why did this happen? After all, you offered a solid structure to create close, authentic community.

Structures are important.

They simply *are not enough*.

Our research indicates that leaders need to stop assuming that programs alone are going to foster close relationships.

In our analyses of the terms young people and adults use to describe their own churches or parishes, we noticed repeated words such as *welcoming, accepting, belonging, authentic, hospitable,* and *caring*. We began to call this the *warmth cluster*. Across the board in statistical analyses, the warmth cluster emerged as a stronger variable than any one program. And while 6 out of 10 interviewees mentioned group practices like small groups, youth group, and retreats when they talked about why their church is thriving, what seems important about those practices is that they create space for people to be together and nurture relationships.

So should your congregation develop a small group structure that works? Absolutely. Just be careful not to depend on small groups themselves to remedy the social isolation often felt by teenagers and emerging adults. Nor can you rely on whole-church events. Or put all your eggs in the basket of age- and stage-based programming. Warmth often lives much deeper than your programs and structures—it's the lifeblood coursing through the veins of your church body.

"Warmth resonates, especially doing ministry in an urban context. For kids growing up without biological fathers or being raised by an aunt or in foster care, the church has to stand in the gap and be family. That means much more than a programmatic approach. Young people have to experience, 'This is where I belong, where I'm affirmed, where I'm pushed and held accountable.' This is a hopeful finding for a small church in the inner city or a rural area. You too can make a significant difference with young people. You can get in the game." —Efrem Smith, World Impact

Ironically, it is possible that your church actually might be working against warmth by offering a myriad of programs. In churches growing young, many young people shared that their church culture is moving away from unnecessary busyness. A deprogramming strategy sometimes helps to elevate relationships by opening up time and space where they can flourish. Young people can then do life together through shared meals, shared transportation, shared service in the community, or shared child-care. In churches growing young, warmth trumps programs.

When asked which age group their church is most effective in reaching, respondents in our study named college-age students less often than teenagers or adults from ages 24 to 29. Yet when those ages 19 to 23 who *are* connected to a church were asked why they stay involved, 45 percent pointed to personal relationships (nearly doubling the response rate of adults over age 30), *not programs.*

Warm Is the New Cool: Authenticity Trumps Worship Style

When someone says the name of your church, what image comes to your mind?

A building?

A worship service?

If you were a teenager or emerging adult in one of the churches in our study, your answer might be different. For young people today, church means much more than a worship service or a place to gather. Despite how much energy, money, and other resources we pour into making Sunday spectacular, the worship service may be less important to young people than we think.

When we asked young people how they would describe their church to a friend, only 12 percent talked about worship, and only 9 percent mentioned worship style.

Similarly, when we asked, "What makes your church effective with young people?" only a quarter mentioned worship at all, and only 12 percent mentioned anything about music (that figure dropped to only 3 percent when we isolated the top third of churches most effective with young people).

So what *do* they talk about when they describe their church? Overwhelmingly, nearly 1 in 3 share about its *warmth*. Also telling, in evaluating church effectiveness with young people, twice as many pastors as young people name worship music as a vital factor. This reflects a gap between what pastors think young people care about and what they actually care about. One pastor who understands this gap confessed, "We can hire and buy cool, but we can't hire—or fake—warmth." Cultivation of warmth requires much more than staffing or planning in order to attract young people to your services.

In site visits, we couldn't help but notice that some churches are moving away from the models of attractional worship and highly polished, timed-to-the-minute experiences. More than one research team noted that what a particular church lacks in physical resources or flashiness, it makes up in warmth, authenticity, and hospitality. As it turns out, *warm* is indeed the new *cool*.

However, these statistics don't mean that worship planning no longer matters. It may be that for young people, worship is a potential turnoff but not necessarily a turn-on. In other words, our worship style or elements of our service may have potential to repel young people or prevent youth engagement, but simply making our music better does not seem to ensure their involvement.

Or as one young person at The District Church in Washington, DC, shared, it's one thing to watch a worship performance—you can just do that online. In contrast, "The internet can't help you move to your new apartment. Only a close community will do that." Well said.

Warmth Is in the DNA of the Church Family

By suggesting that churches need to grow warmer, we don't mean adults should be nice to young people. Nice does not cut it. It isn't how Jesus responded to people, and it falls short of the depth we saw in congregations.

Warmth is more than superficial community. It's like family. In fact, the phrase "like family" surfaced as the most common term young people used to describe their church in our interviews and field visits. One youth ministry volunteer explained, "This is life. It's not just church life, it's *life* life. It's hard, it's busy, but we're in it together. We're like a family." A high school senior shared, "This is family here. It's natural, I guess."

This metaphor of family is rich with images of hospitality, welcome, and unconditional acceptance, all of which emerged in church descriptions. This shouldn't really surprise us, given the developmental need of young people to discover where and with whom they belong (see chapter 3). It turns out that they are looking for warmth not as an add-on but in their church's very DNA.

The warmth young people seek isn't usually clean and tidy. That's just fine, because family isn't neat. It's messy. And *messy* is a good word to describe what young people want from a congregation. They desire not only to share their own messiness but also to walk alongside the authentic messiness of others.

Warmth Helps Young People Find—and Stick with—a Church

As young people are choosing a church, warm community is often a stronger draw than belief. When we asked what keeps people involved in their church, the highest response was personal relationships (named by 1 out of 3), and warmth was almost equally mentioned. In fact, beliefs comprised only 6 percent of responses—and more telling, 12 percent of leaders but only 3 percent of young people mentioned beliefs.

In other words, you may think young people are staying because of beliefs, but it's more often about finding an experience

This experience of being enfolded into a family echoes the ancient Christian practice of *hospitality*. Much more than our thin image of welcoming people who may share our life stage or interests into our homes and communities, hospitality in Scripture and the Christian tradition *always* includes welcoming *the stranger*.[1] When we consider the young people within and beyond our congregations who may feel like strangers in our gatherings, these words of theologian Christine Pohl ring especially fresh:

> In hospitality, the stranger is welcomed into a safe, personal, and comfortable place, a place of respect and acceptance and friendship. Even if only briefly, the stranger is included in a life-giving and life-sustaining network of relations. Such welcome involves attentive listening and a mutual sharing of lives and life stories. It requires an openness of heart, a willingness to make one's life visible to others, and a generosity of time and resources.[2]

that feels like family. For teenagers and emerging adults, depth of relationship opens the door to deeper exploration of belief. First relationship, then formation. First belonging, then belief. And eventually these blend into one fluid movement.[3]

The first time Grant showed up at Thursday night youth group, his demeanor sent one message: he wasn't happy to be there. His sister had encouraged him to attend her new church to try to make friends, but he didn't appear interested. At one point, he declared to his small discussion group that he was an atheist.

Committed to warmly welcoming all young people—even those like Grant who aren't eager to connect—the volunteers at this West Coast church reached out and attempted to get to know him. He mostly shrugged off their advances, keeping to himself and quickly disappearing at the end of the evening. The youth ministry team never expected to see Grant again.

So the youth pastor was surprised later that week when he received a message from Grant's sister. She shared that lately Grant had been hostile to everyone around him, and understandably so. Their dad had passed away a few years back, their mom was now in a toxic relationship, and Grant had moved in with his sister to escape. But when he visited the church group that night, he came home and told his sister, "That was awesome. There was *love* there." He felt like some hard part of him had begun to crack open. This response came as a total shock to the youth pastor, who had assumed Grant found little of interest in their gathering.

What's more, Grant came back week after week. He still wasn't sure about God, but he felt drawn by the community. He often pushed boundaries as if to test whether this church was really willing to accept him. One night after the youth ministry had become an especially safe place for Grant, he shared with a volunteer leader, "Maybe there's more to this God stuff."

Grant's journey is nowhere near neat and tidy. He has been in and out of church over the months since his first visit. But the youth ministry team insists that the church's emphasis on acceptance and welcome leads to stories like Grant's. They affirmed, "The first message students hear and experience is, 'You belong here.'"

Honest Relationships Build Belonging

"I can just be myself."

We repeatedly heard this phrase (or a close counterpart) from teenagers and emerging adults in warm churches. As one young person described, "It feels so safe to be part of a community that isn't afraid of or offended by the ugly parts of my life." When the research team listened to the way young people talk about their churches, we were surprised by how much it matters to them to have a church family where they can be authentic.

The youth leaders at one congregation of under 200 want honesty and authenticity to be hallmarks of their ministry. These adult volunteers made a pact with one another that they would simply *be there* for teenagers and emerging adults no matter what, without judging or criticizing them. They didn't tell the young people about this; they just tried to live it out. Through our interviews and focus groups on site, it became obvious that

"When I lost my grandfather to cancer, I was able to talk about that in front of other high schoolers and . . . [gets choked up] . . . that really helped me to get through that time, to have the support of my church and to be able to share and work through that and to grow in my faith. I think that is the feeling a lot of people get from the youth group, that they can talk about things that you don't normally talk about in the school cafeteria." —Ginger, age 18

*"Some of our older couples are, like, in their seventies, and the
first time or two that someone new comes to worship, these older
couples will invite them over to their house for Sunday dinner. It's
a homemade dinner, and so the young people will go and tell their
friends, 'Hey, come to this church. You know what? There are people
who will invite you over for dinner!'" —Titus, age 19*

the young people feel like they can trust these adults enough to
be honest about their struggles. One young woman affirmed,
"The adults here actually listen to us."

In other words, the pact worked!

Young people also expect others—including their leaders—
to be real about struggles. As discussed in chapter 2, keychain
leaders share openly about their shortcomings as opposed to
pretending they are immune to failure. This reciprocal authenticity warms up the whole church.

Warm Intergenerational Relationships Grow Everyone Young

Much of American youth and young adult ministry tends to
be devoted to building relationships with age-group peers. While
peer friendships are crucial, a variety of analyses suggest that
intergenerational relationships are also incredibly important.
Specifically, churches with close intergenerational relationships
show higher faith maturity and vibrancy, as well as more examples of the six core commitments in action.

While intergenerational relationships can develop naturally,
two primary avenues through which churches strategically integrate generations are mentoring and worship. *Mentoring* often
develops through one-on-one discipleship, vocational guidance,
or shared ministry work. A common example of shared work
is adults and teenagers serving together in some skill-specific

Where does traditional "relational ministry" show up in churches that grow young?

Strategic one-on-one ministry is parallel to what youth ministry has historically called "relational ministry" or "contact work," meaning leaders go to the places students spend time each day—schools, ball fields, and local hangouts.[4] This approach is still alive and well in churches growing young; in many cases, ministries are shifting the responsibility for contact work from one paid leader to a diverse team of volunteers, mentors, and the church community. Some churches that emphasize contact work reduce ministry programming in order to focus on meeting students around town. In this way, they're able to engage even more young people in relationship.

One parent misses structured church events even while sharing her appreciation for this kind of outreach: "The leaders probably do not do as many programs as I would like, but they are high on relationships. They will put together a school calendar of events that students are part of, and they attend many of them. So when my daughter is in a play, they come watch. Another girl plays volleyball, and they come watch. But they don't come alone. When they show up, they bring three or four or ten other teenagers with them."

task in the church, such as kids' ministry, technology, or music. Some mentoring structures are more formal than others, but most include a level of intentionality in matching young people with adults who share interests and talents.[5]

"Intergenerational worship" has become a catchphrase of the Sticky Faith movement over the past handful of years. We discovered in our previous research that involvement in all-church worship during high school is more consistently linked with mature faith in both high school and college than any other form of church participation.[6] As we studied churches growing young, we found a variety of valued and effective intergenerational worship practices. At St. John the Evangelist Roman Catholic Church in Indianapolis, the masses are fully intergenerational. All ages attend, and young people are involved in various roles. One mom of young twins shared, "My kids are soaking in Jesus. They know the Lord's Prayer and so much of what we say in mass together."

Just because intergenerational relationships are important doesn't make them common. One participant shared that he "loathes" the peer-based small group model in which he has always been forced to participate. He lamented, "As a 29-year-old I want a small group led by a 45-year-old with 60-year-olds and 15-year-olds and both genders. I want to learn from a high school freshman and an 80-year-old grandmother and everyone in between. We do not have any avenues for that."

Many churches that are growing young still struggle with intergenerational relationships.[7] After participants in our study had rated their church on several characteristics, we asked them to give a story or example of one of the characteristics at which they thought their church was *weakest*. The highest response (by far) was "Helps people from different age groups get to know each other," mentioned by a quarter of interviewees.

Perhaps the best response to the systemic abandonment described in chapter 3 is systemic *support*, where a warm, family-like community embraces young people as fully participating and fully needed members of the body. The good news is that when we bridge generation gaps, *everyone* grows young. Cross-generational discipleship is beneficial not only for young people but also for older generations who need the vitality of the young to inspire their faith just as much as the young need wise elders to ground theirs. Faith, after all, is not just passed *down*. It's passed *around*.

Fostering Peer Friendships Fosters Spiritual Formation

We wanted to get your attention about the importance of intergenerational relationships, but guess what? Peer friendships at church also strengthen faith. You may have guessed that, but now we have research to support it.

Specifically, when we asked young people about church friendships, those who report more close friends at church also show higher faith maturity. As the number of close friends gets closer to five, so does the likelihood that a young person attends church and regularly participates in worship with others, takes time to read and study the Bible, talks openly with other Christians about their faith questions or struggles, serves others in need locally and/or globally, and sees their faith as an influence in their friendships.

This benchmark of five close friends isn't magic, but it sure seems to help.

Becoming a Body Drives Warmth

At the end of the day, increasing warmth in your church is not only about growing young. It's also about good theology.

Theologian Miroslav Volf draws on the warm communion of the Trinity to undergird warmth in the church. He contends that "We are the church" doesn't mean "We meet occasionally" or "We cooperate in a current project." Instead, we actually *become part of one another*.[8] This sounds like Paul's exhortation that "each member belongs to all the others" (Rom. 12:5).

This kind of ecclesiology—our theology of church—pushes against the societal trend of hyperindividualism, in which churches envision themselves as loosely affiliated groups of spiritual persons having simultaneous, individual spiritual experiences.[9] In contrast, we are adopted into *one body*.[10] That

"We do life together. I always feel like I am part of a family, a collective member of it. I just feel like I am a part of something really big, something important, and I do not feel complete unless I go. It's like a chunk of my week is missing." —Timothy, age 28

means smelly teenagers and jaded emerging adults are connected tendon-to-bone with great-grandparents of the faith as they work out community together.

Jesus' own life illustrates how young people can be welcomed within the faith community. You may remember the scene in Luke 2:41–52 in which Jesus at age 12 (the only time we meet him as an adolescent in Scripture) travels with his parents to Jerusalem. After the Passover celebration, his parents begin to journey back toward Nazareth with extended family and friends who have traveled together. At the end of the first day, his parents realize that they each assumed he was traveling with the other (it was customary for the men and women to travel in separate groups, with the children passing back and forth between them). They race back to Jerusalem and after three days find him sitting among the teachers in the temple, listening and inquiring.

There are a few questions we don't often hear asked about this story, but they have the potential to be game changers for churches that want to grow young.

Where did Jesus sleep?

Who made sure he was safe?

And maybe most importantly, *who fed this boy?* Have you ever attempted to keep a 12-year-old boy fed? I (Kara) have, and it's not a small feat!

We can give a spiritualized answer to these questions, and perhaps God simply watched over and provided for Jesus those three days. But odds are good there is also a communal answer.

Our hunch is that the faith community saw this young person, embraced him, and welcomed him to their table. Both two thousand years ago and today, churches that grow young find adolescents and emerging adults who need our welcome and embrace.

One senior pastor of an African American church in our study embodies the type of community Jesus found in Luke 2. He doesn't wait for young people to show up and ask for connection; he goes to them. Each year this sixty-something leader takes a week to participate in a high school camp. He leads some of the teaching, but he goes beyond that. He plays games, eats meals, and even stays in cabins with students and youth ministry leaders rather than lodging somewhere more peaceful. He has realized that with teenagers, he has to gain enough trust through real relationships before he can speak into their lives. Like his whole church, this leader is growing young.

Ideas for Action

As you review the following ideas, perhaps make notes in the margin. Mark if the idea is a fit for your church, who should implement the idea (you or another leader), and whether it can happen now or later. Please don't try to do everything—instead, aim for two or three ideas that *you* can act on now. Then at the end of the chapter, use the strategic questions to guide your church toward a specific plan to fuel a warm community.

Take Your Congregation's Relational Temperature

Warmth isn't generated through simply being polite. By our definition (from young people themselves), the qualities of a warm church include authenticity, hospitality, caring,

Sometimes close communities become closed communities. How do warm congregations continually enfold new people?

One of the potential pitfalls of closely connected groups is that over time they can become shut off to outsiders. Shared life creates such strong bonds that newcomers can feel alienated and intimidated by a communal narrative that doesn't seem to include them. This can be especially true in smaller churches in which everyone seems to know each other, or in larger churches with well-established friend clusters or historic small groups that appear impenetrable.

Warm churches keep watch for the unhealthy tendency to grow inward. In some cases, this can manifest as resistance to growth; congregants feel threatened by new people and greater numbers. If that's happening to your church or parish, consider when particular groups or the whole body needs reminders to reach beyond cloistered in-group dynamics and cultivate fertile soil where new relational seeds can germinate. *Small* need not be an idol that prevents hospitality.

welcoming, accepting, and belonging. Consider asking a handful of young people to gauge the relational temperature of your congregation based on this definition of warmth.

On a scale of *icy, cool, room temperature*, or *fireside warm*, what rating would they give your community? Ask why they think the temperature is what it is and what ideas they have for fostering more warmth.[11]

Take their insights to your leadership team and wonder together what it might look like to get beyond *nice* to true warmth. Consider these questions: What if young people really felt like they belonged in our church community? What would we gain if we took the steps it would take to be warmer? What would we lose?

Help Newcomers Land Smoothly—and Soon

With your ministry team, assess your church's approach to visitors, perhaps thinking specifically about different age groups and life circumstances (e.g., single adults, families with kids, or college students).

- What is it like to walk into your building for worship or other ministries?

- How warmly are newcomers greeted? How are they oriented to the building and to the service or program? If you ask guests to stand or raise their hands during worship services, how does that feel to them? How can you make that kind of recognition warmer and less awkward?

- How does the language and direction—or lack of direction—given in worship feel to an outsider? Are there particular phrases that need to be explained from time to time? Are transitions handled in a manner that keeps new people oriented or leaves them confused?

- How easy is it for a newer person to access smaller gatherings, groups, or classes in which they might find relational connection? What is the balance of "open" versus "closed" groups in your congregation right now?

- Do you host any kind of new visitor or new member connection event, like a monthly meal just for recent attenders? If not, what might feel natural and within your capacity to create?

One church-planting friend of ours shared, "We see our job as creating the environment where relationships can happen. We have programs, yes, but more importantly, we build the platforms where people connect. Our strategy has been to create an environment that screams, 'Stay here!' after worship. Every week we have food, things for kids to do (all within eyesight of parents), and a football or baseball game on a big screen nearby. We see the time after the service as just as important as the service itself."

Create a 5:1 Ratio of Adults and Young People

One of the most practical ways churches and families can boost intergenerational relationships is to rethink our ratios. Often in ministry we say we need one adult for every five children or teenagers. But what if we flipped that ratio and sought out five adults for each young person? That vision, sparked by Chap Clark's research, has inspired leaders and parents nationwide to surround young people with a team of at least five supportive adults.

Who are those five? We're not suggesting that you now need to recruit five small group leaders for every young person. One may be a small group leader or Sunday school teacher, another a mentor, and still another someone who simply knows that young person's name and commits to pray for them. Coaches, favorite aunts, and the parents of close friends all carry 5:1 potential. We can tap into that potential to release a flood of support around each young person.

Fellowship Memphis used to look primarily to the "Paul and Timothy" model of one-on-one discipleship, but given the

"During the summer we have a thing called S'mores Sundays that the pastor holds in his backyard on Sunday nights. Everyone is invited. We roast hot dogs and people bring salads and chips, and we play lawn games and maybe sing some songs. We just get to bond with other Christians outside of the church. It's different than just going to church on Sunday and talking to people afterward. It's something that young people kind of look forward to, or at least I look forward to!" —Henry, age 15

transient nature of our society and the research that supports bringing a cluster of adults around young people, they now talk about the 5:1 ratio as building "greenhouses of formation." They hope that a committed group of adults will provide a rich, warm ecosystem of discipleship for each young person within their church's influence.

Another senior pastor shared that his church fosters this 5:1 vision as students enter sixth grade. The ministry leaders work with parents and students to identify five adults who commit to walk with them through middle and high school as mentors and prayer partners. Just last year, the first group of former sixth-graders graduated from high school. When the congregation celebrated this milestone, each student stood at the front of the sanctuary along with their team of five adults. With great emotion, these adults prayed for the young people they had been cheering on over the last seven years. This blessing doesn't just inspire the graduates; it changes everyone.

You may wonder at this point whether the quantity or quality of intergenerational relationships is more important. The answer is *both*. One significant adult is better than none. In general, five adults are better than three. Ultimately, it's not as much about the quantity or quality independently but rather the *quantity of quality* relationships.

Explore More Intergenerational Worship

Worshiping together across generations is important but can be tricky depending on your context. Functionally, there are three main categories of intergenerational worship:

- *All-inclusive worship*: Everyone worships together all the time. In some cases, an adjacent room is provided for parents with babies or restless children.

- *Partially inclusive worship*: Everyone worships together some of the time during each worship service. Perhaps children and youth begin and/or end the service with the whole congregation but exit for age-level worship and teaching.

- *Special-occasion worship*: Most of the time everyone worships in age-level programming, but occasionally the whole church worships together in one service. In some cases, this happens as often as once a month or quarter. In other cases, particular holidays are celebrated with intergenerational worship.

With your ministry team, assess where your church falls now on this spectrum. Brainstorm ideas of what a natural next step toward more integrated worship could look like in your setting. One option might be moving from one category to the next; another option might be to look at what you're doing right now and find nuances to make existing intergenerational engagement more vibrant.

Renovate Your Worship Gathering into a Family Room

The temptation to increase the performance value of our Sunday mornings is everywhere. Whether we're focusing on crafting better sermons, staging a well-rehearsed band or choir, or investing in state-of-the art lighting equipment, the drive for polished worship events dominates many leaders' agendas. Often this push is fueled by well-intentioned congregants who want a "professional" worship experience.

Rather than lean into the allure of viewing the worship service like a trip to the theater, imagine it as a gathering in the family room. Whether you meet in a sanctuary filled with pews, a contemporary auditorium, a high school gymnasium, or an actual house, envision your worship experience like a family room.

In some cases, restructuring your physical space in order to see one another more clearly and reduce the distance between worshipers and leaders might help. But you may not actually need to rearrange the furniture. Instead, encourage your worship planning team to look for ways worship can include both vertical (people–God) and horizontal (people–people) encounters. Here are a few practical ideas:

- Weave more personal stories of struggle into sermons that help humanize the pastor as "one of us."

- Add sermon illustrations that include young people or speak to issues they care about.

- If your liturgy is relatively formal, lean into the sacredness of this formality without assuming *formal* has to mean *cold*. Buffer the highly structured parts of the service with elements that exude more warmth. For example, add an informal "passing of the peace" or other greeting into your liturgy. Give people a few minutes to talk to one another, and perhaps provide a question for folks to ask each other to break the ice.

- Include opportunities during or after the sermon or homily for conversation with others sitting nearby or for discussion with the pastor or priest.

- Offer "prayers of the people" that invite congregants to voice their own brief prayers of petition and thanksgiving from where they are sitting, standing, or kneeling.

- Reframe mistakes and awkward moments in the flow of the service as reminders that we gather not to consume a slick show but to worship a great God.

- Invite young people to help write and deliver sections of the liturgy. Better yet, engage young people in your worship service planning or even sermon preparation meetings. One pastor who does this shared, "Teenagers are quick to point out words and ideas that lose them."

* If language differences exist in your congregation, consider which language might feel more like "family room" dialogue to parishioners from different cultural or generational backgrounds. If possible, include prayers, Scripture readings, or songs that reflect the different languages or preferences represented among your people.

* Experiment with a teaching series that spans age groups. Usually this idea means youth and children's ministry take their lead from the pastor or lectionary to decide the passages they will share. But in one medium-sized church in our study, the pastor leads a different way. A question from a seven-year-old girl caught him off guard one Sunday. She wondered why they studied different passages of Scripture in Sunday school and during the worship service. After this, he decided to connect the sermon to Sunday school and used the Sunday school lessons as his lectionary.

Pray Warmly

A logical starting point for churches that want to build greater intergenerational warmth is one of our most basic, but profound, community practices: praying for one another. One Sunday each month in a Minnesota congregation growing young, members share "prayer Post-its." At the beginning of worship, people of all generations write down prayer requests on sticky notes and post them on a wall. Later in the service, others take down those notes and commit to pray for the requests. An interviewee reflected, "It is just really cool to see elementary students put their prayer requests up, and then the college-age kids put theirs up, and they all take notes with them. There is something incredible about the different generations in our church committing to support each other in prayer."

What prayer practices could foster warmth across generations in your congregation? Here are a few ideas to spark your imagination:

- Invite small groups or Sunday school classes to pray for specific youth or young adult events, retreats, and mission trips. Encourage the young people to visit those groups beforehand to share requests and report back in person afterward about how God moved.

- Create prayer bookmarks for adults in the church that feature names, faces, and contact information about college students or graduating high school seniors. Ask them to commit to pray for that student throughout the school year.

- Match elementary students and teenagers in back-to-school pairs to pray for each other during the year.

- Designate a prayer wall where children and teenagers can trace handprints (on the wall or on large sheets of paper) and write their names. Encourage adults to write prayers and passages from Scripture in the handprints.

Generate Tiny Churches

While we can't structure warmth, our structures can work to support it. Small groups represent one of the most common strategies incorporated by churches growing young. At a church in the Southeast, young people describe their small groups this way: "We're not a church *with* small groups but a church *of* small groups." The small group community is so important that it becomes like a tiny church. So much so that

"We are increasingly moving toward a family metaphor for church rather than the corporate America model. We're asking, 'What does it mean to be the people—the family—of God? How do we as a team of leaders function as family?' That's messy, and hard." —Rafi, pastor

people may be willing to miss Sunday worship but not their small group.

While we can't tell you which small group format will work best for your community, we encourage you to consider how what you're doing now fuels warmth through peer friendships and intergenerational connections. Evaluate how your current small group leaders are trained and supported. Gather them and brainstorm improvements to make your small group strategy even more effective for nurturing warmth.

Several churches in our study are experimenting specifically with intergenerational small groups. These groups intentionally bring people together across the life span for spiritual formation. Often this means more emphasis on shared meals, life stories, and prayer requests than on intensive Bible study. In some cases, it means young children join for portions of the gathering but leave during more serious conversation. Other such groups invest in their neighborhoods by serving local needs together.

One larger church preserves both age-level and intergenerational small groups by reducing its overall youth ministry and adult programming. Every teenager is encouraged to participate in a weekly peer-based discipleship group and a monthly intergenerational group (along with their families). In order to make space for that in students' schedules, the youth group meets as a large group only once a month. While this rhythm may not work in your context, consider the small group tempos and structures that can best support the warmth you hope to nurture.

Create Both On-Ramps and Road Trips

Like us, you may live in a community where young people tend to be transitional. How can we create warmth in such highly mobile populations?

In my (Brad's) church—which was independently nominated for this study[12]—we use *on-ramps* and *road trips* as metaphors for increasing levels of commitment to community. Not everyone is ready to jump into a 12-month road trip level of commitment to a small group. For many young adults in particular, shorter experiments in community give them freedom to explore new frontiers until they're ready to settle in more permanent relational territory.

On-ramp experiences may include monthly community dinners open to everyone, 6- to 10-week life groups based on particular interests, service opportunities, or Bible studies. Options range from craft nights to basketball teams to book clubs. Sometimes the group itself is continuous but participation is fluid. For example, we walked through the book of Mark for 18 months in our worship services, and an ongoing group met to reflect on the passage and sermon from the prior Sunday. The leadership of that group was consistent, but there was no commitment level required from participants. This allowed anyone to engage a smaller group experience of studying Scripture without any expectation that they would return week after week. Ironically, this freedom actually led to some highly committed participants who might never have signed on to an 18-month study.

Another successful on-ramp is our annual whole-church retreat. All generations trek to a mountain retreat center over a spring weekend. We exhale city life for a few days and inhale both fresh mountain air and the slow pace of a relaxed schedule. The retreat is intentionally under-programmed, freeing up time for games, hikes, or sitting by the fire. What inevitably emerges are new relationships forged over board games, shared meals, and worship.

Those friendships travel back down the winding mountain road, deepening our shared life from week to week. What starts as a small investment of one weekend yields high relational returns.

A higher commitment road trip might be a six-month group exploring vocation, a yearlong commitment to a prayer group or an intergenerational small group, or participation in a dialogue-based "understanding group" around issues such as human sexuality, immigration, or the formation of a local arts collective. Understanding groups tend to begin without a formal end in place, giving the group the space it needs to do the hard work of exploring culture, tradition, Scripture, and the stories of the people in the community. The resulting deeper understanding is then shared in dialogue with the broader church.

Promote Small Group Leaders Along with Students to the Next Grade

You probably know a volunteer who has served young people in the same age level for years, perhaps even for decades. Families look forward to multiple children experiencing this leader at that particular age and stage. This kind of commitment is to be commended.

What you may have heard less about is an emerging model that encourages small group leaders or Sunday school teachers to move up with students each year. Some churches do this through the elementary years, others through middle and high school. One church described a small group model in which the same students and leaders traverse from fifth grade through senior year together. A volunteer from another parish shared, "My husband and I have taught the same kids' Sunday school group since they were in second grade. And we have moved up with them every year. This year we're freshmen. Now we are in high school."

We love how this woman uses the pronoun *we* when referring to this group. She and her husband see themselves journeying into high school right alongside their students. Talk about warm! In your own context, see if there are a few small group or Sunday school leaders who would be willing to move up with their kids as an experiment at the beginning of the next ministry year. Choose leaders who are respected and whom other leaders would listen to so that if their experience goes well, they can be your champions for a broader experiment.

Support Graduates Well

When students graduate from high school, it can be easy to think our church has done its part in their formation and simply wish them well as they exit the door. While we've written quite a bit about what can be done to change this phenomenon in our churches (see StickyFaith.org for more resources), we couldn't share this chapter on warm communities without pointing out that many churches growing young are supporting graduates well.

An Evangelical Covenant congregation intentionally reaches out to college students—both those from the church and those who have come to their city for school—through "take a college student to lunch days." Adults adopt a college student or two for the afternoon and take them to lunch after worship. Simple. And warm. Looking back on a year of college programming, the ministry leader reflected that it was one of the most effective things they had done to connect with students. In fact, students asked to repeat this event more than any other.

If your congregation includes college students, try a similar initiative. Food is often the pathway to the heart of this age group! For graduates who are far away, encourage adults to send care packages (including snacks or coffee gift cards) and to connect through social media.

Redirect Budget to Facilitate Warmth Whenever You Can

At one multiethnic church, we were struck when volunteer leaders shared that they all have meal budgets. Every small group leader in the youth ministry is encouraged to take students out for meals or treats regularly as part of their formation process. The students trumpeted the value of this investment as well, as you'd expect from teenagers who are getting fed. But it wasn't just about food; when describing their meal conversations, students used many of the phrases common to warm communities that we've discussed in this chapter.

You might wonder how the church manages to carve out budget for this expense. In many ways, it's a trade-off in a ministry that lacks a building and avoids heavy programming. Their entire ministry philosophy is built around volunteer leaders investing in students. Small group leaders meet with young people in homes or public spaces. Since the church has a policy against a leader meeting one-on-one with a student in a home, meeting over smoothies or bagels in public is somewhat unavoidable. The ministry's volunteers cannot all support that kind of expense personally, so every volunteer is extended a meal budget.

That strategy will not work in every church, but it's a fascinating take on rethinking the youth ministry budget. Occasionally, we meet youth and young adult leaders who cannot convince their church board to extend a food expense budget to *them* (as paid staff members), let alone their whole volunteer

> "This church does really well creating a sense of 'This is home.' That actually gives you a fighting chance with young adults. College students are willing to take a risk and show up again, because no matter how long they have been gone, someone will know their name and be glad they came back." —Brandon, ministry intern

team. Whether it's meals or something else, what kinds of budget changes might heat up the warmth in your ministry? What ideas can work well *without* any budget? Who needs to be involved in a conversation about this in your church?

Remember That Warmth Can Be Slow

Warmth may not seem like a big secret. But it does come with a hard truth: warmth is often slow. *Really slow.*

Stability, patience, faithfulness to a local community. These inglorious and unsexy traits give roots to churches that grow young, eventually producing the fruit of warmth. It takes time and commitment to move past the superficiality of lobby hellos into the intimate spaces where authenticity reveals deep pain and loss.

In the name of trying to stay up-to-date and relevant, sometimes churches have forced both *cool* and *community* too quickly. This kind of accelerated progress inevitably backfires. Instead, let's take the time needed to foster community practices that fuel warmth.[13] Slow progress may not look impressive five months from now, but the kind of warmth that forms young people deeply may take five years to cook up.

"This church has stretched my definition of community. Like others, I had an idea of Jesus' love—who it was for and what a Christian community meant. What this church has taught me is far greater than any definition I've heard, because it's truly organic. I would imagine that 'Slow Food' movements encompass completely organic ingredients because time is on their side; this is also true of my church and what makes it so beautiful. Community is not defined; it's a posture toward people that creates space for everyone at the table. Our table always has room." —Tasha, age 23

Chapter Highlights

- Structure is necessary for growing young, but it's not enough. Churches that grow young sometimes actually program *less* in order to free up more space for relational connection.

- Warm is the new cool. More than flashy worship, young people want authenticity and connection. When they talk about their churches, they talk about people and warmth. Regardless of whether you meet in an auditorium or a house, consider how your worship service can feel more like a family room.

- Churches grow young by weaving warmth into their DNA. The most common phrase people used to describe their churches was "like family." Other words describing warmth included *welcoming, accepting, belonging, authentic, hospitable*, and *caring*.

- Honest relationships and the ability to be real or authentic are not only preferences for young people; they also build stronger churches.

- Intergenerational relationships grow everyone young by helping them break out of the silos of age- and stage-based ministry and create connections across generations. Two of the most common ways churches invest in intergenerational relationships are through mentoring and corporate worship.

- Fueling warmth helps us live out good *ecclesiology*, our theology of church. The relationship of the Trinity and the metaphor of the body of Christ remind us that we belong to one another.

Strategic Questions to Help You Fuel a Warm Community

Research Findings

On a scale of 1 to 5 (with 1 being "we're struggling here" and 5 being "we're nailing this"), rate your congregation on the research findings presented in this chapter:

1. Young people describe our congregation as relationally warm (welcoming, authentic, hospitable) overall, like a family.

    1 .... 2 .... 3 .... 4 5

2. We avoid relying on programs and structures alone to build warmth.

    1 .... 2 .... 3 .... 4 5

3. Our congregation fosters honest friendships in which struggles can be shared authentically.

    1 .... 2 .... 3 .... 4 5

4. We intentionally connect generations within the church and support intergenerational relationships.

    1 .... 2 .... 3 .... 4 5

5. Our worship gatherings feel warm and inviting.

    1 .... 2 .... 3 .... 4 5

Ideas for Action

1. What are you already doing to help fuel warmth in your congregation?

2. In what ways does your congregation struggle with relational connection?

3. Given your ranking of the findings in the previous section, as well as the ideas you've read in this chapter, what one or two shifts might you or your church want to make?

4. Who else needs to be part of this conversation?

5. What can you do in the next few weeks or months to move toward these changes?

6. Prioritize Young People (and Families) Everywhere

From Rhetoric to Reality

> Teenagers know they are important because they are involved in ministry. They are treated as full-fledged *members* of the church, not just kids to be entertained.
>
> —Angela, church leader

How much would you and your church give up to reach young people?

One congregation in our study answered that question by deciding they would do *whatever* it took—even a change tied to the heart of the church's identity.

Like many ethnic minority churches in the US, this urban Latino congregation had grappled with challenging cultural questions as they dreamed about growing young. The lifeblood of cultural identity for many ethnic churches, language can also be a source of heated generational conflict. It didn't take long to unearth a pivotal question: What will we do about the language divide between adults and young people?

Second- and third-generation children of immigrant families often struggle to find their place in ethnic congregations that feel like home to their parents and grandparents. These young people may speak English as their primary (or only) language. Sometimes they feel like they are held to a double standard of being "as American as possible" in their everyday lives while also needing to integrate fluidly into their ethnic context when they step through the church doorway.

It can seem like a no-win situation for teenagers and young adults.

This congregation knew that a common solution for immigrant churches that want to prioritize young people is to hire an English-speaking pastoral leader (or recruit a volunteer) charged to develop ministry with young people—sometimes called "English Ministry" to distinguish it from the church's primary language. On the one hand, this helps young people feel heard and supported. They can be themselves—still ethnically distinct but able to speak comfortably. On the other hand, this raises new challenges, since a separate English-based ministry can become a threat to the immigrant church community as it grows. Traditions are lost. Meaning is garbled. Good intentions on both sides are misinterpreted. Most churches with this model find themselves in ongoing tension to maintain not only cultural identity but also unity.

First Baptist Church of South Gate chose a different strategy. This church committed to prioritize young people. But they decided to do it everywhere. Even if it meant some of the congregation's traditions had to change.

Including language.

A predominantly Hispanic congregation located in south Los Angeles, First Baptist knows the language divide well. Reflecting their neighborhood, members represent a mix of first-generation Spanish-speaking immigrants from over 10 Latin American countries. These immigrants worship alongside second- and third-generation young people growing up in the US, some of whom do not speak Spanish fluently. As diversity increased over the years, leaders wondered if language conflict would become a force that would tear them apart.

Instead, they found even stronger glue than language to bond them together.

Rather than dig in their heels, the pastor and other adults in the congregation decided to take a step toward young people. A huge step. They agreed to change their weekly worship service for the sake of young people, shifting up to one-third of every service to English. Now songs, prayers, and greetings alternate between Spanish and English, often led by young people themselves. Teenagers and young adults comprise about half of the worship team.

Despite the level of sacrifice this language shift represents, the community of First Baptist has largely embraced the change. Even though many adults do not understand all the English phrases used, they want to communicate to young people that they are welcome, known, and prioritized in the worshiping community—without having to change who they are.[1]

"We believe the future of the Latina church is to be multilingual, multigenerational, and multiethnic. We believe that an effective Latino ministry today must necessarily focus on the second generation of leaders and congregants who speak English as their first language. The care for the spiritual welfare of our English-speaking children and grandchildren forces us to adapt to their approaches and styles of ministry, rather than insisting that they worship and serve God according to our linguistic and cultural preferences." —Community statement of integration from First Baptist Church of South Gate

What's more, young people are actively welcomed into planning for worship and special events. When it comes to special services, such as Easter, the first question is usually, "What will the young people do?" They serve in all areas of the church, from children's ministry to the weekly food pantry outreach, alongside adults. One 15-year-old girl noted, "If you want to help, they help you help." And it's not just a patronizing kind of help—young people feel *needed* at First Baptist.

In other words, this church prioritizes young people *everywhere*. Even when it means giving up preferences or shifting what in the past may have been considered nonnegotiable. Even when it means relinquishing traditional authority and power in order to embrace the young. Prioritizing teenagers and young adults has made the difference between ailing and thriving—not only for young people but also for the whole congregation.

CORE COMMITMENT:
PRIORITIZE YOUNG PEOPLE (AND FAMILIES) EVERYWHERE

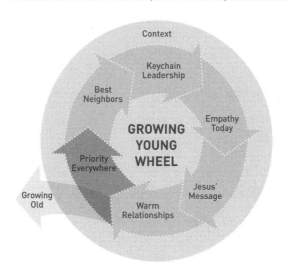

Your church may not face such a blatant generational and cultural divide as First Baptist, but you doubtless have your own tough questions. Regardless of your context, our research has us convinced that the hinge point separating churches that grow old from those that grow young is *priority*. When churches prioritize young people—and their families—everywhere, they take a step beyond both empathy and warmth. They allocate resources, energy, and attention to teenagers and young adults both inside and outside their walls.

We call this a hinge point because while churches who have keychain leaders, empathize with young people, focus on Jesus, and nurture warmth can be lovely churches, they can eventually get comfortable, face inward, and ultimately grow old. If they fail to prioritize young people everywhere and help them live as good neighbors in the world (see chapter 7), over time the congregation will age out. That's why there is an arrow pointing away from the Growing Young Wheel at the juncture between warmth and priority.

Whether you're reading this as a pastoral staff member, parent, volunteer, or some other role, you will not be able to make your church more effective on your own. You need everyone in your church to prioritize young people if you hope to make worthwhile and lasting progress. Simply put, priority is the game changer for churches that want to grow young.

Research Findings

Why Making Young People a Priority Matters More than You Might Think

In all candor, until we began gathering data from churches, we didn't anticipate how much prioritization would surface in the research. In the first stage of research, pastoral leaders

How is prioritization different from empathy and warmth?

These three core commitments emerged separately in the research and can be distinguished as follows:

Empathizing with today's young people means we listen for and seek to understand their developmental journey toward identity, belonging, and purpose.

Warmth is the way we surround them with supportive, accepting, and authentic community.

Prioritization of young people everywhere represents our tangible, institutional commitment to allocate resources and attention—not only for specific youth or young adult programming but also across the life of the congregation.

We found that these three commitments, while distinct, influence and reinforce one another.

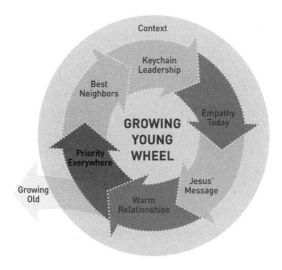

were asked to name up to three characteristics of their church that account for its success at engaging young people. The top response category—tied with leadership—was making young people and their interests a priority in the church. Priority represented half of all responses. Testing this finding in the second interview phase of our study only solidified the place of priority as a core commitment of the Growing Young Wheel.

But what does this prioritization mean? An experienced pastor shared with some hesitation that during his ministry training he was told, "If you want to know the priorities of a church, look at their budget." Initially, this bothered him, but he has come to realize that resource allocation is a helpful indicator of prioritization. Not only budget resources but also personnel, facility space, time, and programming offer glimpses into the level of priority a church places on the young.

However, this resource allocation often looks different than churches expect. A church may think it is prioritizing young people by hiring a youth pastor and setting aside the "youth basement" where teenagers can exercise their dominion. It's a musty dominion, but as long as no one can hear them down there, all is well and they're probably pretty happy.

Not so fast.

Prioritizing young people *everywhere* means more. Much more.

How do churches that grow young make youth and emerging adults a greater priority? When they think about budget, strategy, worship planning, programming, community life, theology, and all other aspects of church life, they think about young people. They intentionally pay attention.

Young people themselves provided the best barometer of prioritization in our study. When we asked how their church makes them a priority, there was no hesitation. Teenagers and young adults were eager to share how churches keep them at the heart of the community. While they may not have named the budget or other resource categories, their intuition was incredibly accurate.

Churches growing young prioritize young people not just for the sake of making young people happy but because the *whole church* benefits. One pastor of over 40 years put it like this: "Everybody rises when you focus on children and teens." Adults in another church reflected, "Young people are like salt. When they're included, they make everything taste better."

Prioritizing Young People Means Prioritizing Families Too

It's impossible to prioritize young people well without also prioritizing their families.

The roots of the Fuller Youth Institute run deep in the three schools of Fuller Theological Seminary: theology, psychology, and intercultural studies. These roots nourish a holistic approach to research that is confirmed by what we found: we can't engage with children and adolescents apart from the systems in which they are embedded—in particular, their families.

Despite decades of practice otherwise, youth ministry today is experiencing a reversal toward an emphasis on partnering with families in faith formation.[2] There are two good reasons for this shift.

PARENTAL INFLUENCE MATTERS MOST

First, parents still carry the most important weight in their kids' faith development. This is true not only in childhood but also through adolescence. Research continues to affirm that the best predictor of a young person's faith is the faith of their parents.[3] That means the role of ministry leaders who care about kids also must include the care, equipping, and formation of parents and families.

*"What I really like about our parish youth ministry is that they
encourage the parents to come. They include the parents in all the
classes that their kids are taking. There's at least one meeting a week
where the parents are invited to share in whatever is going on to
deepen their faith as well as understand where their kids are coming
from. I totally wish I had that when I was growing up."* —Alice, age 19

In studying churches growing young, we found that parents'
participation in church worship and programming correlates
with more mature faith in young people. But that's not all.
According to pastoral leaders, when parents are intentional
about faith building *outside* of church, overall faith maturity
and vibrancy within the congregation rises even more.

After young people graduate from high school, parents' influence predictably wanes, but not as much as often thought.
For 19- to 23-year-olds *and* 24- to 29-year-olds, parents' participation in faith building outside of church ministries is still
significantly correlated with faith maturity.[4]

PARENTS NEED SUPPORT

The second reason youth ministry is swinging back toward
an emphasis on families is that parents today need all the support they can get. Unfortunately, most typical ministry models
fail to adequately provide this care. At one extreme, parents
are invited to outsource their children's and teenagers' spiritual development to the church. At the other extreme, parents
are shamed into believing they are solely responsible for their
kids' faith. The former lets parents off the hook, while the latter
heaps on guilt. Both models isolate parents.

Since parents hold so much influence and need so much support, prioritizing young people must also involve prioritizing

their families. Despite the great need, in our interviews we found that churches' partnership with parents in deepening their kids' faith was one of the lower-rated characteristics of effectiveness. In other words, there are a host of opportunities to reimagine our roles in partnership with one another as a big family of faith.

Churches growing young are doing just that.

My (Kara's) church realized we had become good at the rhetoric of partnering with families but had not put that rhetoric into practice. Resolving to blend words with action more consistently, the student ministry team devised a plan for parent engagement that includes daily, weekly, monthly, and yearly touch points.

Daily: Each day from Monday through Friday, the staff members set calendar reminders to stop and pray for five minutes for parents. Five minutes may not sound like much, but our leaders confessed that before the cues, they hardly prayed for parents at all.

Weekly: The team agreed to communicate with all parents directly once each week in some way—most often through a weekly email to parents—and to communicate with various parents individually through occasional calls, texts, and meetings. This commitment included a promise to respond to parent emails and phone calls within 48 hours.

Monthly: Parent training had been scattered and inconsistent at our church, so the team built a monthly rhythm of resourcing parents directly. Using a variety of means, they offer training parents can access more readily: an online article one month, a parent book club another, and occasionally an in-person training seminar.

Yearly: Taking a cue from schools, our innovative ministry leaders set up annual parent-leader conferences. They schedule

30-minute blocks over the course of a couple of weeks, and the staff or volunteer team member most connected with a student meets with that student's parents for an intentional conversation. The leader shares highlights of the student's growth, the gifts they see emerging, and the ministry's vision of better partnering with parents to nurture teenagers' spiritual formation. Perhaps most importantly, they ask seven golden words: *How can we pray for your family?*

It took time to establish all of these rhythms, but the hard work has paid off over the past several years. Today parents at our church feel more connected and cared for than ever, and the ministry leaders benefit from greater parent buy-in and support.

The Effects of Divorce Require Our Attention

Prioritizing families means we must also respond to a myriad of struggles that burden the families in our congregations. While the divorce rate in America is not as high as often assumed (more reliably in the 20 to 25 percent range than 50 percent),[5] the wounds of divorce are no less critical. Divorce leaves kids permanently conflicted, ping-ponging back and forth between parents in a game they never wanted to play. They end up feeling like they partially belong in both parents' worlds, meaning they fully belong in neither. For young people from intact families, special events such as birthdays, holidays, and graduations enhance a sense of belonging. For teenagers and emerging adults from divorced families, these same events heighten the tensions of standing with one foot in each parent's world.

Lacking a secure sense of belonging at home, children of divorce are three times as likely to feel alone, twice as likely to feel unsafe, and almost four times as likely to disrespect their parents.[6] As they age, young adults from divorced families tend

What does it look like to prioritize young people's families when their parents don't attend church?

For teenagers who make their way into church without their parents, often the church body becomes a surrogate faith family, providing spiritual nurture that may be missing at home. While this ministry is admirable, churches often miss opportunities to connect with those parents on the fringes. In fact, parents can feel threatened by ministry leaders if their kids suddenly want to spend all of their time at the youth ministry or with teenagers and adults from church.

Sometimes we hear ministry leaders write off marginal parents as uninvolved, disinterested, and even uncaring. Research advisor Reggie Joiner, founder of Orange and the ReThink Group, champions a different posture toward parents outside the church. His bias is that the vast majority of the time, those parents—like all parents—love their kids and want to do right by them. So a first step toward prioritizing families outside the church is to start with the assumption that *they* love their kids more than *we* love their kids. Then we make it our job, not theirs, to reach out and initiate relationship. Once we have relationship, we build understanding and empathy toward parents that eventually nurture trust, which in turn can slowly open doors for deeper connection.

to have higher rates of alcohol and drug use, do more poorly in school, and are more likely to be depressed and withdrawn.[7]

The most heartbreaking statistic to me (Kara), a child of divorce myself, is how poorly the faith community supports young people affected by a family breakup. One study found that two-thirds of young adults who regularly attended a church or synagogue at the time of their parents' divorce reported that no one from their faith community reached out to them during that painful season.[8] As a young person's fabric of family is ripped apart, the faith community has the opportunity to weave itself into a young person's relational network. More often than not, we fail to do so.

We witnessed a moving story about the power of the church in the life of a child of divorce on one of our site visits. An 18-year-old African American woman shared a testimony in worship when our team visited her church. She began by explaining that she has two families—her biological family and her church family. Through tears, this high school senior shared about her parents' divorce and resulting pain that contributed to deep struggle. She called out areas where she felt like the church had failed her but also ways they valued her and walked with her. Most notably, she treasured how members of the community saw "something in me I didn't see in myself." Like the pastor who invited her into a leadership role, and the group of women who moved from being acquaintances to adoptive aunts.

The congregation did not sit silently during this testimony. Vocal support emanated from the people as they encouraged, "You can do it," "Come on," and "We're here for you." It was clear they knew, loved, and were committed to this young woman. By the end of her story, tears flowed around the room.

Young People Must Play a Load-Bearing Role

We've already highlighted how First Baptist Church of South Gate underwent significant change in order to prioritize young people. But it wasn't just alternating languages in worship that made the difference. When our research team asked high school students why they keep coming back to First Baptist, they frequently named their responsibilities in the church. Playing in the worship band, serving in children's ministry, helping in the neighborhood—these needs keep them accountable and connected.

When young people in your church and community know they are needed and invited into participation just like everyone else, they sense that they play a *load-bearing role* in the congregation. They become purposeful co-participants in the life of the body rather than junior participants or future members. Their voices, hands, and hearts matter *now* for the ongoing life and work of the congregation, and they know it.

Congregation members in churches growing young notice the value of young people's work too. Asked to name one or two ways teenagers and emerging adults contribute to the church and make it better, over 75 percent of interviewees shared that they assist in worship (especially through music), provide leadership, serve in children's ministry, mentor younger kids, and serve the broader community and world.

ASK FOR PARTICIPANTS, NOT JUST VOLUNTEERS

This emphasis on playing a load-bearing role brings both higher expectations and higher reward. One church in our study frequently uses the language of *participatory church* to frame all of the work of the congregation. For example, rather than ask for a *volunteer* to fill a role, they ask for *participation* in the community. Volunteers feel like they are giving time and energy in order to fulfill a civic duty. In contrast, participants

"Many of our high school kids help with children's ministry, not because they have to but because they love it. One beautiful thing that we do is set out a prayer chair in our kids' ministry. You can sit in the prayer chair and tell God whatever you want. When we do the prayer chair, the high school kids all want to sit in it too. It warms my heart that they are modeling prayer for our younger kids." —Susan, ministry volunteer

contribute work essential to the life of the church, work that binds them to other members of the body.

This model increases young people's connection to the church but also increases the level of risk. A task may not get done, or done as well, as it would if a paid staff member or a qualified adult simply did the work. But it's essential for moving from a consumer mindset (in which the church provides goods and services to young people) to one of participation in covenant relationships in which all members bear the load.

Small churches tend to have an upper hand here, because they truly *need* everybody to do the work. First Baptist is a church of under 200 members, with a slim staff. But large churches can also be successful at empowering teenagers and young adults to serve if they are careful not to lean too heavily on a staff-driven ministry model. Across the breadth of church sizes in our study (100–10,000 members), we found young people fully engaged in meaningful work of all kinds.

BUT BE CAREFUL TO SEE THEM FOR MORE THAN WHAT THEY DO

In the midst of this emphasis on inviting young people into significant work, we need to beware of focusing only on what young people *do*. Prioritizing young people because of what they can do for us can inadvertently degenerate into using them for cheap work. In the pastoral survey stage of the research, leaders were asked to describe three to five characteristics of a young person who has a vibrant faith in Jesus Christ. Only half of responses described internal characteristics, while two-thirds of the responses described behaviors. Similarly, nearly half described vibrant faith as participating in church-related activities (e.g., worship service, small group). These descriptions of vibrancy lend themselves toward an emphasis on *doing* versus *being.* While we are glad young people are valued as contributors, we can't help but wonder if some churches forget how young people contribute simply because of *who they are.* They thrive when treated with honor and dignity as full members of the body.

In site visits, however, this emphasis on participation played out encouragingly. A Presbyterian pastor we interviewed intentionally communicates that young people are "just like everybody else" in the congregation, including what's expected of them. The community anticipates that young people will contribute "time, talent, and treasure" like every other congregant. But they are not guilted into this service. On the contrary, the church invites young people to serve where they are gifted and to discover their gifting as they serve. Offering young people a load-bearing role doesn't mean we assume that their best (or only) role in weekend worship is to cover the toddler room. It means we actively incorporate their gifts across the congregation, from the maintenance team to the deacon board.

Ella is a young person in another congregation whose church valued her enough to carve out a special niche for her. Feeling as though she had "aged out" of her church's youth group by 14, she didn't simply fade away. Instead, she redirected her investment to an area that felt natural: the church choir. This all-adult group (until now) was not attempting to attract young people. They were a traditional choir in every way, right down to the graying heads above the blue robes.

"Students are invited by the staff of the church to learn a skill or to use a skill they already have to directly participate in the church body. My son was taught how to do some technology that involves the screens, for example. The youth are woven into the fabric of the church, not so siloed off." —Deborah, parent

"I may have hinted at this, but I think what really makes our church effective is our commitment to young people. I mean, it sounds so simple, but it is not easy to just replicate commitment. There is such a passion for young people, and it is just part of the culture, the environment, the emphasis of the church. It's a dedication."
—Tara, age 24

Not discouraged by this reality, Ella appeared at choir practice one Wednesday and quickly made herself at home amid the group. She was an avid singer, and her voice boosted the spirits of the vocalists as much as her warm smile and easy laugh. Choir became not only Ella's place to serve but also her primary community within the church. When her mother endured the trials of breast cancer a year later, one elderly couple (who had been giving her rides to and from choir practice each week) faithfully stood by Ella in a way that bonded them like family. Now in college a few states away, Ella makes a point to visit this couple when she's home on breaks because they made such an investment in her during high school. What's more, she found a church in her college town and again joined the choir as her portal to community. Worshiping and serving with adults became her model for how church should be. As churches have prioritized Ella, she has in turn prioritized church.

Myth: Good Leaders and Programs Automatically Lead to Priority

I (Brad) like running, and early mornings are typically when I can work it into my schedule. Around Pasadena's Rose Bowl stadium loops a pathway where a broad spectrum of citizens exercise. At any given time, easily a hundred or more people make their way around the track. Yet everyone does it differently.

People walk, run, sprint, and skate. Some cycle at the speed of light; others meander along casually. A high school cross-country team warms up before hitting the adjacent trails. Babies cruise in jogging strollers, and elderly couples shuffle with walking sticks. One man hobbles along shouting, "Hello!" to everyone he sees.

Oh, and there are the dogs. Big dogs dragging their owners along at a trot, little dogs getting carried, dogs in strollers (I try not to judge), four dogs on one leash, and the occasional coyote wandering down out of the mountains.

All this at six in the morning!

While the working definitions of "exercise" vary widely around the Rose Bowl loop, all of these people share one thing in common: the commitment to get out of bed early in the morning to work out. It's a priority. If you show up around the same time a few days a week, after a while you begin to recognize many of the faces (and dogs!) of folks who prioritize their morning workout enough that it becomes a lifestyle.

This is the level of priority we witnessed in churches that grow young. Not the occasional "If I feel like it in the morning, I'll get up and run tomorrow," but the steady commitment that sets out clothing the night before, checks the alarm clock, and makes it happen day after day, week after week. These churches have made prioritizing young people a lifestyle commitment. And the young people know it. It only takes about five minutes in a circle listening to their stories to hear their confidence that their church is crazy about them. Clearly it's reciprocal.

But there's a myth about how churches reach this level of prioritizing young people. If a member at an average congregation were asked to guess what it takes to prioritize teenagers and emerging adults, they might talk about strong programs and good leaders. While they would not be completely wrong, they would be missing something critical.

That "something" is congregational culture, and it's more important than most church members think. Culture cannot be defined by a list of programs; it's much deeper. We heard this both from leaders and from young people. When talking about their church's effectiveness with young people, 2 out of 3 pastors named their church's attitudes and attributes, not specific programs. This is because pastors and youth ministry leaders see how deeply their church culture influences whether priority takes root and grows. In short, even a great leader can't force priority if the church culture doesn't support it. Similarly, young people in our study whose congregations make them a priority talked less about their church's programs *for* them and more about their church's culture—specifically its relationships, traditions, and rituals.

As the arrow departing from the Growing Young Wheel suggests, a failure to prioritize young people typically sends churches on a trajectory toward growing old. Often this is

GROWING YOUNG VS. GROWING OLD

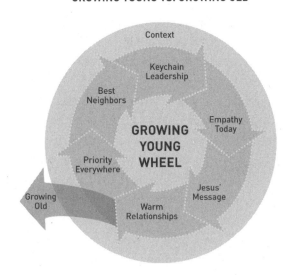

because surface-level changes are made without deeper shifts in church culture. When it comes to young people, culture change means building an overall ethos of investment in teenagers and emerging adults. Like the dedication to get up and run, over time a commitment to intentional prioritization becomes a natural, faithful movement in congregational life.

Myth: Good Intentions Are Enough

There's a saying in the business world that culture eats strategy for breakfast.[9]

In other words, you might articulate a strategic plan for your organization, but the actual culture of your organization trumps the stated strategy every time. Or more simply, who you *really* are overrules who you *say* you are. When it comes to prioritizing young people, we might translate this maxim, "You can't fool young people into thinking your church has made them a priority."

Here's why. If leaders try hiding the congregation's real priorities and give lip service to teenagers and young adults about how much they matter, they'll roll their eyes right out the door. Young people in every generation—but perhaps especially today—can sniff out a fake in no time.

Most church leaders' motives are not so insidious. It's not so much that we are trying to hide the truth from young people. It's just that while we think we are doing what we can to prioritize them through strategy and resource allocation, our church culture is working against us. Good intentions are not enough.

This dynamic emerged in our initial survey of 373 pastoral leaders. The survey asked senior pastors/priests and youth or young adult pastors to rate their church on a number of characteristics. Each characteristic was evaluated using four-point

How does a church make young people such a big priority without excluding other groups?

Prioritizing young people and their families does not mean that a congregation ignores senior adults or sidelines the missions committee. But sometimes it does mean tough choices about re-source allocation. Based on stories from churches growing young, when big decisions are made about dedicating more funding, staff, or space to young people, these changes are made by multiple generations who share a common commitment to teenagers and emerging adults.

We asked one group of high school students in a 150-year-old congregation why the senior adults in their church care about them so much that they are willing to make changes to welcome them. They replied, "The older people see that we *want* to be here, so they want us to be here." Here and in other congregations, we saw a mutual respect and mutual need that permeated conversa-tions with young and old alike. Adults weren't forced to focus on young people; they chose to do so.

scales for the following measures: how important a particular characteristic is to the leader, how intentional their church is in enacting that characteristic, and the percentage of their congregation that actually participates in that practice. For example:[10]

How *important* is it to you that your congregation cultivates rela-tionships where peers can share honestly with each other?

How *intentional* is your congregation in planning activities that cul-tivate relationships where peers can share honestly with each other?

What percentage of your congregation *participates* in relationships where peers can share honestly with each other?

Overwhelmingly and nearly across the board, *intentionality* trumped importance, and *participation* trumped both importance and intentionality. When we ran correlations with vibrancy, higher faith maturity, and a host of other variables, the story was clear. It's one thing to say a practice is important, another thing to be intentional to think and talk about it, but when we put our hands and feet to work, that's when churches change.

IMPORTANCE < INTENTIONALITY < ACTION

We found evidence of this shift from importance to action in a Nazarene congregation. Despite good intentions to focus more on children and youth with special needs, the church realized that it had not really prioritized kids with disabilities. Unwilling to allow this group to go unnoticed, the church began to make changes.

When our team visited, we were moved by the way both young people and adults shared how this church has moved from *saying* kids with disabilities are important to *doing* something about it. For example, kids and teenagers with special needs are now paired with buddies for regular programming. One young adult who originally connected to the church because of its special needs ministry shared about making friends with two girls who have cerebral palsy. At a recent youth group outdoor game night, a leader asked two other students to push these girls around in their wheelchairs for a game of whiffle ball. Everyone cheered as the students worked together to help the girls bat and then roll around the bases. This youth ministry is putting priority into action and is shifting the culture of the entire church.

While culture change is rarely easy, in chapter 8 we'll learn from churches that stretch to focus on young people without falling apart at the seams.

We Follow Jesus' Lead When We Prioritize the Young

The day wasn't turning out quite like they hoped.

Jesus' disciples were accustomed to crowds, endless days of teaching and healing, and demands from the most unlikely people seeking a hearing with Jesus. They were used to Jesus going out of his way to heal children specifically (Mark 5:21–43; 7:24–30; 9:14–29). They had already been admonished by Jesus

Does the building matter?

Yes and no. Some churches that are growing young meet in local public schools on purpose so that their financial resources are not tied up in building ownership and maintenance. Young people often help set up and tear down each week in these mobile environments. A parent in one such congregation affirmed, "The church doesn't just put resources into a building but into people. We've been to churches with better facilities, but we've never been in a healthier environment."

Other congregations keep very simple buildings. In still other cases, elaborate buildings—some old and ethereal, some new and hip—contribute to the church's effectiveness with young people.[11] Yet if we take young people's responses across the study as a whole, when they describe their church to their friends, they rarely mention the building.

However, designating physical areas *specifically for* young people especially high school students—appears to be important. In several of our site visits, it was clearly significant to high school students that they feel ownership of a particular space. One church that meets in schools on Sunday mornings rents a more consistent location where the youth group can meet regularly on Sunday evenings and midweek. Another church offers a simple, unimpressive room to young people, but just knowing the space is theirs makes a deep impact.

about the value of children, both in this world and in God's kingdom, as he took a child in his arms and declared, "Whoever welcomes one of these little children in my name welcomes me; and whoever welcomes me does not welcome me but the one who sent me" (Mark 9:37).

Yet the disciples were still struggling with how Jesus talked about and interacted with children. Could Jesus really have meant that welcoming children is a way to welcome Jesus, and by extension the Father? Surely he had been speaking hyperbolically.

While children were treasured in Old Testament Judaism, by the first century AD, children were not viewed as equal in value to adults. At best, childhood was seen as a training ground for adulthood, not a significant stage of life in itself.[12] Jesus, however, eagerly welcomed young people to come close to him, at the expense of adults who thought they had the upper hand in access to Jesus, his ideas, and his power.

Whether the disciples didn't understand Jesus or did not yet believe him, on this day they made a choice that apparently crossed a line. "People were bringing little children to Jesus," the text reads (Mark 10:13). *Not more children!* These parents and grandparents wanted Jesus to touch the children—to give a touch of blessing or perhaps a touch of healing. But this irritated the disciples. Jesus needed space. They did too. Jesus needed

"There is an older gentleman in our congregation who gives large sums of money to support the youth ministry. But it is not about the income. It is about the statement that they are important. The fact that he is saying with all this money that youth are important—other people get on board with that. That's a lot more powerful than the youth pastor trying to convince people that teenagers are important."
—Daniel, church leader

to attend to more important matters, more important people. So the disciples "spoke sternly" (NRSV) to them.

That aroused Jesus' attention.

> When Jesus saw this, he was indignant. He said to them, "Let the little children come to me, and do not hinder them, for the kingdom of God belongs to such as these. Truly I tell you, anyone who will not receive the kingdom of God like a little child will never enter it." And he took the children in his arms, placed his hands on them and blessed them. (Mark 10:14–16)

Jesus' actions must have astounded not only his disciples but all of the people gathered, children included. It was not the first time Jesus had held a child in order to make a point (Mark 9:36). But this time Jesus moved from a command to *welcome* children to a command to *become like* children, receiving God's kingdom as children do.

This command sounds strikingly like an invitation to grow young.

By saying we must become like children, Jesus was not suggesting a reversion to immaturity. He was making it clear that not only are children eligible to receive the kingdom, but they are actually exemplars of what it means to do so. Some have suggested that children's sincerity, willingness to trust, and dependence make them so exemplary. According to Roman Catholic theologian Karl Rahner, children model to the entire community an "infinite openness" to the infinite.[13] Maybe it's that very nature that inspires us all to grow young. In other words, we need them as much as they need us.

Theologically, we stand on solid ground when we prioritize young people everywhere in our congregation. Jesus led the way for us in his shocking attention to children and his reorientation of the community around them. It was a *disproportionate* prioritization. What would it look like if your church took the same approach to children, teenagers, and young adults today?

Ideas for Action

As you review the following ideas, perhaps make notes in the margin. Mark if the idea is a fit for your church, who should implement the idea (you or another leader), and whether it can happen now or later. Please don't try to do everything—instead, aim for two or three ideas that *you* can act on now. Then at the end of the chapter, use the strategic questions to guide your church toward a specific plan to prioritize young people everywhere.

Rethink the Numbers

Congregations often use attendance numbers to evaluate success, which makes sense. But additional numbers can help us assess what God is doing in and through our ministries with young people. Consider evaluating the following numbers and see what picture emerges:

- The percentage of young people ages 15 to 29 in your congregation (you might break that into high school, college-age, and 24- to 29-year-olds).

- The percentage of young people in your broader community and how that's reflected in your church.

- The percentage of your budget currently allocated toward ministry programming with young people.

- The percentage of your staff and/or building resources allocated toward ministry with young people.

Evaluate these numbers with your leadership team, and determine if the numbers feel right or if adjustments need to be made.

Assess Everywhere

Using a "red-light, yellow-light, green-light" metric, gather others and list current ministries of the church (be as inclusive as possible). Assign a color to each based on how much young people are prioritized in that area.

A green light means high priority, a yellow light means medium priority, and a red light means low priority.

Lead a follow-up discussion identifying why young people have, and haven't, been prioritized in particular areas. List clearly what needs to happen to move from red to yellow or yellow to green lights wherever feasible.

Ask a Simple Question

When any new ministry begins—ideally while it is still in the dreaming phase—intentionally ask the question, "How could young people be part of this?"

At my (Brad's) church, a new kind of prayer group was launching to practice contemplative forms of prayer together. I wondered aloud whether this group might be open to interested middle or high school students. No one had thought of that, but no one objected. So the groups were opened to everyone, and my teenage daughter joined one of them along with my wife. Sharing in prayer regularly with these adults has been a highlight of their spiritual journey over the past year. This has made our church wonder whether young people have been unintentionally excluded from other ministry opportunities simply because we haven't asked.

Hire Purposefully in Youth and Young Adult Ministry

Sometimes congregations rush to put a youth pastor in place to fill an empty spot or to create a role they assume must be part of their staffing structure. Churches growing young often take a more thoughtful posture toward hiring.

One Methodist congregation shared that their turning point in effective youth and young adult ministry was hiring a stable leader. After a chain of one- to two-year youth directors who were cool but not consistent, they realized they needed a youth ministry veteran who was willing to commit to the long haul. That meant a salary that could support someone with more experience. This investment in stability translated into a team of both paid and volunteer leaders who are now skillfully mentored and supported by this experienced leader. He is currently wrapping up his first decade in the congregation. The senior pastor recently reflected, "Yes, it was more expensive to hire someone with experience. But to be honest, I would wager that we've more than made up for it financially because of the families who have stuck around and new families who have joined because of this leader."

As you think about staffing decisions and resource allocation, what changes could you make to help support greater longevity in youth and young adult ministry?

Revisit Who Fundraises—and for What

Youth ministry fundraisers are a bit of a double-edged sword. On one side of the blade, laboring to raise money instills values and a work ethic in young people, fighting the common tendency toward entitlement or lethargy. In our research, stories about youth fundraisers were unanimously cast in a positive light by both students and adults. They seemed to work because they were framed as opportunities for the whole church community to come together in both vocal and tangible support of teenagers.

On the other side, when young people need to raise money for every opportunity, it can feel degrading and demotivating.

Not to mention the weight on parents, especially when kids are also participating in endless fundraisers for school and extra-curricular activities.

While we don't have a simple solution for this dilemma, one of our pastoral advisors wondered if prioritizing young people means lessening the burden on them to raise so much of their own funding. He mused, "We don't send out senior adults to raise funds for their own ministry or mission trip. Why do we do it with students?" Good question.

Evaluate the fundraisers at your church. Who leads them? Whom and what do they benefit? Which fundraisers involving young people reinforce the church's prioritization of them, and which ones might communicate that young people are on their own to raise money? Which adults participate in youth-based fundraisers, and are there fundraisers for other causes that young people take part in as supporters? Plan out the fund-raising year with every ministry of the church in mind, and consider what might need to be reimagined or cut altogether.

Address Family Pain and Brokenness through Support

Prioritizing young people and their families means being ready to empathize with and address the deep pain and broken-ness within family systems. This aspect of pastoral care often relies heavily on pastors, mentors, Sunday school teachers, and small group leaders, but we found congregations growing young offering more opportunities for support.

A San Francisco church in our study offers both professional and lay counseling opportunities and support groups for the array of struggles in its community: anxiety, addiction, divorce, grief, miscarriage, abuse, and chronic pain. In order to foster more member-led care groups, the church created a lay coun-seling program that provides nine months of training and a

"My church has loved me like God loves the church. This congregation has not seen me as the 'divorced person' but has loved me for who I am today because of my past. They have opened my eyes to a love that gives and a love that commits." —Ginger, age 29

supervised practicum prior to becoming a group leader. While lay groups are not meant to take the place of professional therapy when needed, the church hopes to foster a community in which more members are equipped to support one another through life's darkest places.

Evaluate your congregation's care for others through both structures (programs, staff, and groups) and relational culture (an environment of warmth, acceptance, honesty, and support). What could it look like to prioritize young people and families by offering more support for family pain and brokenness?

Prioritize Partnering with Parents

At FYI we are big fans of our colleagues at Orange, a ministry committed to "engaging churches and families to influence the faith and character of the next generation."[14]

The premise behind Orange is tied to the color itself. When you take yellow, representing the light of Christ in the church, and mix it with red, representing the heart of the home, you get orange. The two influences combined make a greater impact than either by itself. But this mixing doesn't happen simply because families attend your church. It requires intentional partnership that honors, equips, and helps parents win in their own family's spiritual formation.

In your work with youth ministry leaders, try taking a few intentional steps to move churches and families closer to one another:

- *Review your ministry calendar.* Look for youth and children's programs or events that compete with families for time and energy or that cause tension within families because of the ways calendars collide with—rather than complement—one another. Consider realigning your schedule and maybe even cutting events.

- *Create rhythms of engaging parents.* Look at your ministry's daily, weekly, monthly, and yearly engagement with parents and create touch points that feel sustainable in your context. Better yet, ask parents how much and through what channels they would like to hear from your ministry.

- *Partner with adult education.* Since parents are the greatest influence on their kids' faith, the discipleship of adults has a direct impact on the discipleship of young people. Partner with whoever leads adult spiritual formation in your church to better equip parents to talk about and live out faith every day.

- *Offer parent training when it works for parents, and feature topics they care about.* Sometimes youth ministries plan meetings and training events that are poorly attended (and attended primarily by those parents who least need the training). Instead, thoughtful ministries have shared with us two strategies: First, tap into times when parents are already on campus (during your youth group gathering, just afterward, during Sunday school, or immediately following church—providing lunch and childcare). Second, give them valuable help with topics they care about and might be anxious about, such as digital technology and social media, the transition into middle or high school, and learning to talk with kids about sex.

- *Invite parents to volunteer.* Tap into the gifts and skills of parents so they can serve in youth ministry directly rather than watch from the stands. Think beyond tasks like organizing meals or driving to events, and look for opportunities for parents to be involved in formation through mentoring, leading small groups, or discipling younger ministry volunteers.

Ditch Youth Sunday—Involve Young People Every Week Instead

Youth Sunday is a long-standing tradition in many congregations. It's the one Sunday of the year when the youth group takes over the worship service and leads everything from the music to the preaching. Some members of the congregation love it, smiling approvingly while teenagers display their abilities. Others avoid this Sunday, preferring to skip a week rather than endure loud music and awkward moments. For teenagers themselves, Youth Sunday can be a mixed bag. Some enjoy the opportunity to share with the congregation, while others feel pressured by leaders and parents to participate in something that feels unnatural, like being put on display.

For many churches growing young, Youth Sunday is a thing of the past. Not because they do not want to give teenagers opportunities to participate and lead; quite the opposite. A New England church told us they ditched what had been called "Teen Sunday" because they were dissatisfied with including teenagers only one day out of the year. Now teenagers are involved every Sunday. From leading parts of the worship service, to running the sound board, to helping with children's ministry, young people play a load-bearing role in the church's Sunday ministries.

With your church leadership team, dream together about your weekend gatherings becoming what young people look forward to most throughout their week. Where could young people be more integrated? What would it take to integrate them? How much would you be willing to change in order to make that happen?

Leverage Technology, but Don't Obsess Over It

Young people are digital natives—born into a world where the internet has always been an active presence in their daily lives and smartphones are more common than microwaves. Rather than lamenting the role technology plays in the lives of young people, churches growing young leverage technology for connection and yes, even discipleship. It's possible that young people can lead our congregations forward in surprising ways through digital technology if we let them.

However, leveraging technology does not mean we need to embrace every new gadget or social media platform in order to reach young people. Remember, they want a warm community more than a flashy one. Also be careful not to use social media solely for event promotion. One college ministry leader confided that they stopped promoting events as much on social media and instead started celebrating them afterward, believing that what's celebrated gets repeated. They share photos, quotes, and highlights as avenues toward community and trust rather than as marketing tactics.

Further, young people do not necessarily want to connect with adults in the same space where they connect with their friends. Ask young people in your congregation how they think your church could improve its use of technology and social media. Also ask where they do *not* think more effort is needed. Specifically ask what social media platforms they do and do not want to use to interact with church members or to discuss faith questions.

Diversify to Meet 24- to 29-Year-Olds Where They Are

Chapelgate Presbyterian has worked to adapt to the needs and realities of twenty-somethings in their community, and it has paid off. Their ministry to young adults offers a variety of opportunities to accommodate those in different life stages—whether single, married, or with young families.

Anchor is a Bible study that meets twice a month, centered around a shared meal in the home of adults in the congregation. Pub Theology meets at a local bar each Tuesday, offering conversational Bible study in an environment where young people feel comfortable inviting their friends who may not be willing to explore faith in a church building. Chapelgate also offers traditional Sunday school classes for this age group, and many are involved in other ministries of the church beyond young adult–focused programming. Chapelgate doesn't want young adult ministry to become Youth Group 2.0 but wants to engage emerging adults where they are and help them discover their place and purpose—both in the church and in the world.

Gather a few of the young people in their mid to upper twenties in your church and ask them to share both what they appreciate about what your church does now to connect with them and ideas for better addressing the needs of their age group. Do not assume that they will want a programmatic response. In some contexts, we found no specific ministry program targeting post-college young adults. They seamlessly integrated into the life of the congregation. See what surfaces when you share the goal of prioritizing young people everywhere. You might even find that young adults are willing to create structures and launch ministries or initiatives themselves. Just be sure they receive adequate support from leaders as they do.

Thank Adults Who Sacrifice Personal Preferences to Prioritize Young People

In many cases, prioritizing young people everywhere means adults put aside some of their own preferences for the sake of younger generations. For the adults at First Baptist in South Gate, giving up an all-Spanish service meant more than preference—it meant risking a loss of identity. While adults in your church may not have as much to lose, these sacrifices still should be named and celebrated. One pastor shared, "We constantly express gratitude to adults from the platform by acknowledging they are very likely giving up some of their preferences around dress, music, and formality in order to reach younger people. We thank them for that gift."

Sacrifices for the sake of young people can lead to rich relational rewards. Tony is a dad who shared how putting aside his own desires for the sake of his son deepened an otherwise ordinary practice: the daily commute to school. In the car, six-year-old Alex began requesting track 11 on his favorite worship album. Tony hated track 11. The first few times his son piped up, he ignored the request. Eventually, Tony gave in and was surprised at what happened next. Alex knew *every word* of the song. As he belted out the lyrics from the back of the car, Tony was transformed in the driver's seat. Hearing Alex's sincerity and passion flipped Tony's opinion about track 11. It's now his favorite song.

The adults in your congregation may or may not experience the same emotional response as Tony when asked to give up some of their preferences for the sake of young people. And in the spirit of true community, at times young people similarly need to forsake their own wants for the good of the whole. Regardless of which generation is paying the price, let's thank them for making "track 11" sacrifices that help *everyone* grow young.

Chapter Highlights

- Churches that grow young are willing to make young people a priority not just in rhetoric but also in daily reality. These churches don't assume it will happen automatically; they emphasize young people in their overall philosophy, worship gatherings, staffing, and budget.

- Prioritizing young people means prioritizing families. Parents are the strongest spiritual influences in their kids' lives, but they need the support and partnership of the church.

- Young people need load-bearing roles in the community, meaning they contribute through serving and using their gifts.

- Good leaders and programs do not automatically lead to prioritization, nor are good intentions enough. Prioritizing young people everywhere often requires a congregational culture shift.

- Jesus invites us to grow young as we both welcome and become like children, who are exemplars in receiving the kingdom of God.

Strategic Questions to Help You Prioritize Young People Everywhere

Research Findings

On a scale of 1 to 5 (with 1 being "we're struggling here" and 5 being "we're nailing this"), rate your congregation on the research findings presented in this chapter:

1. Our congregation actively prioritizes young people well across the collective life and ministries of the church.

   1 ⋯⋯ 2 ⋯⋯ 3 ⋯⋯ 4 ⋯⋯ 5

2. Our congregation specifically invests in programming and staffing for ministry with young people (consistent with our size and resources).

1················2················3················4················5

3. Parents and caregivers in our congregation feel supported in raising kids and nurturing their spiritual growth.

1················2················3················4················5

4. Young people in our church serve in significant roles and know they are needed throughout the congregation.

1················2················3················4················5

5. Our congregational culture supports the prioritization of young people everywhere.

1················2················3················4················5

Ideas for Action

1. What are you already doing to help prioritize young people everywhere in your congregation?

2. What evidence do you see that your church culture prioritizes young people?

3. How does your church intentionally support and partner with parents?

4. Given your ranking of the findings in the previous section, as well as the ideas you've read in this chapter, what one or two shifts might you or your church want to make?

5. Who else needs to be part of this conversation?

6. What can you do in the next few weeks or months to move toward these changes?

7. Be the Best Neighbors

Loving and Shaping Your World Well

Christianity is about the restoration of how it is all supposed to be. We have been given hope, we have been redeemed, and we have been empowered by the authority of God to go out and change this world. —Isaiah, age 20

College degree freshly in hand, Alexis moved from the Midwest to Washington, DC, convinced that she was going to change the world. Like so many young professionals, she was drawn to our nation's capital by its high concentration of nonprofit organizations and the chance to influence national and global policy.

"Doing good" was at the top of her to-do list.

Finding a church?

Not so much.

During Alexis's first weekend in town, she heard music coming from a festival in a nearby park and decided to check it out. She strolled through the grass, thrilled to find dozens of community organizations offering opportunities to make a difference.

Alexis was particularly drawn to a simple table with a large banner that read "Foster the City." "Foster the City's aim," the two young adult volunteers shared, "is to reverse the foster care waitlist in our city. We're going to line up more families who want to adopt than the hundreds in DC's foster care system who need a home. It's a huge problem and a huge goal, but we've been making steady progress."

Alexis was ready to sign up and help however she could. She wasn't in a position to adopt, but she was willing to donate and share the need with others.

As the three continued their conversation, Alexis eventually learned that these volunteers weren't just part of a nonprofit organization—they were part of a church. The District Church.

This new church plant lived to be "a church for the city"— that was actually its motto. The church coordinated not only Foster the City in DC but also several other social justice initiatives in the surrounding neighborhoods. The more Alexis asked about the activities and overall spirit of the church, the more she felt like this was a church she could imagine joining.

While finding a church was nowhere on Alexis's list initially, The District Church leaped to the top because of how it incarnated Jesus in its community.

One year later, when we visited her church, Alexis was deeply involved as a worship leader and small group member. When asked what she loves about her congregation, Alexis reiterated its involvement in the community. "I love that I met these people at a festival," she said. "I didn't need to be looking for Jesus or a church to find them. They were *out there* doing their thing as opposed to a lot of churches that try to get you to come to *their* events in the church building."

The church's primary focus at the festival was not to promote its Sunday service but to make its city a better place.

Alexis continued, "Everyone in our city wants to change the world, but this church makes that tangible in a manner I have never seen before in a church. It teaches you how to apply your faith to the culture so you can interact with the world as God intends."

The District Church sacrifices neither depth nor theology as it positively engages with culture and makes a difference in the world. Alexis is hooked, and so are hundreds of young professionals and adults. Like many others that grow young, this church loves its neighbors well.

The District Church highlights how churches growing young strive to be the best neighbors, both locally and globally. They wisely maintain a delicate balance as they interact with our culture and world. On the one hand, they do not simply mimic the surrounding culture, indiscriminately patterning their lives and activities after what they see around them. On the other hand, they are not so different or separate from the world that they lose their ability to relate.

CORE COMMITMENT: BE THE BEST NEIGHBORS

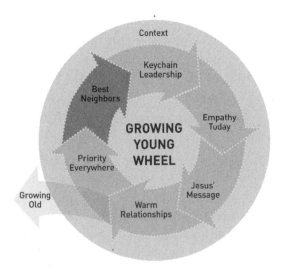

What do we mean by "the world" and "culture"?

Since Christian traditions use the terms *the world, culture,* and other synonyms broadly, we want to briefly explain our working understanding of these two important terms.

The world: We are *not* using this phrase with a negative connotation or as something bad that Christians should avoid. Instead, when we say "the world," we mean almost anything that is located or takes place outside of the church walls (or, if your church doesn't have walls, what takes place outside of formal church gatherings).

Culture: Our use of this term includes values and ideas, ethnic and gender identity, pop culture (such as media, art, fashion, technology, and music), politics, and heated issues (such as gay marriage and immigration). We've been helped by author and FYI research advisor Andy Crouch's definition of culture as "what we make of the world."[1]

Instead, churches that grow young recognize the careful dance that values both fidelity to Scripture's commands for holiness and knowing and graciously loving their neighbors. This dance affects how they serve, pursue social justice, help teenagers and emerging adults find their calling, interact with popular culture, and respond to heated cultural issues. Much more than developing detailed policies or releasing theological position papers, these churches train and infuse their young people with an integrated discipleship that enables them to thrive in our complex world.

This sounds simple enough, right?

In reality, we found that offering young people a thoughtful path to neighbor well is anything but easy, even in exemplary churches. When leaders of churches that grow young were surveyed about the biggest challenges their church faces in ministering to teenagers and emerging adults, 1 out of 3 named challenges navigating culture. The most frequently named cultural obstacles included the difficulty of keeping their church relevant and the pressure on young people to conform to popular cultural norms.

As you read about churches that aim to be the best neighbors, please remember (as explained in chapter 1) that the order of core commitments in the Growing Young Wheel is flexible. In some churches, this commitment serves as an entry point to growing young; in others it comes later. Just because this is last in the Growing Young Wheel does not mean it will be last in *your* church. Regardless of the timing of this commitment, we've discovered several postures common in churches that neighbor well.

Research Findings

The Best Neighbors Ask, "Who Is My Neighbor?"

Churches that intend to be the best neighbors, and that train young people like Alexis to do likewise, try to adhere to the example set by Jesus. In Matthew 22, when an expert in the law asks Jesus to identify the greatest commandment, Jesus replies by citing Deuteronomy 6:5: "Love the Lord your God with all your heart and with all your soul and with all your mind." Moving beyond this familiar Jewish command, Jesus then adds

"All churches must understand, love, and identify with their local community and social setting, and yet at the same time be able and willing to critique and challenge it."[2] —Tim Keller, pastor of Redeemer Presbyterian Church, New York City

The young people in my church don't seem to reflect or even respect our views on cultural issues today, especially human sexuality. Does our congregation have to choose between either keeping our teenagers and emerging adults or throwing out our convictions?

Our culture is changing at what feels like an exponential rate, and it's difficult for most of us to keep up. A quick skim of young people's social media accounts is all it takes to reveal that their approaches to cultural issues may be a little different from, or even completely opposed to, those of older congregants.

While there are no quick or easy answers, we recommend that congregations view these differences (and this chapter) through the lenses already shared about empathizing with today's young people (see chapter 3) and fueling a warm community (see chapter 5). Loose associations of individuals who only gather for worship and teaching will likely melt apart in the face of heated debate. Instead, churches can grow young by viewing this season as an opportunity to draw closer to one another in relationship and do the hard work of sharing life together across different generations and perspectives.

a second "greatest" command that references Leviticus 19:18: "Love your neighbor as yourself." For Jesus, love of God and love of neighbor are inseparable.

The obvious question that follows is, "Who is my neighbor?"

Thankfully, Jesus responds to this question in the famous parable of the Good Samaritan in Luke 10:25–37. When a Jewish man traveling from Jerusalem to Jericho is violently attacked, robbed, and left to die, two religious authorities (a priest and a Levite) see the man but pass by. The man's life is saved when a Samaritan traveler stops to help. Despite being an enemy of the Jews, the Samaritan bandages the stranger's wounds, takes him to an inn, and pays for his expenses. Unlike the religious but aloof travelers, the Samaritan enacts true neighboring.

Churches striving to be the best neighbors reflect this selfless mercy toward the people outside their congregations—whether those neighbors are friends, strangers, or enemies. They demonstrate compassion and forgiveness, even when it is within their power to turn away or inflict harm. Churches that grow young practice this mercy in a myriad of forms—in their service and social justice efforts, in their political engagement, in discussions about race and ethnic identity, and in response to pop culture. Doing so earns these churches a hearing in a culture that often otherwise dismisses them as judgmental or closed-minded.

Asking "Who is my neighbor?" helps ground young people's response to the needs and culture around them in more than self-congratulatory benevolence. When we posture our work in the redemptive narrative of Jesus, good deeds are repositioned within Good News. Twenty-seven-year-old Tina summed up how theology shapes her congregation's action in the community: "Our church has more than just a *desire* to do good. We understand that this good, this need for justice, comes from our understanding of the gospel. It's grounded in who Jesus is, who God is, and what life is all about, not just an add-on."

Like Tina, Alexis and hundreds of other young people are drawn to The District Church due to this rich understanding and application of the gospel. While Washington, DC, is often characterized as a city of polarization, this church trains emerging adults to engage in a careful dance, demonstrating mercy to all people—whether they be Democrats or Republicans, rich or poor, gay or straight, conservative or liberal, or any other friends or strangers who enter their neighborhood.

Hospitable Neighbors Honor What's Good

Day after day, news headlines shout that the world is not as it should be. This reality is not lost on young people. If anything, social media relays global strife with an immediacy unknown to prior generations.

Given the pain and brokenness around us, there are times when evil needs to be called out, challenged, and overcome. While churches that grow young don't deny the problems of the world, they consistently look to emphasize the good and to embody that good in faithful living. They understand young people are tired of congregations that define themselves by what they are against rather than what they are for.

When leaders in our study were asked, "What do you believe accounts for your church's success at engaging young people?" nearly 1 in 3 pointed to its inclusive and open attitude toward other people and the overall culture. In addition, when teenagers, emerging adults, parents, and church volunteers were asked to name why their church is effective with young people, equally as many named this positive posture. As one pastor from Alabama described, "We definitely try to stay connected to culture. Philosophically, we don't fear culture or treat it like the enemy."

One twenty-something from a church in New York City wanted us to know, "The girl that I am dating was raised Muslim and was agnostic for the most part. The first time I took her to my church, I was a little nervous because I did not want her to think that it was crazy or anything like that. But it was actually a really incredible experience. The whole tone at our church is more about understanding than about doctrine, while also not pushing the doctrine aside. . . . She actually started crying in the service because she was so touched."

Congregations that aim to be the best neighbors keep their radar tuned to the good they find in culture and those outside their church. This doesn't imply wholehearted acceptance or that your church should pretend real differences do not exist. However, hospitable neighbors maintain both dialogue and relationship, especially when they disagree. The churches in our study did not have much trouble finding enough common ground to at least begin to have a conversation, even about controversial cultural issues. After all, as Psalm 24:1 declares, "The earth is the LORD's, and everything in it."

Compassionate Neighbors Make Their World Better

Churches that become the best neighbors don't stop with naming what's good around them; they also focus on *doing* good, both in their neighborhood and around the world. While most leaders might guess this is important, we can't say strongly enough how vital it is for churches to engage in service, acts of compassion, missions, and social justice.[3]

When interview participants in our study were asked what makes their church effective with young people, nearly 60 percent named service practices, missional practices, or generally being outward oriented. Further, when we asked leaders, "What is a practice in your congregation that indicates commitment from or growth in young people?" nearly 70 percent named young people serving in some way.

Participants in phone interviews from Trinity Church in Miami regularly repeated the phrase "we're committed to our

God is not at all surprised at the abundance of good to be found in the world. As the Dutch theologian Abraham Kuyper proclaimed, "There is not a square inch in the whole domain of our human existence over which Christ, who is Sovereign over all, does not cry: 'Mine!'"[4]

community." As our team prepared to visit this large church in person, we wondered if the words would hold true or if it was merely a well-worn slogan. However, shortly after the drive from Miami's wealthy and flashy South Beach to the understated city of Miami Gardens, where the church is located, we realized the phrase was indeed embodied by the congregation.

The pastors explained their church's strategy: "We don't separate spiritual needs from physical, emotional, and social needs. We want to see this whole community flourish, so we do whatever it takes to make that happen." Trinity Church invests in the local community through multiple initiatives geared to provide holistic support. Its Peacemakers Ministry provides a food pantry for neighbors (many of whom are immigrants), tutoring and counseling for children of prison inmates, and assistance with job development. The church also hosts an annual daylong event called Hope Jam that offers haircuts, dental services, healthcare enrollment, and food to thousands.

Another pastor at this church growing young emphasized, "We've always had a heart to get out of the church building and serve the world—but sometimes we also want to bring positive parts of the world into the church." The congregation accomplishes this goal by renting part of its office space to government organizations and other social service agencies. Anyone who comes through the church doors during the week can receive support from the appropriate agency. This pastor continued, "When someone shows up to Trinity Church, they know we not only address their spiritual needs, but they can receive food, talk to a social worker, and have other practical needs met."

This church's approach to its neighbors has changed the lives of many, including Alejandro, a young person we interviewed whose family emigrated from the Caribbean when he was seven years old. With no father at home and a mom busy with multiple

*"An emphasis on our role as neighbor as part of our identity . . .
[reminds] us of our shared cultural and geographical spaces and the
fact that proximity brings responsibility. Even apart from Jesus' call
to love our neighbor, we know that our common flourishing depends
on one another."*[5] —Makoto Fujimura, artist, writer, and director of
Fuller Seminary's Brehm Center for Worship, Theology, and the Arts

jobs, he tried drugs for the first time at age nine. By seventh grade, he was dealing. In eighth grade, he was bullied at school and even attempted suicide. After giving his life to Christ in a mental hospital and completing an Alcoholics Anonymous program, he returned to high school for his freshman year. Thankfully, he was immediately connected to a Christian club that meets on the school campus and is led by students from Trinity Church.

Within a few short weeks, Alejandro was regularly attending Trinity's worship services and was connected to a Christian mentor. "I love this church, man," he shared with our research team. "Trinity has shown me I can let go of all the negative images I've held of myself, because God loves me no matter what. Anyone could show up to this church on their worst day and it will turn your life around."

Now a young adult, Alejandro has a healthy self-image, is doing well in school, and serves on the church's hospitality team. He keeps his eyes open for other hurting young people and supports them through listening and encouragement—just like the church did for him years ago.

Patient Neighbors Respect the Journey as Much as the Destination

When participants in phone interviews were asked how they would describe their church to a Christian friend, 43 percent focused on the church's accepting nature. This was confirmed during our site visits, as Alexis and nearly 200 other young people from the 12 congregations we observed unpacked how their church interacts with cultural issues. Teenagers and emerging adults consistently described how much they care about their church's process or journey for arriving at particular beliefs, positions, and statements. Especially when it comes to heated cultural issues like politics, interreligious dialogue, or homosexuality, a church's predetermined agenda can become hard for young people to stomach. When churches seem closed to dialogue, young people often look elsewhere for more palatable conversations about issues that matter most to them.

While the churches in our study are anything but theological lightweights, they often demonstrate a generous spirit when it comes to differing opinions. When interview participants describe their church, they are eight times more likely to mention the diversity of beliefs in their church than the similarities.

At Flood Church, young people were quick to share that they feel comfortable bringing their friends because they know the teaching will proclaim biblical truth without judging people who are not yet ready to embrace that truth. "Our youth pastor is big on saying, 'Come as you are.' That makes it easy to promise our friends they won't be judged for not being Christians yet," one high school junior shared. No matter where churches growing young fall on the theological spectrum, they place emphasis on essential beliefs that can be shared rather than exaggerating various differences. In this way, those whose

"If you don't understand restoration, you won't understand the next Christians. They see themselves on a mission, partnering with God to breathe justice and mercy and peace and compassion and generosity into the world."[6] *—Gabe Lyons, author and founder of Q Ideas*

beliefs do not match the church's at least feel welcome to join the conversation.

Interestingly, we heard from several young people who do not completely align with their church's stance on one or more controversial issues but nevertheless remain part of the church because they respect the process by which decisions are made. One 18-year-old from Minnesota shared, "We talk about the big social issues . . . we definitely engage those. But we don't tell people what to think about them. And that is what I really love. I have never felt awkward asking one of the leaders, 'What do you think about this?' because I know they're not going to tell me exactly what to think. Instead, they engage me in conversation. And then through that, we can derive together the ways that we should live out our beliefs."

More conversations. Less conclusions.

Respecting the journey seems particularly vital when navigating two of the most fiercely contested topics in US churches today: sexual identity and gay marriage. While it is beyond the scope of this book to suggest a resolution to these debates, they were subjects of discussion in almost all churches growing young.

While the churches in our study landed on all "sides" of these complex issues, they were united in their commitment to informed, respectful, and thoughtful dialogue. For instance, one church began every discussion on same-sex questions with a reminder of every person's common need for the grace of God. Another church publicly asked forgiveness from the same-sex community for its past quick judgments and lack of grace, emphasizing the God who is bigger than any conflict or debate.

Furthermore, leaders of churches growing young are sensitive to making a decision or taking a particular theological stance that is perceived as shutting down discussion. Rather than make decisions in a leadership vacuum, they recognize the tensions that swirl around these issues, especially for young people who may interact every day with those who identify as LGBTQ or who may identify as having LGBTQ tendencies or attraction. These church leaders avoid making blanket statements and instead try to honor all people involved as created in God's image. They make space for safe and honest dialogue so that everyone—both young and old—can share their questions, beliefs, and experiences.

Courageous Neighbors Embrace Ethnic Diversity

Ethnic diversity is on the radar of teenagers and emerging adults, possibly even more so than for other age groups. When asked to describe their church, 1 out of 5 young people ages 24 to 29 mentioned ethnic diversity. However, only 1 in 10 church leaders or older adults within these same churches chose to highlight diversity.

As we shared in chapter 3, racial and ethnic diversity are an everyday reality for today's young people. Yet most denominations and churches in the US represent an overwhelmingly monocultural tribe.[7] Given young people's awareness of racial and ethnic diversity, as well as the lack of this diversity in many

"The American church needs to face the inevitable and prepare for the next stage of her history—we are looking at a nonwhite majority, multiethnic American Christianity in the immediate future. Unfortunately, despite these drastic demographic changes, American evangelicalism remains enamored with an ecclesiology and a value system that reflect a dated and increasingly irrelevant cultural captivity and are disconnected from both a global and a local reality."[8]
—Soong-Chan Rah, North Park Theological Seminary

"Racial reconciliation is not the goal. The goal is the gospel. The gospel is to love the people in your neighborhood, at work, and at the gym. Those are the people we're asked to engage with as we live out the gospel. At our church we are asked, 'What does your dinner table look like? Who are you inviting into your home?' Life change comes when your table has people who are different from you. Reconciliation is part of the gospel." —Jamar, age 29

churches, our research team was encouraged that almost one-third of the churches in our study were multiracial.

At Fellowship Memphis, an intentionally multiethnic congregation that is growing young, every conversation traces back to two topics: the gospel and racial reconciliation. The second is never mentioned without the first.

Young people nationwide are often confused and frustrated when they look around their school or their favorite coffeehouse and see others who look different but then show up to a church service where everyone looks the same. At Fellowship Memphis, the diversity of church members mirrors the diverse city of Memphis. As one high school student from the church noted, "In my public school, everyone's integrated. But when it comes to churches, there's so much segregation in town. Our church is more like the school. When I bring a friend, they're like, 'Oh wow, this is different than *my* church.'"

ETHNIC DIVERSITY AND EFFECTIVENESS WITH YOUNG PEOPLE OFFER A COMPLEX PICTURE

When we explored the effectiveness of churches with higher levels of diversity, the findings were complex. Across various analyses, diverse churches in our study (those with 80 percent or less from the same ethnicity, meaning at least 20 percent come from one or more additional ethnicities) fare *better* than non-diverse churches in ratings of church health as well as the faith maturity of young people.[9] However, as churches achieve greater than 80 percent diversity (moving closer to only 70 percent or 60 percent of the congregation representing the same race), they report incrementally *lower* levels of health and faith maturity.

Our interpretation of these results is that when a congregation is less than 20 percent diverse, something important is lost—at least when it comes to engaging young people. But as a church increases diversity and gets closer to half (or less) of congregation members representing one primary racial/ethnic group, the work of church life and ministry gets harder. When we talked with our project's non-White advisors about these findings, they resonated with the challenge that as diversity increases, so does complexity.

For example, one founding pastor of a multiethnic congregation in our study noted that while their congregation began about 70 percent White and young, over time that population shifted to represent more of the church's predominantly African American neighborhood. Having an African American pastor helped bridge this gap. But the more multiethnic the church became, the more issues of race, class, immigration, and language surfaced. This pastor reflected, "You can't separate a deep commitment to discipleship from a deep commitment to reconciliation. If a leader can't handle that level of tension, they'll talk about *unity* and *harmony* without going really deep into reconciliation for fear of implosion. This limits how much you can bear one another's burdens." While there are understandably many challenges with significant levels of diversity, we're encouraged by the increasing number of churches and church leaders who pursue this diversity and recognize it as a practical extension of the gospel.

RACIAL INJUSTICE: AIM FOR UNDERSTANDING
FOLLOWED BY ACTION

Informed by social media, young people today are often immediately aware of racially charged acts of violence or potential racial injustice when it bursts onto the public scene. Teenagers and emerging adults long for space to dialogue, speak honestly about hard issues, and lament and pray on behalf of those directly affected. When young people's churches (especially predominantly White churches) say nothing in response, that silence speaks volumes.

As we talked about diversity with our project's advisors, there was a fair amount of confusion, with some members of the conversation feeling frustrated—and even convicted—that despite their intentionality, their ministries weren't as diverse as they desired, or as our nation is. The discussion turned a positive corner thanks to an insight from Dr. Virginia Ward, former New England Black Campus Ministries Director for InterVarsity Christian Fellowship who is now Director of Leadership and Mentored Ministry at Gordon-Conwell Theological Seminary. Virginia wisely offered, "We know that you do not get it. We are waiting for you to know that you do not get it. Come to us and say, 'Help me understand.'"

As you think about ways you "do not get it," as well as people who can help you "get it," how might you practice this posture in conversation in the next few weeks?

"Our church talks about how the Bible highlights all the tribes worshiping together in heaven. My church is a reflection of that. It's so diverse, it's not even a thing. You're a person, I'm a person. There are no barriers." —Dawson, age 18

Equitable Neighbors Seek Socioeconomic Diversity

Churches growing young don't stop at ethnic diversity; they also pursue socioeconomic diversity. As one Roman Catholic leader commented, "What I love about our parish is that during a recent mass, in one of the back pews sat a man I know who is homeless. Sitting right next to him was the vice president of one of the largest pharmaceutical companies in the country. One is a multimillionaire and one has next to nothing, but they're in the same pew. That's what our parish is all about."

While the 12 congregations we visited in person each pursued socioeconomic diversity in different ways, it was a demonstrated value in nearly every church. Churches that want to be the best neighbors seem especially aware of their ministry to, and inclusion of, the poor.

Wise Neighbors Help Young People Discover Their Calling

As chapter 3 highlighted, today's 25-year-olds can often seem like 15-year-olds, and vice versa. When it comes to discovering their purpose, young people often struggle to find the right paths for both their vocational calling and their calling to serve their community. Like a GPS app offering six potential routes to a destination, life gives teenagers and emerging adults an overwhelming array of options that prove difficult to sort out. In the midst of that confusion, we believe the church is much better positioned than a school guidance counselor to help young people discover all God has for their future.

Churches that grow young provide this vocational guidance by helping teenagers and emerging adults locate themselves and their work in light of a grand narrative.[10] This narrative gives their lives greater meaning and purpose than simply "finding a job that pays the bills." Many of the 200 Christian young people we interviewed in our church visits highlighted how the Christian story is giving shape and context to their biggest questions and dreams. It helps them step away from hyperindividualism and consumerism and toward participating in what God is doing in our world. This story also provides teenagers and emerging adults with guidance about why their plans might not always work out to their satisfaction, guarding against the negative effects of jaded realism.

Tonya, a 24-year-old recent college graduate, shared, "My church makes me feel like being a young person is not just important but *crucial* in the body of the church. It communicates, 'You are important and your time now matters maybe more than ever.' That message has stayed with me and is a good voice I need in the back of my head when I feel like I am just waiting for my life to start. It has changed how I see my life and purpose as a young adult."

Churches like Tonya's recognize the gifts of emerging adults and serve as mentoring communities where young people can discover their identity, nurture a sense of belonging, and find purpose. They help young people identify their particular vocational fit during a time of seemingly unlimited options. One medium-sized suburban church in our study accomplished this by turning its young adult Bible study into a small group that explored questions of vocation and calling. Another small congregation developed a 10-week series on similar topics that they repeat yearly, inviting new young people to journey alongside more seasoned adults as they discover purposeful work.

The Best Neighbors Avoid Common Pitfalls

When it comes to engaging with our world, churches that grow young successfully avoid four common pitfalls that often trip up other congregations.

AIMING FOR PERFECTION

When interview participants in our study were asked to rate how true particular statements are of their church, one of the lowest average ratings (3.72 out of 5) was "teaching people how to interact with cultural and societal issues." Even in churches that are strong and healthy, participants feel there is room to grow in their cultural engagement. However, when asked how true it is that their church emphasizes social justice or serving others in need, respondents ranked their congregations at 4.47 out of 5.

Young people seem to appreciate their church's good intentions and initial action in neighboring well, even when not done perfectly.[11] One emerging adult from the Northeast shared, "My friends and I *need* more than the cynicism we're offered by the world and wider culture. Our church offers more, and that's why it's attractive to younger people."

COPYING AND COMPETING

Given young people's high value on authenticity and their uncanny ability to sniff out someone or something that's fake, churches that grow young do not attempt to copy the culture around them or compete with the entertainment industry. That's wise given that young people in our survey expressed skepticism about churches that try too hard to be relevant.

Grace, a youth pastor from Florida, reflected, "We resist the temptation to *entertain* them simply because we are in an entertainment culture. If we were trying to entertain our young people, they would sense some inauthenticity and likely leave the church. There are such better forms of entertainment out there."

CONDEMNING AND CRITIQUING

Teenagers and emerging adults today know what their church is against. Trust us. The so-called Christian mantra to "love the sinner but hate the sin" has more than done its job . . . at least when it comes to the second part of the statement.

While condemning and critiquing might occasionally be useful, churches that grow young seem to take that posture sparingly. Research advisor Andy Crouch envisions a more positive strategy: "The only way to change culture is to create more of it . . . something that will persuade our neighbors to set aside some existing set of cultural goods for our new proposal."[12]

This approach of creating "more culture" is certainly true of The District Church. Given its location in Washington, DC, it is surrounded by groups that condemn and critique each other. Rather than enter the endless debates as one more negative voice, the church seeks to listen to what is happening in the wider world. They next ask what unique contribution a Christian community could make, and then try to make that response a reality. This posture is certainly what has drawn Alexis and other young people to the church.

FINDING THE ONE "RIGHT" PROGRAM, CAUSE, OR SOCIAL JUSTICE ISSUE

When we presented these findings to a group of leaders, we were asked a logical question: "When it comes to making a difference in the world, does your research show that it's better to serve locally or globally? And does it matter what cause or justice issue churches choose?"

The short answer is no.

The longer answer is that while the churches in our study were nearly universal in talking about the importance of service, exactly how they serve is all over the map. Literally. Churches practice being good neighbors through participating in global and local mission trips, volunteering inside the church, serving outside the church, raking leaves for the elderly, volunteering in a soup kitchen, building houses, leading advocacy work and immigration support, coordinating anti–sex trafficking efforts, practicing racial reconciliation, caring for the environment, picking up trash in their city, and exploring social entrepreneurship.

More important than finding the "right" cause is that the issue is meaningful to those involved. The leaders of churches growing young are able to discover what is meaningful because they listen to those in their congregation and community. They pay attention to statements like, "I really care about this issue," or, "I felt alive when I was serving there."

By listening to what's meaningful to their own people, churches that grow young strategically avoid adding endless new causes to an already full church calendar or budget. They also allow their people's interests to sprout new ministries without feeling like they have to support vast infrastructure. These catalytic churches empower their members to launch additional causes at a grassroots level or to get involved with organizations in the community that are already doing great work. Justin, a 23-year-old from a nondenominational church, shared, "At our church, everybody has something they care about, and the church doesn't need to rubber-stamp your passion before you can do it. We want the kind of environment where people are empowered and released to pursue what they care about and bring people around them to get involved. So we have an anti-trafficking small group, HIV/ AIDS small group, and much more."

Ideas for Action

As you review the following ideas, perhaps make notes in the margin. Mark if the idea is a fit for your church, who should implement the idea (you or another leader), and whether it can happen now or later. Please don't try to do everything—instead, aim for two or three ideas that *you* can act on now. Then at the end of the chapter, use the strategic questions to guide your church toward a specific plan to be the best neighbors.

Know Your Neighborhood

Being the best neighbor begins by understanding who your neighbors are. Luckily, the US census provides an in-depth and regularly updated overview of your neighborhood. Visit Census. gov to tap into a big-picture understanding of the demographics of your city or zip code. Pay attention to your neighborhood's household income, ethnic and age diversity, and poverty and education levels. Does anything surprise you? How do the results match the demographics of your church? Based on the data about your community, what do you wish was different about your church?

Gather a group to study your community more intently based on what you learn through census data. Host gatherings with neighbors, informally survey members of the community about their needs, meet with local government and law enforcement workers, and catalog existing services via nonprofits and other local ministries. All this data can build a more complete picture of your community's existing assets and biggest needs.

Pursuing diversity at a level that matches your surrounding community is not just a good thing to do—it's likely critical for the future of your church. Not convinced? As of 2012, over half of children younger than age one in the US were non-White.[13] These kids and their parents will be ready to join your children's ministry, youth group, and church in the near future—but will they feel like they fit?

Diversify Your Contacts

Would you like your church to have greater diversity but aren't quite sure how to reach that goal? Instead of focusing on your church, first focus on your own circle of contacts. Take out your cell phone and scroll through the contact list. Write down the number of people you have talked to in the last week or two who come from an ethnic group other than your own.[14]

If the number is lower than you hoped, create a plan to help you build relationships with people from other ethnic groups. Consider aiming for at least five friendships as a starting point (or adjust higher based on your context). Perhaps there are other church leaders in your city or denomination you could connect with who are of a different ethnicity. If you're a parent, maybe you could have coffee or dinner with the parents of one of your own children's friends.

Brush Up on Culture through Systematic Listening

Do you still own a VCR?

Have you ever used a phone that wasn't "smart"?

When someone says "cookies," is the first image that comes to your mind edible?

If you answered yes to any of those questions, your perspective on today's culture might need a bit of freshening up. Churches that grow young are marked by their regular and systematic practice of listening to the world around them. They not only practice listening as individuals but also gather other leaders and volunteers to reflect upon what they have heard in various conversations. Here are a few suggestions to get you started:

* Listen to a few of the most popular songs in the country right now—alone or with others. What do they tell you

"As a pastor, you need to know your Scripture and theology, but this can create a natural disconnect from people. You need to know people, listen to people, and form your theology in the streets and not just behind the desk." —Eugene Cho, Quest Church

about our culture and what's important to the millions who listened to these songs in the last week? If it feels natural, try referencing an artist's name during your next sermon or small group—you might be surprised by how quickly young people perk up!

- Take a 45-minute walking tour of the neighborhood around your church property with a journal or note-taking app on your phone at the ready. Who are your neighbors? What seems to be important to them? How might your church better connect with them?

- Spend some time at the mall. Not just as a customer, but as a cultural detective. Park yourself on a bench near the food court around dinnertime and simply observe. Enter a few stores you typically pass by, especially those that cater to youth culture. What do the signs, fashions, and topics of conversation around you communicate?

Survey Says . . .

Conduct a survey of your congregation. One of the churches in our study does so every year, especially because its population consists of transient young professionals so its community is constantly shifting. For any congregation, survey results can offer guidance on preaching and small group topics, staffing, and program offerings.

This was the case for Sam, the associate pastor of one church growing young:

We conducted a church-wide survey and were shocked when we realized how many single people are part of our community. Most of our preaching and programming was targeted to married couples with kids. As a result, we hired an additional pastor who can better address the needs of single people and that ministry is growing. Our pastor also adapted how he preaches, now including single people in his examples. We also realized we needed to talk more about sex and dating, which we did. For that series, we had four times the number of people show up as normal. It was a lesson for us that too few churches are talking about topics like these.

There are plenty of companies you can pay to conduct a survey for you, or get a team together and design your own. If there is a young person in your congregation who is a marketing major in college, they might even be able to coordinate it for class credit. Whatever method you choose, gather personal demographic information such as age, gender, education level, ethnicity, marital status, income level, and birthplace. Other potential questions include:

- How long have you attended our church?
- How often do you attend our church?
- In what programs/activities do you participate? What do you value about them?
- What attracted you to our church (friend/family member, internet search, preaching, worship style, service opportunity, reputation in the community, or something else)?
- What are your favorite aspects of our church?
- What would you like to change or improve about our church?
- Is there a story you could share about how our church has made a positive impact in your own life?

Craft a Theology of Culture

Are you aware of your theology of culture and how it contributes to your church's interactions with the world outside your doors? The teenagers and emerging adults in your church can sense your theology, even though they may never use the term.

Gather your leadership or volunteer team (and maybe a few teenagers or emerging adults also) to discuss three critical questions:

- What do our current actions and public communication (website, position papers, etc.) reveal (either explicitly or implicitly) about our posture toward culture and the world around us?

- What do we actually believe about how our church should interact with culture and the world around us? (As you answer this question, engage with our emphasis on *story* in chapter 4, pages 138–40.)

- As we compare what we actually believe to what we currently communicate, what are two or three shifts our church needs to make in order to be the best neighbors?

Tackle a Difficult Topic with Grace

What's a difficult contemporary topic that you don't want to talk about with your small group, volunteers, leadership team, or overall church . . . but know you need to? In some churches we visited, it was money. For others, it was immigration reform. While the topics vary, churches that grow young don't sidestep these issues; they make sure their conversations are flavored with the unity that comes only through our bonds in Christ.

One way to emphasize this unity is to take time to share the Lord's Supper (also known as Communion or the Eucharist) together before jumping into the discussion.

The pastor of a church I (Jake) used to attend advocated for Communion before any potentially divisive discussion. He reasoned there was no greater unifying activity than sharing the body and blood of Christ together, recognizing our common sin and the source of our salvation.

Designate one member of the group to remind everyone of the unity we have in Christ. As difficult topics are tackled, if tensions start to boil over, pause. Have the designated person remind everyone of the ritual you have just shared together. Even when conversations get heated, our common solidarity, demonstrated through Communion, outweighs the differences among us.

Take a few seconds of silence so everyone can reflect on the uniting power of Jesus Christ.

Then continue the discussion. Repeat as necessary.

Start Locally: A Research-Driven Church Strategy, Not Just a Popular Slogan

While young people like Alexis value mission trips to faraway places and tend to be globally aware, they also value making a difference in their own backyard. So much so that even when we as researchers thought that the churches we visited were doing amazing work in their local communities, the teenagers and emerging adults in those churches often wished their congregations were doing even more.

One large parish channeled their young people's passion to serve their local community into an extensive ministry to feed and clothe neighbors who are homeless. This focus on those who are homeless is now much more than a simple program or ministry strategy. It has shaped the psyche and relationships of the church as a whole. A young adult shared that one of his church friends who was homeless attended his wedding ceremony at

"The secret to reaching the world is first reaching your world. When you reach your world, it's amazing how your world starts expanding to reach the world." —Erwin Raphael McManus

the church. A friend from work (who did not attend the church) approached the groom and commented, "Did you see that a bum is here at your wedding? Can you believe that?"

The groom responded, "He's not a bum. He's one of us."

Your church might have neighbors who are homeless whom you could get to know and serve. Or you could take students on a mission "trip" where you stay and work in your own town. No matter what you choose, make your decision based on carefully listening to your local neighborhood.

Expand Globally: Mission and Justice as a Two-Way Street

While starting locally is important, being the best neighbors also includes our worldwide neighbors. Your church likely has plenty of requests coming to you from global churches or international mission and aid organizations. Based on our research, we want to offer one piece of advice as you pursue this service.

Make your mission and justice work a two-way street.

When we discussed this topic with our project's advisors, several leaders highlighted the "savior complex" prevalent in many of our churches. We talk and act as though *we* (who have things all together) are going to save *them* (who are desperately in need of our help). We who want our churches to grow young should adopt an opposite posture. We need to be honest with all generations that Jesus is the One who saves and that we often end up benefiting more than those we serve.[15]

As you prepare a team to travel globally, reflect on the following questions:[16]

- How do we move service beyond "spiritual tourism"?

- How can our service work be part of God's kingdom justice?

- What are the most important theological threads that should weave their way through our service?

- How does service contribute to teenagers' and emerging adults' identity development?

- What does it look like to develop true reciprocal partnerships with those we're serving?

Partner Up

If your church is running all of its own community service efforts, you're likely putting undue pressure on yourself and potentially offering a lower quality of service than if you identified strategic partners. One church in the Pacific Northwest wanted to provide practical training for parents on topics ranging from handling tantrums to planning for college. Rather than launch the entire training program on their own, they recognized that the local YMCA shared a similar mission. They now partner with the YMCA to offer six weeks of parent training several times per year. Parents from the community often feel more comfortable attending training seminars at this neutral location, and the church staff and volunteers still have the chance to build relationships with their neighbors. Further, both parents and church staff gain significant knowledge from the YMCA teachers on areas outside their own expertise.

As you dream about how to be the best neighbors, instead of launching a brand-new ministry on your own, spend time with the members of your leadership team or mission committee brainstorming local social organizations with whom you could partner. Better yet, consider having each member of your team join one local board, task force, or school council in order to enter on the ground level of the needs of your community.

One multiethnic church that is growing young has met in a local school for the past 10 years. The pastor shared that they're soon planning to launch a building campaign, but not to build a church. They want to build a community center in which the church will *rent* space. Six days out of the week, the building will host community-based activities. Sundays and occasional slots during the rest of the week will be dedicated to the church's activities. In this way, the church will keep its identity as a guest rather than an owner. The pastor sees this mindset as vital to preventing their church from getting too comfortable. It also helps blur the line between "inside the church" and "outside the church" and keeps the congregation connected to the local community.

Another large congregation that holds worship services in a high school auditorium sees its school partnership as critical to being good neighbors. The pastoral staff and school administration have built strong relationships—so strong that the principal actually provided a location for one pastor to hold regular on-campus office hours! The church donates back-to-school supplies and provides parking volunteers for graduation. The church and high school even co-sponsor a weeklong summer sports camp for elementary kids staffed by high school students and church members, many of whom take vacation time to lead one of the most meaningful ministries of the year. The church's pastor of global impact reflected, "Sometimes young people are drawn to things that surprise us. We never would have guessed that being good neighbors in the community through hosting a summer camp with the high school would be so important, but young people name it as the thing they love about our church."

Launch a Vocation Group

Like many churches, you might struggle with getting people in their twenties to show up for your ministries.

Especially that Sunday 7:30 a.m. Bible study on the book of Numbers. It hasn't grown young in over a decade.

Given emerging adults' desire to land on a vocation, as well as their simultaneous tendency to float from job to job, churches that grow young talk explicitly about vocation and calling. One creative church in our study hosts these conversations through *vocation groups*. In the midst of the confusing messages young people receive about calling, gifts, career, and vocation, these groups help sort through the clutter and bring clarity.

Rather than telling teenagers and emerging adults, "You can be anything you want to be," journey alongside them and help them discover what God has called them to be and do. Ideas to get started include:

- Be intentional about the time commitment. Some churches growing young purposely seek a long-term commitment from young people, believing it leads to deeper impact. Instead of asking young people to make such an extended commitment, others initially aim for six to eight weeks. They believe it's long enough to establish a rhythm and provide value but short enough that it's easy for busy or hesitant emerging adults to say yes. Groups always have the option of continuing after the time elapses. One suburban church in our study began to offer these groups and quickly attracted young people from the community outside their church who were desperate for career support and guidance. Find whatever pace feels right for your church and start there.

- When it comes to curriculum, spend time studying passages in Scripture that address calling or different vocations.[17]

Share hopes and fears and pray about them together. As an alternative, the book *Called: The Crisis and Promise of Following Jesus Today* by Fuller Seminary president Mark Labberton is another great starting point. Labberton grounds the idea of calling in Jesus' words to "Come, follow me" and then provides practical next steps for people to accept and live out Jesus' invitation.[18] Whether you use a book, study Scripture, or develop entirely different content, make sure you give time and space for group members to share honestly, and pray together that you would experience God in the midst of your vocational adventures.

- Encourage teenagers and emerging adults to share their testimonies, and help draw out aspects of their stories that hint at how God has wired them for different careers and ministry interests. Invite adults from a variety of professions to share their own stories as well. Perhaps create short-term or long-term mentoring relationships by matching these adults with young people who share the same vocational interests and dreams.

- Offer paid or unpaid internships at your church. Internships give emerging adults valuable tastes of vocational ministry during times of natural transition (e.g., the summer after they graduate from high school, summers during college, and immediately following college graduation). One nondenominational church in our study provides free housing for any young person who raises their own financial support for a one-year internship at the church. Another intern program thrives because of the access these college and graduate students have to mentoring from the pastoral staff. One young woman shared, "We're given real responsibility. We're trusted."

Give Them a Why

Many of the young people in your church or parish want to make a difference. Your congregation has the power to help them understand *why* they feel this passion by locating it in God's redemptive gospel narrative. For an upcoming sermon or small group series, think through how to help teenagers and emerging adults connect their passion for being the best neighbors with what God intended in the beginning of creation, as well as God's future new creation.

A pastor of The District Church did just this during the weekend we visited. The title of the sermon was "Why Church?," and he recounted why the church was founded and its hopes for the future. The thirty-something pastor shared that the big lie people in DC believe is that they can change the world outside of Christian community. In contrast, he argued that as difficult (or near impossible) as it may be to change the world on our own, it is best attempted through the defining, sustainable, Spirit-empowered work of a community of believers.

Based on the nodding heads of Alexis and hundreds of young adults in the congregation, it felt like he had struck a chord.

We're inclined to agree.

Chapter Highlights

* Churches that grow young strive to be the best neighbors both locally and globally. They recognize the careful dance that values both fidelity to Scripture's commands for holiness and knowing and graciously loving their neighbors.

* Offering teenagers and emerging adults a thoughtful path to neighbor well is not easy—36 percent of churches in our study named challenges navigating culture as one of their

biggest barriers in ministering to young people. In the midst of this gap and confusion, we discovered several common postures of churches that aim to be the best neighbors.

- Being the best neighbors means congregations reflect mercy toward the people outside their walls by adhering to the example set by Jesus in Matthew 22:34–40 and Luke 10:25–37.

- Churches that grow young neighbor well by honoring what's good, making their world better, and respecting the journey as much as the destination. These congregations show a neighbor love that is greater than differences in ethnicity and socioeconomic status.

- Right at the crux of young people's vocational exploration, churches are uniquely positioned to provide mentoring communities that help teenagers and emerging adults discover their calling and become good neighbors.

Strategic Questions to Help You Be the Best Neighbors

Research Findings

On a scale of 1 to 5 (with 1 being "we're struggling here" and 5 being "we're nailing this"), rate your congregation on the research findings presented in this chapter:

1. Our church intentionally trains young people to be the best neighbors by modeling the selfless mercy taught and exemplified by Jesus.

    1   2   3   4   5

2. Our church's posture toward culture honors the good while working to improve the world around us.

    1   2   3   4   5

3. Our congregation focuses on the process, or journey, for arriving at our positions and conclusions as much as on the conclusions themselves.

1 .... 2 .... 3 .... 4 5

4. Our church is satisfied with the level of ethnic and socioeconomic diversity present in our church community.

1 .... 2 .... 3 .... 4 5

5. Our congregation helps young people discover their calling in the world.

1 .... 2 .... 3 .... 4 5

Ideas for Action

1. What are you already doing personally to stay in touch with the culture around you?

2. What are some of the positive and life-giving steps your congregation is taking to be the best neighbor to the world outside its doors?

3. Given your ranking of the findings in the previous section, as well as the ideas you've read in this chapter, what one or two shifts might you or your church want to make?

4. Who else needs to be part of this conversation?

5. What can you do in the next few weeks or months to move toward these changes?

8. Growing Young in Your Context

How to Create a Plan for Change

Our church knows we need to reach out and change, or we'll die.

—Kristin, executive pastor

This is a changing church, and we're part of a changing world.
I've learned that I need to be big enough to change with it.

—Hank, age 76

St. John the Evangelist Catholic Church knows that growing young is not just *optional* but *essential*.

Founded in 1871 as the first Roman Catholic parish in Indianapolis, St. John's has a rich history. Located in the heart of the downtown business district, its towering steeples have been a landmark of the skyline for over 140 years. The church has stood the test of time with 18 priests who have served at the helm, a handful of whom led for more than three decades.

But in the 1980s and 1990s, the future of the parish looked bleak.

St. John's had been heavily affected over the preceding three decades by the nationwide trend of residents moving from downtown areas to the suburbs. By the 1980s, membership had declined. Most attendees were commuters who worked in the city and attended midday mass. One church leader remembered, "Thirty years ago, the doors were unlocked for mass and then locked again after mass." There were hardly any children or younger people involved, leaving a sparse mix of senior adults and business professionals.

St. John's, like many churches, was growing old. This was true of its buildings and physical campus. Even more disconcerting, the average age of the membership was migrating higher and higher.

One bleak year, the church almost closed its doors. For good.

Then in 2009, the parish turned a corner. Unwilling to concede that the people were too old, the road too difficult, or the timing too late, the church resolved to grow young.

In a move of support, the Catholic Archdiocese decided to prioritize young adult ministry at St. John's. The downtown area had recently been redeveloped, making it the ideal time for a parallel revitalization of the congregation. Father Rick, a wise and gifted leader, was recruited to serve as the campus chaplain at one of Indiana University's campuses, located just a few blocks from the church. New activities were initiated for young adults, including a Sunday evening mass and midweek gatherings designed to integrate them into the community.

Slowly, younger people started to reengage with the church. Overall attendance began to increase, average age began to decrease, and ministry grew both deeper and wider.

St. John's was growing young.

Understandably, this movement toward growing young did not come without its trials. Several of the longtime older members felt undervalued; others found it challenging to connect with this younger population.

One older parishioner named Gladys recalled, "It felt like they were scared of me, or like they didn't want to talk to an older person."

Thankfully, she felt comfortable voicing these concerns to Father Rick, who helped her and others empathize with the young people and their search for identity, belonging, and purpose. Growing young was not easy; it took a significant time investment from both the young people and the older parishioners. The leadership team of the parish was steadfast, though, and mixed the age groups in membership committees, small groups, and service teams. They also started an "adopt a student" program that matched adults with college students who shared similar vocational interests or hobbies. Gladys and other parishioners continued to look for ways to reach out, and eventually cross-generational relationships grew deeper.

Too often, however, the church felt like it was split in two. Father Rick, still serving as the campus chaplain, expressed this dilemma to the church's leadership. In response, he was appointed as the head pastor of the church and was charged with the work of merging the two communities. The church also hired a few part-time college staff members so that Father Rick could maintain his role as college chaplain while focusing the majority of his time on the congregation as a whole. It wasn't easy, but Father Rick and his team were determined to unite their parish as *one body*.

Their team strategically targeted social events, such as weekly minor league baseball games, that older parishioners attended regularly. They encouraged young people to attend both the game and the traditional pregame cookout in the church's courtyard. As a result, church attendance at the games tripled. Even more importantly, the younger and older parishioners were able to connect in nonthreatening and fun environments.

Emerging adults were especially drawn to the social justice efforts of the church, including a powerful ministry to their downtown neighbors who are homeless. The young people joined an already consistent group of volunteers who fed dozens of hungry people daily.

The church's dynamic young adult community soon evolved into a mixture of singles and married couples, many of whom met at St. John's. As the couples began having children, the congregation responded over time by developing training and small groups to help young families adapt to this new life stage.

A few years into these incremental changes, an arsonist broke into the church and set it ablaze. While the fire was miraculously extinguished quickly, the flames still consumed the church entryway, and the suffocating smoke that filled the sanctuary caused over $400,000 in damage.

It was a defining moment for St. John's.

Rather than express hatred and anger toward the arsonist, as a twenty-something remembered, "the leaders of the parish called us not to be mad but to pray for that person and to demonstrate the gospel." The church came together to host a "Tested by Fire" fundraiser to refocus on its mission and rebuild its damaged building. As the members weathered this tragedy, their shared passion to restore the church transcended generational differences and further united the church as a family.

Today St. John's is a thriving parish that exemplifies what it looks like for a church to grow young. Like every church, it has its share of ongoing obstacles and bumpy patches. However, as one national Roman Catholic representative commented, "St. John's is one of the most vibrant parishes I've ever seen." Indeed, there are over 1,500 members, nearly 1,000 of whom are teenagers or young adults.

Not bad for a church that was close to shutting its doors.

The Six Core Commitments Fleshed Out in St. John the Evangelist Catholic Church

Throughout the previous chapters, you've received an in-depth treatment of the six core commitments common to churches growing young. Notice how each was embodied in St. John's, catalyzing the church to grow young:

Unlock keychain leadership. Father Rick was a capable leader but not controlling. He empowered people in his church to use their gifts to fulfill the vision of the congregation.

Empathize with today's young people. At first, Gladys and others in the congregation did not connect with young people. However, they eventually developed relationships by listening carefully and appreciating the challenges navigated by today's teenagers and emerging adults.

Take Jesus' message seriously. St. John's talked about Jesus' message consistently and applied faith to the here and now. Rather than respond to the arsonist with anger and condemnation, the leadership preached and modeled grace and restoration.

Fuel a warm community. Instead of relying on the power of church services alone to draw the church together, the leaders also strategically planned social events to connect the whole church in relationship.

Prioritize young people (and families) everywhere. The Archdiocese made the decision to prioritize young adult ministry at St. John's and also instated campus minister Father Rick as its priest. In addition, the congregation developed training and small groups geared to help young families entering a new chapter of parenthood.

Be the best neighbors. As just one example of its commitment to serve the marginalized, the church fed—and continues to feed—dozens of its homeless neighbors every day.

Great News for Your Church: Change Is Possible

The story of St. John the Evangelist, while remarkable, doesn't have to be uncommon. The thousands of US churches growing older have good reason to be concerned.

But they don't have to admit defeat.

Perhaps your congregation's future looks dismal, and that's what led you to read this book.

Or maybe your church isn't in danger of closing its doors, but you know it has so much more potential. It may not be growing old, but it's not growing young or benefiting as much as possible from the energy and vitality of young people.

If you can relate to either scenario, this final chapter helps you move beyond *what* needs to change by helping you plan *how* your church can change. For many congregations, this question of how to bring about change is actually more difficult.

THE ROLE OF CONTEXT

Context

Keychain
Leadership

Best
Neighbors

Empathy
Today

GROWING
YOUNG
WHEEL

Priority
Everywhere

Jesus'
Message

Growing
Old

Warm
Relationships

In the Growing Young Wheel, the outside rim labeled "context" is now shaded. This is because your church—and every church—needs to understand how to embody these six core commitments in your own particular setting. While you can certainly learn from the experience of other congregations, what works for them might not work in your town or with your young people.

Nor will it work to cherry-pick a few ideas from each chapter and expect to bring about sustainable change. The six core commitments will not help that much if you apply them haphazardly; instead, we want to help you apply them *strategically*.

As the powerful story of St. John's illustrates, the six core commitments require more than a quick fix or list of easy steps. But the good news is that your church isn't left guessing about how to develop your own unique plan; you can build upon our research and the collective wisdom of leading experts on organizational leadership. In addition, our team has observed and worked with hundreds of churches that have successfully pioneered lasting change in their programs, systems, and overall church culture.[1]

In tandem with the research our team conducted in this project, we had the privilege of working closely with Dr. Scott Cormode, the Hugh De Pree Professor of Leadership Development at Fuller Theological Seminary. Scott's writing, teaching, and conversations with our team significantly informed this entire project but especially these principles about contextual change.

Given our goal in this chapter to help you weave together and implement the core commitments from the previous chapters, its format is a little different. The "Ideas for Action" normally placed at the end of a chapter are instead already woven into the research. Our hope is that as you work your way through this research on transition, you'll fold your insights and ideas from previous chapters into a comprehensive plan that empowers your congregation to grow young.

The overarching great news is that deep and lasting change *really is possible.*

The churches involved in the Growing Young study prove it. When interview participants were asked whether their church had always been effective with young people, many admitted that their church had not been effective from its inception. Of those young people and adults who knew the history of their church, more than one-third reported that their church had undergone significant change to become more effective with young people.

Making this bold move to more fully embody the six core commitments benefits churches on multiple fronts. As we've highlighted, the biggest benefit is vitality. Young people's energy, excitement, and passion can electrify churches and propel them forward into a more hopeful future.

However, there are also real dangers for churches that make shifts to grow young. A church may risk upsetting a large portion of its membership (perhaps even those who provide your church's financial backbone). Perceived failures may cause church members to become more disgruntled and frustrated with those in leadership. Leaders may even lose their jobs. It is certainly wise to count these potential costs before jumping in and making adjustments.

But at the end of the day, the decision to grow young is not rooted in statistics or strategies (even though, as you can tell by now, we love both). It's rooted in prayerfully seeking God's call for your congregation. So gather your church's staff, volunteer leaders, and anyone else who cares about teenagers and young adults as you prayerfully ask God for guidance. Take courage in the fact that millions of churches in the last 2,000 years have successfully navigated significant obstacles to adapt to new realities. Your church can too.

Three Myths about Churches That Change to Grow Young

Before we explore how leading churches initiate change, we need to dispel three common myths that will *not* help your church grow young. In fact, relying on any of these myths can stall or sabotage your church's efforts to embrace the six core commitments.

Myth #1: There Is a Single Silver Bullet

There is neither one easy step to take nor one common problem to fix that will lead your entire church to grow young. When participants in our study were asked what they might want to change about their church, their responses varied greatly. No single area was mentioned by more than 10 percent of congregants. While this can free up churches to experiment and learn, it also puts more pressure on leaders to listen to their context as a compass to help chart their own particular course.

Myth #2: Bigger or Well-Resourced Churches Can Change Faster and Easier

Possessing a big building, the latest technology, a significant number of staff, or a surplus of cash positions a church to make shifts quickly, right?

Not according to our research. In fact, when hundreds of pastors were asked in our surveys about their biggest challenge to becoming more effective with young people, only 1 in 10 mentioned the church's lack of material resources. This wasn't because all the churches are well-resourced. Some of the most innovative and exciting churches in our study are fairly small and lack a big budget, a large staff, or a fancy building.

Myth #3: Hiring _____ Will Solve the Problem

Many roles could fill this blank.

A new pastor. A youth pastor. Someone outgoing. Someone young. Someone experienced. An expensive consultant.

Hiring can certainly help, at least in the short term. But most of the real revision that needs to happen in a church cannot be imposed from the outside or from the top down. It needs to be owned and implemented by the entire church—usually from the inside and sometimes from the bottom up.

Creating Your Church's Plan for Change

You likely have a sense for where your church is currently (represented by the image on the left side of the diagram)—it might be stalled, growing old, or doing well but not reaching its full potential. By now, you probably also have some picture of what your church would look like if it were growing young (represented by the right-hand image). Your goal now is to create your plan for change to get from "here" to "there." The following sections on listening, storytelling, and tools for change empower you to embody the six core commitments and create your own contextual plan.

CREATING YOUR CHURCH'S PLAN FOR CHANGE

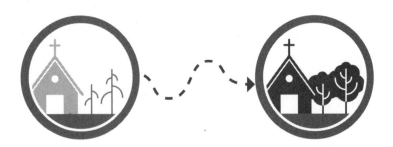

Aim for Adaptive Change in Order to Grow Young

The reason these myths don't work is because the type of changes required to grow young are *adaptive* challenges. As coined by Harvard leadership professor Ronald Heifetz, *adaptive* challenges involve shifts in attitudes, values, and behaviors that require leaders to learn new ways to solve problems. Heifetz contrasts *adaptive* challenges with *technical* problems in which leaders can resolve their dilemmas through current know-how.

Think of a technical problem as someone with a broken arm. A doctor can set the bone and apply a cast, typically solving the problem in a handful of weeks. While activities like driving may become a bit more difficult, significant changes in behavior and values are not required. Adaptive work is more like trying to convince someone to stop smoking. A doctor can provide guidance about the risks and suggest ideas that might help the person stop smoking, but they cannot stop smoking for the person. Further, a spouse, friend, or even therapist cannot stop smoking for the person. The ultimate decision depends on a major modification of the values and behaviors of the smoker. Applying this principle to organizations, Heifetz writes, "The single most common source of leadership failure we've been able to identify—in politics, community life, business, or the nonprofit sector—is that people, especially those in positions of authority, treat *adaptive* challenges like *technical* problems."[2]

After studying hundreds of churches and witnessing the complexity of their systems, structures, and culture, we are strong advocates for the power of adaptive change. Most of the important obstacles faced by churches that want to grow young involve a shift in the attitudes, values, and behaviors of the people in the congregation. Throughout this entire book, we have sprinkled in principles of adaptive change that we believe best position your church to grow young. We'll specifically revisit more thoughts about adaptive change in the section "Tools to Help Your Church Change" later in this chapter.

Leadership Begins with Listening[3]

Since the six core commitments in the Growing Young Wheel have already illustrated *what* we should do, it's tempting (especially for those of us with type A personalities) to launch into action steps that help us feel like we're making progress. We're inclined to immediately make a formal announcement from the platform, develop an elaborate strategic plan, or hire a new staff member. But if leaders move forward before carefully listening to their congregation, they're implying that they already know and understand what their congregation needs. Forward momentum, while critically important to leading change, must first be tempered with appreciating the particular obstacles and opportunities of our own unique church context.

If we don't listen to others, we are prone to a common mistake, namely, equating the health and needs of our church with the "three Bs" that have often been used to measure congregations—building, bodies, and budget. While these can provide one helpful picture, there is so much of a church's past, present, and future that falls outside these simple categories and must be incorporated in our growing young plan.

Churches that grow young move past such reductionist categories; they take time to understand and respond to the needs of their own young people. In fact, when pastors were asked, "What are the three biggest challenges your church faces when it comes to ministering to young people?" nearly half (45 percent) of respondents highlighted young people's general busyness or transience. Recognizing this, those churches that began

"Students are consumed with school and homework and extracurricular activities and sports and all that stuff. I feel like some churches try to force too much and put the pressure on. One thing that our church does well is we try to just listen." —Trevor, age 27

listening well revamped their ministries to adapt to teenagers' and emerging adults' unique schedules.

This focus on listening is certainly true in the case of St. John's. When asked to describe Father Rick, participants referred to him as "very in touch, relatable" and said "his connection to people is evident."

HOW DO WE START LISTENING WELL?

Begin by gathering a team that commits to listening well. Resolve together that if your church truly desires to grow young, you won't get far without understanding your current context and reality.

Every congregation is different when it comes to how much time should be spent listening before crafting a plan. However, consider spending at least two months listening well before you decide on any further action steps. Rather than create an inflexible timeline, evaluate your progress along the way. You and others on your team will likely know when you've listened long enough.

WHO SHOULD WE LISTEN TO?

Here's a starter list. Undoubtedly, you will think of additional individuals or groups relevant to your church.

- *God.* You guessed it—listening to God is nonnegotiable. Spend time as a team in prayer, consult Scripture, or engage in other spiritual practices to help you hear God's voice.

- *Young people themselves.* This is also nonnegotiable. Don't try to make any shifts without sitting down with at least a few young people (or 20) to gain their perspective.

- *Your own heart.* Spend time exploring your own thoughts and feelings about helping your church change and embrace the core commitments. Keep a journal for a few weeks, or spend time in a team meeting discussing the viewpoint of each person at the table.

- *Research about young people.* Chapter 3 gives you access to the best scholarship on this generation's search for identity, belonging, and purpose. If you're feeling particularly motivated, dive deeper into the books and resources referenced throughout that chapter.

- *Parents, Sunday school teachers, and youth/young adult ministry volunteers.* Given their unique interest and role in developing young people, include at least a few parents, teachers, and small group leaders in your listening tour.

- *Older generations.* Some of the most successful churches we've observed capture the passion and support of older members of their church and channel it toward younger people. This often happens best by listening to and honoring those seasoned members.

- *Your church's neighbors.* Depending on your goals, this might be beyond the bounds of this exercise. However, careful listening to those outside your faith community can provide valuable insight as well.

WHAT'S THE BEST METHOD FOR LISTENING?

The method you use to listen well is entirely up to you. Some churches in our study utilize the power of detailed surveys. Others rely primarily on one-on-one conversations or focus groups. Another church holds a newcomers' dinner in which the pastor hosts a meal in her home twice per month. Recent visitors are invited alongside long-standing members to share stories and perceptions of the church. Try one of these methods or experiment with your own even better ideas to see what works well for your congregation.

"We don't really focus on innovation or change but simply on listening to our kids through relationship. The rest just follows naturally."
—Tony, youth ministry volunteer

Whatever path you choose, you might want to work with your team to develop a list of common questions that everyone can use in their various conversations. To help you get started, consider the following:

- How did you hear about our church?
- What drew you to our church?
- What do you like best about our congregation?
- What do you like least about our congregation?
- What is one idea you have to improve our church?
- What's something exciting that has happened in your life recently?
- What's something difficult that has happened in your life recently?
- If there was one story from your life that would help me understand who you are, what would it be and why?
- What is something that you hope for or dream about?

As you begin to approach others, listen as if the future of your church depends on it. Because it does.[4]

WHAT SHOULD WE LISTEN FOR IN RESPONSE TO OUR QUESTIONS?

In your listening, aim for more than surface-level conversation. Ask about people's hopes and dreams. Listen for the pain in their lives and the questions that keep them awake at night.

By doing this work in your own context, your church will be positioned to respond to the longings and losses that really matter to your teenagers, emerging adults, and families.[5]

Afraid teenagers won't want to talk to you? Think again. Try talking about something they actually care about, such as stress, dating relationships, or learning to hold down a job. Or enlist an adult young people know well to partner with you when you meet with them.

In addition, listen for ideas about what your church could *be* or *do*. Discern their expectations for your church, especially when you hear words like *should*. Pay attention to what sparks their interests or passions. Consider listening for the presence (or lack thereof) of the six core commitments: pay attention to people's hopes and frustrations related to leadership, empathy toward young people, understanding Jesus' message, community support, priorities of the church, and being good neighbors.

Perhaps most importantly, *listen for stories*. Reflect on what the stories convey about your congregation's attitudes and values, along with the implications for your journey to grow young.

HOW SHOULD WE USE WHAT WE HEAR?

During one of your team meetings, invite each person to recount the key themes heard during your listening. Identify and reflect on the implications of topics or phrases that are either particularly vivid or repeatedly mentioned.

WHEN DO WE STOP LISTENING?

Never.

You will never finish listening.

Even when you feel like you have completed this first phase of listening and can start creating a specific action plan, listening should weave its way throughout your entire transformation process. In fact, we recommend that you occasionally loop back to the above groups at whatever time intervals seem right for subsequent rounds of questions and story gathering.

Vision Is a Shared Story of Future Hope

Church leadership conferences and books over the past few decades have hammered home the importance of vision. Our research on churches that grow young affirms that vision is a wise place to invest time and energy. When asked about the history of their church, 31 percent of those who said their church changed to become more effective with young people attributed that shift to a change in the church's vision or strategy. This was the second highest response, only slightly behind shifts in church staff.

While having a vision is important, churches' definition of "vision" and understanding of what qualifies as a "vision statement" vary widely. Bringing helpful clarity to the topic, Scott Cormode defines vision as "shared stories of future hope."[6] This definition encompasses three crucial elements of a generative vision: *shared*, *stories*, and *future hope*.

The first crucial element, *shared*, implies that the vision does not emerge from the mind of one person—or a few people—alone. The third crucial element, *future hope*, signals that Jesus brings Good News for the whole world and, as a result, any church can grow young over the next few months, years, or decades.

THE SIGNIFICANCE OF STORIES

What makes this definition so potent is the second key element: *stories*. God's story, your story, and your church's story are connected and lead to something powerful: *our story*. Connecting vision to stories enables the vision to immediately connect with an individual and sweeps up that individual into a story much larger than any one person alone. Stories challenge, encourage, and lead people deeper into the redemptive gospel narrative of what God is doing in the world.

Your church, your family, and the fans of your favorite sports team all tell stories that give them a unique identity. When it comes to churches, sociologist Nancy Ammerman suggests:

> Stories, then, provide us both with the common elements that allow us to make connections with each other and the unique identities that keep us anchored in the midst of our diversity. They can be told over and over, linking us to our past, while evolving with each new telling. . . . Active, intentional storytelling is the basis on which all communities have always been built, and that is no less true today when communities are so fluid and fragile.[7]

Take a moment and think of a person from your church (or from a church you've been connected to in the past) who has a vibrant faith. Envision a young person, or even an older person, whose identity is rooted in the grace of God, who knows they belong in the love of Christian community, and who passionately lives out their God-given purpose through a mission-oriented life. Now think through the story of that person's life and experiences that shaped them into who they are today.

Now dream on your own or (even better) with others, "What would our church look like if we wanted today's young people to have these same experiences?"

At St. John's, the leadership team could have chosen the story of an older parishioner like Gladys. Gladys grew up in the church in the 1940s and 1950s when the parish was thriving. Perhaps keychain leaders recognized her potential and gave her opportunities to lead because they prioritized young people and families, including hers. Maybe older adults in the congregation empathized with her hopes and concerns, looking past some of her teenage quirks and enveloping her in a warm community. Her deepest passions were possibly awakened and fueled by the Jesus-focused messages in the church's vibrant teaching and small groups. It could have been these passions that led her to help start the church's ministry to its neighbors who were homeless. It's likely that all of these core commitments are the reason she is still part of St. John's today.

Following this exercise, the leadership team could then ask, "How can these experiences that were formative in Gladys's life be manifested in the lives of today's teenagers and emerging adults?" Yes, some of the packaging and delivery needs to be updated to match the church's current culture and context. However, as leaders recognize the dominant themes in the stories of people like Gladys, all ministries and programs of the church become rooted in a cohesive whole.

PUTTING STORIES TO WORK IN YOUR CHURCH

Based on what your team heard in your listening, consider drafting a short (one- or two-page) story of what you hope your church will be like in the future. You might find it helpful to begin by first writing stories that focus on individuals.

Previously, you unpacked the real-life stories of one or more people with vibrant faith. Now it's time to brush up on your creativity skills and imagine a future for either a real or fictional young person. What do you hope or dream will happen in the life of that person as a result of your church? How do you hope that your church's embodiment of the six core commitments shapes their faith and life?

Try writing a short (one- or two-page) story about one young person. Or maybe about a few. Once you've developed the right story or stories, tell them over and over in every part of your congregation.

When another leader catches you in the hall after worship and asks what you're excited about, share a story.

When you are invited to give a report to your church board, share a story.

When you meet with someone new to your congregation and want them to understand your greatest dreams for the future, share a story.

These stories might be actual accounts of what God has already done in your young people or your visions for how God intends to work in your community in the future. Either way, watch as these stories become contagious and transform the culture of your church.

Tools to Help Your Church Change

Your team has listened well to understand where your church is now.

You've crafted shared stories of future hope to paint a picture of what your church will look like as it grows young.

If you've done these first two aspects well, this will make the final step of developing a plan for change easier.

Not easy.

But *easier*.

Based on our research, our team recommends the following four guiding principles to help your congregation navigate the peaks and valleys of your growing young journey.

BEGIN WHERE YOU HAVE THE MOST INFLUENCE

We asked leaders of churches growing young to identify the major challenges that prevent them from reaching young people more effectively. We hypothesized they might point to traits of youth culture, or qualities of young people's families, or the attributes of today's young people.

CONGREGATION'S GREATEST CHALLENGES
IN REACHING YOUNG PEOPLE

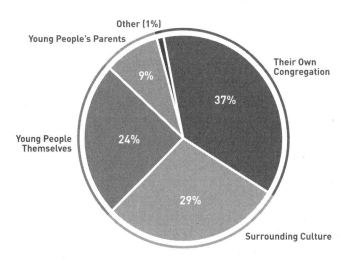

Other (1%)

Young People's Parents

Their Own
Congregation

9%

37%

Young People
Themselves

24%

29%

Surrounding Culture

TOP CHURCH-RELATED CHALLENGES
(ranked in order)

1. A generation gap
2. Inconsistent or nonexistent volunteers
3. Lack of effective church strategy
4. Lack of material resources
5. Lack of willingness to change
6. Worship style
7. Other generations assume the worst about young people

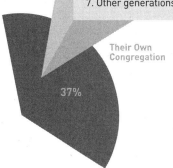

Their Own
Congregation

37%

All of these challenges were named, but they weren't at the top of the list. The top class of obstacles was *their own congregation*. As indicated in the diagram, leaders felt most hindered in their congregation by a generation gap, inconsistent or nonexistent volunteers, and the lack of an effective church strategy.

While these hurdles may seem daunting, we've been impressed by the way many churches that grow young—even those that are large and complex—maneuver them with agility. Rather than focus on those obstacles that are largely outside the church's control (like the impact of the surrounding culture), effective leaders focus on what they can influence inside their own congregation, such as their own keychain leadership or uniting the church around a common vision.

CONSTRUCT A HOLDING ENVIRONMENT

Earlier in this chapter, we distinguished adaptive challenges from technical problems. Heifetz believes leaders can best solve adaptive challenges by creating and managing a "holding environment."[8] Similar to the doctor who cannot force change on a patient who smokes, church leaders cannot force their congregants to change their deeply held attitudes, values, and behaviors about their church.

But that doesn't mean leaders are helpless. They can create holding environments to nurture and encourage major shifts. A holding environment is a space that keeps attention focused on a problem in a way that is uncomfortable enough to promote change but safe enough that the church's anxiety about change isn't too acute. The role of the leader is to carefully raise the heat so that the problem is taken seriously but then lower the heat when tensions rise too high and threaten to boil over.

Whether or not leaders knew the term *holding environment*, many of the churches we studied demonstrated a keen intuition about how to drive change at a pace their context could tolerate. For example, most of the congregations did not prioritize young people at all levels of the church right away. Instead, they slowly raised the heat by highlighting in their preaching, meetings, and one-on-one conversations that the church was in danger of growing old and irrelevant if it didn't change.

Sometimes those shifts come so fast and furious that churches need to lower the heat. One church in our study launched so many new ministries and changed the worship format so often that the congregation experienced change fatigue. Recognizing this growing exhaustion, the leaders in this church gave their congregants a chance to recuperate by pausing to celebrate, intentionally waiting several months to introduce anything new.

EXPERIMENT ON THE MARGINS[9]

As you introduce the core commitments in your context, it is tempting to immediately and publicly roll out a new campaign in front of the whole church. Consider starting with a less overt approach. Rather than launching change from the inside out, try saturating your congregation from the outside in. In other words, look for opportunities to implement shifts that start on the periphery rather than at the core of the church. Trying a new idea first with a Sunday school class, small group, handful of students, or anywhere not on display to your entire congregation qualifies as an experiment on the margins. For most churches, changes in the main worship service do not.

But there are strategies to help you experiment on the margins even with changes in your worship service. The leadership team of one rural church in our study knew that tackling music style head-on could spark a long and messy battle (many of you are nodding your heads along with them). So as an experiment on the margins, they encouraged the emerging adults to start a worship band that practiced immediately after the regular Sunday worship service. While the congregation shared coffee and cookies, they could see and hear this group rehearsing.

Before long, some of the members who would have been most opposed to a drastic and immediate adjustment in music style asked if these young people might be allowed to play one or two songs for the main worship service. Slowly but surely, the church embraced a newer style, which has been a generative step in its journey to grow young.

MAINTAIN DISCIPLINED ATTENTION

When I (Jake) was in my early twenties and fresh into ministry as a youth pastor, I thought that changing our church would be quick and easy. As I participated in several daylong strategic planning sessions with our church's leadership team, I wondered impatiently, "What is everyone waiting for? Why won't they just change faster?" Over the next five years, I watched the church commission one outside consultant and two executive pastors to lead the charge, with few significant results. Like many, I was shortsighted about the time and care it takes to implement lasting transformation.

For many churches, the main barrier to initiating change is not a lack of desire but a lack of the long-term dedication and discipline needed to make the transition a reality. Churches that grow young successfully fight against distractions or other pitfalls that threaten to derail them by *maintaining disciplined attention*.[10] Leaders who maintain disciplined attention intentionally keep themselves and their team focused on the tough questions and difficult shifts ahead through five key strategies.

Develop a growing young team and start meeting. As your church prepares to take steps to grow young, create a guiding coalition that is separate from your church board or leadership team. Recruit a variety of respected stakeholders to serve on this team, including staff, elders or deacons, congregation members, parents, young people, and anyone else who should be represented. Meet every three to four weeks, making sure that each time you identify the next steps your team plans to take, who's in charge of making sure those steps happen, and when those steps need to be completed.

Create a plan to conquer conflict. In one of your early meetings, discuss how you will handle (or are currently handling) conflict. It is an unavoidable aspect of change. When you find yourself mired in conflict, rely on the vision-filled stories you've crafted to remind yourselves why you're pursuing these adjustments in the first place. Practice your best listening and lean into the unity in Christ that holds your church together. At the end of the day, keep hold of the shared stories of future hope to which God has called your community.

Treat failure as a door to learning. Great organizations fail frequently. So do great churches. The key is not to avoid making mistakes but to learn from those mistakes as quickly as possible so you can head in a better direction. Lean into a gospel of grace not just as individuals but as an organization. As you marinate in a sense of God's grace, love, and mission, you might find your church's tolerance for organizational failure increases.

Leverage the power of small wins. Rather than focusing on a single marker that will tell your church it has "arrived" and has grown young, identify several smaller victories your team can measure and celebrate along the way. If your team continues listening well, there will be ongoing stories of positive life transformation you can celebrate. Theresa, a 25-year-old small group leader, emphasized, "Our church tracks *BUT NOW* statements. We know we're making progress and people are growing

> We want to continue to be part of your journey toward growing young, especially as you hit roadblocks or if you're not making progress as fast as you'd like. For tips on how to deal with setbacks in your journey, please visit ChurchesGrowingYoung.org. There you can access a free assessment survey and a host of practical resources and consulting and training options, as well as find other leaders who are on the same road toward growing young. You might also consider joining a Growing Young Cohort, a community of innovative churches committed to growing young together.

in their faith when they say things like, 'I was going to do ____, but now I'm going to ____.' We celebrate that!"

Think long term. While many of the churches we've studied witnessed exciting movement within their church in a few months or a year, broad culture change in a church typically takes several years. While you'll understandably need to focus your initial plans on the next few weeks or months, keep your church's long-term trajectory in the back of your mind. Perhaps schedule a daylong meeting for one and two years from now in order to celebrate progress and address obstacles impeding your progress.

Leading Change in Practice: Growing Young in Volga, South Dakota

When this study began, our team did not anticipate that one of the most exciting and change-friendly churches we would encounter would be a largely volunteer-run congregation located in Volga, South Dakota.

Volga is a rural town of just 2,000 people. During our visit, it was often referred to as a bedroom community of the nearby city of Brookings. This sleepy label did not seem to cast the town or Volga Christian Reformed Church (CRC), a congregation of 100, as a hotspot for young people. There were few restaurants or coffeehouses, no nightlife to speak of, hardly any pop culture, and not much else often believed to draw teenagers and emerging adults. In many ways, the town and church seemed well positioned to grow old.

And it was. Just like the community, much of the congregation was over 60. Most of the church programs and ministries catered to this older generation.

But then the leaders and people at Volga CRC decided to shift their trajectory.

In the midst of a pastoral transition, Vonda, a 20-year youth ministry volunteer, decided to help the church grow young. Having been raised at the church, Vonda knew the congregation's culture and cared deeply for its young people. Her job as a teacher at the local public high school gave her an on-the-ground understanding of the hopes and challenges of teenagers and young adults. Further, given that she was closer in age to the older contingent in the church, she was able to empathize with their needs as well.

Working with a team of volunteers, Vonda launched a quiet campaign nearly 10 years ago to bridge the two generations and create one unified church. She didn't consult a master plan or request a three-month sabbatical so she had time to strategize. Instead, she shared with our team that young people "are creative, motivated, and innovative. If we hope to change, we need to listen to them."

From this listening, the team members recognized that they wanted to help younger and older generations mix with each other in hopes of nurturing a warm community. To encourage the generations to develop organic relationships in relaxed settings, the team began holding youth group gatherings in the homes of older congregants. Next, Vonda and her team organized "Bridge Sundays" in which young people led an all-church Sunday school class every month there was a fifth Sunday. Doing so ensured that the needs and interests of young people were regularly kept in front of the church. After the class, the whole church gathered in the basement for a good old-fashioned church potluck during which teenagers shared personal updates and stories.

Since youth leadership of the Sunday worship service would have been too big of a jump for Volga CRC initially, this first step of having youth lead a Sunday school class was an opportune experiment on the margins. This experiment was so successful that before long, the young people were invited to begin leading music for the main worship service.

In addition, Vonda took more direct steps to connect the congregation's various generations. She invited Trudy, a 90-year-old golfer, for a round with some of the teenagers in the youth group. While at first skeptical of Trudy, the teenagers eventually lightened up once they saw she was quite the skilled golfer. When she sank a 30-foot putt on the seventh hole, the high school students went nuts. That story quickly spread throughout the rest of the church.

Over the years that this church sought to grow young, Vonda and her team also continued to invite young people to take Jesus' message seriously. Their method was not particularly innovative, consisting mostly of Bible study, prayer, and sharing life together. She explained to our team that at the very least, she wanted young people to know that "Jesus died for you, loves you, and you are good enough no matter what." The volunteer team personalized this message to each teenager as much as possible, based on each student's unique hopes and struggles.

The major breakthrough, however, came two years ago in a way that no one could have planned. Given his background in youth ministry, the new pastor, Bryan, shared Vonda's vision to bridge the generations and looked for opportunities to do so. During a prayer service, as the prayer requests came in, Bryan handed some important keys to young people by asking them to volunteer to pray aloud.

The congregation was not prepared for what they heard as the young people prayed. Teenagers and emerging adults prayed passionate, fervent, mature prayers. While they prayed, it became apparent to the older members that these young people were not disinterested in God or church. They were fellow believers who took their faith seriously and desired to have a place at the table. The older adults in the church were floored and began to look at the younger generation in a new light.

When we visited the church, every group we interviewed told us this story. One of the older adults teared up as he recalled, "I was very proud of our youth in that moment."

The young people themselves recounted how they had earned a new level of respect after that prayer service. "It was like the older generation now knew that we actually wanted to be part of the church," one teenager shared. From that point on, the church began to prioritize young people at all levels of the church.

Now young people regularly help lead worship. The pastor has committed to periodically attend youth group gatherings, retreats, and other activities. The church's elder board has upped its commitment to young people, most notably through adjustments to the church budget.

The most important fruit of this prioritization is that every young person now feels welcomed, loved, and known in their church. One high school student gushed, "Walking through the doors on Sunday morning is *the best*—I get a happy feeling whenever I think about it." Volga CRC is that warm. Because of their church's magnetic community, several high school students now plan to go to the local college rather than move far away.

Another teenager commented, "I feel like I have 20 grand-parents at my church."

In addition to the handful of young people whose families attend the church, a dozen teenagers who live in the surrounding community now participate in the life of the church. They show up even though their parents are not Christians, because by being the best neighbors, Volga CRC has demonstrated something compelling that these young people want to be a part of.

As a result of this unparalleled sense of community, Volga CRC is growing young. Its ministry is not flashy, its facilities are pretty basic, and it has only one full-time staff person (and it's not Vonda!). However, the church is now a place where young people love to be and where they are growing in their faith.

Volga CRC also benefits from the life and energy emanating from its young people. As one senior adult shared, "Seeing so many young people around the church brings a smile to my face."

The church is growing in numbers too and is seeking ways to keep up with the increase in attendance. Perhaps most importantly, this church, which once faced the possibility of growing old and dying, is now excited about the bright future that lies ahead.

A future that feels young.

Chapter Highlights

- Any church can change to grow young. Nearly 1 in 3 research participants noted their church had undergone significant shifts to become more effective with young people.

- Churches do not change to grow young by pursuing a silver bullet, relying on their size or large budget, or hiring staff to solve their problems.

- A crucial early step in a congregation's journey toward growing young is to understand its unique context through careful and systematic listening to all generations.

- By sharing stories of future hope, congregations can both develop and communicate their vision for growing young.

- Changes toward growing young are made easier by beginning where you have the most influence, constructing a holding environment, experimenting on the margins, and maintaining disciplined attention.

Strategic Questions to Help Your Church Develop Its Own Plan to Grow Young

Your Church Now

- Who are the key people from your church who should be part of the leadership team or guiding coalition to help your church grow young?

- To whom does your leadership team need to listen? Make a list of individuals or groups, noting the names of those from your leadership team who will do that listening.

- What are the four to six major themes that stand out?

- Go back through this book and review your ratings and answers to the questions at the end of each chapter. Based on what you noted and what you've heard from your congregation, which two of the six core commitments need to be the focus of your church's time and attention in this next season? Perhaps make notes about where you want to focus on the Growing Young Wheel below.

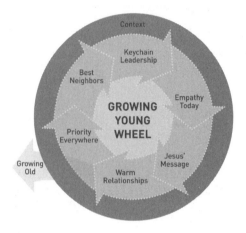

Your Church Growing Young

- What is one inspiring story your team heard during your listening?

- Imagine and write a shared story of future hope that focuses on your hopes or dreams for one young person in your congregation.

- Imagine and write a shared story of future hope that focuses on your hopes or dreams for your congregation overall.

- Given the stories you've discovered and developed, how can you share them with your congregation in such a way that inspires the church to want to grow young? With whom can you share stories, and when?

Your Plan for Change-

- For the first core commitment you want to improve on, what two or three steps could your team take in order to make progress? Who needs to be involved in those steps, and when will they take place?

- For the second core commitment you want to improve on, what two or three steps could your team take in order to make progress? Who needs to be involved in those steps, and when will they take place?

- What potential areas of conflict or roadblocks might you encounter? What is your plan to move past those roadblocks?

- What are small markers along the journey that your church can pay attention to and celebrate? How will you celebrate them?

Appendix

Research Method and Procedures

The findings presented in this book emerged from the Churches Engaging Young People (CEYP, pronounced "keep") Project, conducted from 2012 to 2015 by the Fuller Youth Institute (FYI) at Fuller Theological Seminary. This appendix provides an *abbreviated description* of the research method and procedures. For a more in-depth treatment of the research method, including the survey instruments and scales, interview protocols, and other more detailed research documents, please visit Churches GrowingYoung.org.

Based on extensive preliminary work and literature review, the research team identified one primary question and two secondary questions for study.

* Primary research question: What congregational practices lead to effective engagement of young people?

* Secondary research questions: How does engaging young people contribute to a thriving church? What are next-step

processes for congregations that want to enact changes toward more effective ministry with young people?

Early in the project, a working definition was formed to clarify "effectively engaging young people." An effective church was defined as one that is involving and retaining young people in the congregational community, as well as helping them develop a vibrant faith in Jesus Christ. While involving and retaining were much easier to operationalize, the team employed a variety of methods to understand and measure a vibrant faith in Jesus Christ.[1]

Building on a review of the existing literature, the research team also developed an initial working list (prior to beginning Stage 1 research) of characteristics that seemed likely to be present in churches that are effectively engaging young people. Both quantitative and qualitative items were developed to explore, assess, and revise these characteristics across the three stages of the research.

Nomination Process

In order to understand how and why churches are effectively engaging young people, it was critically important to first identify churches that fit this description.[2] Over 35 nominators (described on page 30) were invited to submit names of up to 15 noteworthy churches via an online questionnaire from June through November 2013.[3] Requirements included that churches be located within the US and that the pastors be able to complete a survey and potential subsequent surveys or interviews in English. The nominations were based upon the following criteria:

- Churches that are effectively engaging a growing number of young people[4] (ages 15 to 29) or are effectively engaging a large number of young people in relation to the size of the congregation. (Up to 10 churches per nominator.)

- Churches that seem to have something *exciting* or *missional* going on with young people but their numbers aren't large or growing. (Up to 5 churches per nominator.)

Nominators provided basic demographic information about each congregation, as well as a brief explanation of why the congregation was being nominated.[5]

Based on this nomination process, names of 363 noteworthy congregations were submitted for study.

Research Method and Procedures

Stage 1 Research

OVERVIEW AND INSTRUMENTS

A pastor and youth/young adult leader (either paid or volunteer) from each church was contacted by the research team via email and/or phone beginning in November 2013 and invited to participate in the study. Participating leaders completed a quantitative and qualitative survey that was delivered through an online questionnaire. Participants were assured of the anonymity of their responses and were offered a $50 gift card for their involvement.

The Stage 1 surveys included questions about the church's size, attendance, growth patterns and presence of young people, socioeconomics, ethnic diversity, and the leader's definition of spiritual vibrancy (and evidence of vibrancy among young people). In addition, a scale was developed to rate the presence of the eight congregational characteristics predicted to be associated with effective engagement of young people,[6] as well as a scale gauging the faith maturity of young people in the congregation.[7] Open-ended questions invited leaders to describe characteristics they believe account for their church's success with engaging young people, challenges they face when it comes to ministering to young people, and ways they have seen young people contribute to the health or growth of their congregation. Slightly different versions of the survey were administered to the pastors and youth/young adult leaders, in particular the exclusion of the faith maturity measure from the senior pastor survey, assuming the pastor may have less awareness of young people's spiritual maturity.[8]

PARTICIPANTS

Stage 1 data collection concluded in February 2014. A total of 373 church leaders from 259 nominated noteworthy congregations participated. See chapter 1 for detailed demographic information of participating congregations. In addition, as for socioeconomic diversity of congregations (as described by reporting churches), 7 percent indicated they were primarily upper class, 41 percent primarily upper-middle class, 41 percent primarily middle class, 8 percent primarily lower-middle class, and 3 percent primarily lower class.

Please see ChurchesGrowingYoung.org for a detailed description of data analysis methods for each stage of the research.

Stage 2 Research

OVERVIEW, SELECTION PROCESS, AND INSTRUMENTS

Based upon the results of the analyses in Stage 1, the research team identified several questions for further exploration in Stage 2. This research began in April 2014, consisting of one-hour interviews with 535 young people, parents of teenagers and emerging adults, church staff, and youth/young adult ministry volunteers across 41 exemplary churches from the 259 congregations that participated in Stage 1 (up to 20 interviews were conducted per church). The 41 exemplary congregations that participated in Stage 2 were selected through the following process.

Group 1: Fifteen churches were selected that had the highest combined score based on the percentage of young people participating (total number of 15- to 29-year-olds divided by total number of people participating in the church) and faith maturity ratings of young people. A formula was created that gave equal weight to each of these two criteria, and then the top 15 churches were selected for inclusion in Stage 2.

Group 2: The next 15 churches were selected based on those with the highest combined scores related to average ratings across all of the eight church characteristic questions.[9]

Group 3: Next, 14 remaining churches were selected that scored highest on each of the individual eight characteristic questions. Two churches were included for each characteristic, excluding the characteristic related to "communicating the gospel."[10]

Group 4: Finally, 14 churches were chosen by expert qualitative analysis based on the team's examination of the narratives of the Stage 1 surveys and unique or exemplary features of these churches.

The team invited 58 exemplary churches to participate in Stage 2 of the research, and 41 churches agreed. A point person from the congregation was selected by each church and was responsible for working with the congregation's leaders to identify congregants to participate in an interview. Using an online nomination form, this point person identified young people ages 18 to 29,[11] parents of teenagers and emerging adults, church staff, and youth/young adult ministry volunteers, up to a total of 40 people per church. Invitations were sent to nominated congregants until up to 20 agreed to participate in an interview. FYI's research team, including the primary researchers and 14 graduate students from Fuller Seminary's Schools of Theology, Psychology, and Intercultural Studies, conducted the approximately 60-minute structured phone interviews. Interviewers received extensive training by the project's senior research advisors. All interviews were recorded, transcribed, and coded.

Stage 2 interviews were conducted individually and included several questions regarding demographic information of the participant, areas of involvement in the church, a description of the church, the participant's perspective on why the church is effective with young people, how young people contribute to the church, Likert scale ratings and open-ended questions based on the church characteristics identified in the literature review,[12] Likert scale ratings and open-ended questions about the participant's beliefs and faith practices,[13] and an opportunity to share any other information the participant deemed important. Participants were assured of their anonymity and the removal of personally identifiable information from the transcripts. One interview template was created for use with young people, while a slightly different version was used with parents, volunteers, and church staff.

PARTICIPANTS

Over 14 denominations were represented in Stage 2, in addition to 7 congregations claiming no denominational affiliation. The largest 5 specific traditions represented were Baptist (7 churches), United Methodist (4), Roman Catholic (4), Nazarene (3), and Evangelical Covenant (3). Churches ranged in size of active congregational participants, including 100 or fewer participants (2 percent of churches), 101–250 (20 percent), 251–500 (17 percent), 501–1000 (24 percent), 1001–3000 (20 percent), over 3001 (17 percent). In terms of census regions of the US, they were distributed among the Midwest (29 percent), West

(29 percent), South (27 percent), and Northeast (15 percent). In terms of ethnic diversity (based on reporting churches), 48 percent of churches identified as "mostly White," 34 percent were "multiracial" (meaning the congregation included 20 percent or more from two different ethnic/racial groups), 8 percent were "mostly African American," 5 percent were "mostly Asian," and 5 percent were "mostly Hispanic/Latino." Regarding socioeconomic status (based on reporting churches), 37 percent reported primarily upper-middle class, 49 percent primarily middle class, and 14 percent primarily lower-middle class.

The following churches participated in Stage 2 and gave permission for their church to be named in association with this project (congregations also participating in subsequent Stage 3 research are marked with an asterisk [*]):

1. Centenary United Methodist Church, Winston-Salem, NC
2. Chapelgate Presbyterian Church, Marriottsville, MD*
3. The Church at Brook Hills, Birmingham, AL
4. College Church of the Nazarene, Nampa, ID
5. Covenant Congregational Church, Boston, MA
6. The District Church, Columbia Heights parish, Washington, DC*
7. Epic Church, Fullerton, CA
8. Faith Lutheran Church, Lacey, WA
9. Fellowship Memphis, Memphis, TN*
10. Fellowship Monrovia, Monrovia, CA
11. The First Baptist Church of Chicago, Chicago, IL*
12. First Baptist Church of South Gate, South Gate, CA*
13. First Covenant Church Minneapolis, Minneapolis, MN
14. First Presbyterian Church of Berkeley, Berkeley, CA
15. First United Methodist Church, Tulsa, OK*

16. Flood, Kearny Campus, San Diego, CA*

17. Frontline Community Church, Grand Rapids, MI

18. Ginghamsburg Church, Tipp City Campus, Tipp City, OH

19. The Highway Community Mountain View, Mountain View, CA

20. The Hills Church, North Richland Hills Campus, North Richland Hills, TX

21. Holy Apostles Episcopal Church, St. Paul, MN

22. Holy Trinity Orthodox Church, San Francisco, CA

23. Immanuel Church of the Nazarene, Lansdale, PA*

24. Lifeway Church, Indianapolis, IN

25. Mars Hill Bible Church, Grandville, MI

26. Metro Community Church, Englewood, NJ*

27. Millennium Revival Center, Raleigh, NC

28. Mountainside Communion, Monrovia, CA

29. Our Lady of Mount Carmel Church, Ridgewood, NJ

30. Our Lady of the Immaculate Conception, Dayton, OH

31. Redeemer's Church, Reedley, CA

32. Saints Constantine and Helen Greek Orthodox Cathedral, Richmond, VA

33. St. Andrew United Methodist Church, Highlands Ranch, CO

34. St. Francis of Assisi Parish, Fulton, MD

35. St. John the Evangelist Catholic Church, Indianapolis, IN*

36. St. Paul's Episcopal Church, Fayetteville, AR

37. Sugar Creek Baptist Church, Sugar Land Campus, Sugar Land, TX

38. Trinity Church, Miami Gardens Campus, Miami, FL*

39. Trinity Grace Church, East Village parish, New York, NY

40. Upper Room, Edina, MN

41. Volga Christian Reformed Church, Volga, SD*

Of the 535 individual interview participants in Stage 2, 60 percent were male and 40 percent were female. Reported age or role in the church (based on the reason they were nominated for the study) was distributed as 18 years old (6 percent), 19–23 years old (17 percent), 24–29 years old (21 percent), youth/young adult ministry volunteer (19 percent), parent of a teenager or young adult (14 percent), and church leader (23 percent). In terms of racial/ethnic diversity, interview participants identified as Asian/Asian American (10 percent), Black/African American (6 percent), Hispanic/Latino (6 percent), Causasian/White (73 percent), Pacific Islander (0.4 percent), and from multiple races (4.6 percent). Regarding highest education level completed, participants reported less than high school (1 percent), high school (9 percent), some college (18 percent), college degree (41 percent), master's degree (27 percent), and doctoral degree (4 percent). In terms of household income,[14] 2 percent reported "far below average," 16 percent "below average," 38 percent "average," 38 percent "above average," and 6 percent "far above average."

Stage 3 Research

OVERVIEW, SELECTION PROCESS, AND PROTOCOLS

In spring 2015, the research team selected 12 churches (from the 41 in Stage 2) to serve as illustrative case studies for deeper analysis in Stage 3. This analysis consisted of participant observation, document analysis, interviews, and focus groups. In order to select these 12 churches, the team began by eliminating 10 churches that had the lowest number of interview participants in Stage 2 or that were not well positioned to participate in this final stage of research.[15] Next, the research team eliminated two churches in which less than 14 percent of their overall church population consisted of young people. A formula was then created that assigned a numeric value to each church by combining the percentage of the overall church that was made up of young people and a composite score based on three questions from the Stage 2 interviews that indicated the church included a high percentage of people with a vibrant faith.[16] These weighted values were used to rank the remaining 29 churches.

This process resulted in a pool of potential churches displaying both high vibrancy and high participation of young people. In order to select churches that might serve as a diverse sample for the sake of the illustrative case studies, the research team created multiple categories deemed important for representation. This included a variety of denominations, ethnicities, socioeconomic statuses, and church sizes. For each representative category, the church with the highest vibrancy/participation weighted rating was selected. A total of 14 churches were invited in order to identify the final 12 that participated. Churches agreed to forego anonymity in this stage of the study, but individuals interviewed were assured their identities would not be used without further permission.

Teams of two or three researchers conducted the site visit to each of the 12 churches. While each visit was customized to the congregation's unique context, a typical site visit took place over one weekend. Before the visit, each team reviewed the church's online survey responses, interview transcripts, church website, printed documents sent by the church's point person, several sermons, and any other information that was publicly available. The church point person set up interviews and focus groups with church staff, high school students, young people ages 19–23, young people ages 24–29, parents of teenagers and emerging adults, youth/young adult ministry volunteers, congregants who could speak to the church's history, and others as deemed necessary. The research team also attended all possible church activities and programs, including services, youth/young adult gatherings, Sunday school, and any other weekend programming. During all visits, interviews and focus groups were recorded and extensive field notes were kept.

PARTICIPANTS

Over eight traditions were represented in Stage 3 research, in addition to two churches indicating no denominational affiliation. The makeup of this stage included three Baptist churches and one church each that identified as Assemblies of God, Evangelical Covenant, Christian Reformed, Nazarene, Presbyterian, Roman Catholic, and United Methodist. Churches ranged in size of active congregational participants, including 100 or fewer participants (1 church), 101–250 (2), 251–500 (1), 501–1000 (4), 1001–3000 (3), and over 3001 (1). In terms of census regions of the US, they were distributed among the Midwest (3 churches), West (2), South (4), and Northeast (3). Ethnic diversity included four churches that identified as "mostly White," four "multiracial" churches, two "mostly African American" churches, one "mostly Asian" church, and one "mostly Hispanic/Latino" church. Regarding socioeconomic status, five churches were primarily upper-middle class, five churches primarily middle class, and two churches primarily lower-middle class. Participating Stage 3 churches are marked by an asterisk (*) in the list of Stage 2 churches in the prior section.

DATA ANALYSIS

The Stage 3 site visits concluded during the summer of 2015. An average of 60 pages of field notes were generated from each visit, for a total of nearly 720 pages across all Stage 3 churches.

After each visit, the two or three research team members met to combine their notes into a comprehensive report. The core FYI research team read and reflected on these reports, both while the visits were being conducted and again after they were complete.

This on-the-ground research from Stage 3 was used alongside the quantitative and qualitative analyses from Stage 1 and Stage 2 and became a lens through which the data from earlier stages was interpreted. The core research team was also in regular dialogue with the advisors from the project regarding potential interpretation of the findings. The eight church characteristics were narrowed down to a list of five that stood out as most common and important across the churches in the study. Upon further reflection on the site visits and ongoing data analysis, the research team added a sixth and final characteristic of "empathizing with today's young people." Also at this time, the research team chose to describe these as the six "core commitments" of churches that effectively engage young people.

During the summer and fall of 2015, the core research team sent detailed reports of the project's findings to each member of the senior research advisors, Expert Advisory Council, and Pastor Advisory Council. These 30 advisors provided feedback through one-on-one and group phone calls or meetings.

In addition, the core research team presented select findings to a group of scholars and practitioners at the Association of Youth Ministry Educators conferences in fall 2014 and fall 2015, as well as to a group of over 50 church leaders at a fall 2015 Engaging Young People Summit at Fuller.

Assumptions and Limitations

While the research team made every effort to ensure that the CEYP Project was as academically rigorous, practically accessible, and generally thorough as possible, no research (ours included) is without assumptions or limitations. Following are just a few of the assumptions made and associated limitations of the study.

Our context as researchers. The research team understands our context as researchers to be both a strength and a weakness. The Fuller Youth Institute is located within Fuller Theological Seminary, one of the largest seminaries in the world. Given Fuller's multidenominational makeup and overall diversity, it has served as a wonderful and unique home in which to conduct this research. However, we recognize our location in Southern California, our own ethnic backgrounds, our middle-class socioeconomic status, and our level of education have undoubtedly shaped the way in which the team approached this research. Significant effort was made to include other voices from a variety of contexts and backgrounds to provide the widest perspective possible.

The importance of church participation. In forming the foundations for the CEYP Project, the team assumed that church participation is important for all Christians. As a result, the research team chose to study church participation directly rather than starting with the question, "What helps a young person grow in their faith?" The CEYP Project did not ask questions about the detailed spiritual experiences of young people but rather focused on their experiences of church.

Reliance on perceived effectiveness. Though the core commitments were found to be common across a variety of churches, the CEYP Project was largely reliant on what various leaders and congregants perceived to be effective. There are undoubtedly some variables that may not have been examined, such as those that did not come to mind during interviews or those that were unnoticed by participants.

A study of those who are involved. Since a key aspect of the study was to focus on churches that are actually effective in their ministry to young people, this project did not study the thousands of young people who have disengaged from and are no longer part of church. While their voices are important, less research has been conducted on the reasons why some stay involved in the church.

Generalizability of results. The CEYP Project's findings will not apply to all people, at all times, in any setting. Rather, this study focuses on a particular group of exemplary churches in the US. Undoubtedly, some churches will find the research difficult to apply to their unique context.

Correlation versus causation. The research team does not claim to have demonstrated a causal relationship between these core commitments and a church that is effective with young people. However, we're confident that the CEYP Project has identified six core commitments demonstrably present (through a variety of methods of data collection and analysis) within churches that grow young. The particular expression of each core commitment will vary based on the church's context. In the end, our desire is that this research will initiate helpful and life-giving conversations among church leaders. We're also hopeful that other scholars and researchers will review, test, and build on this work.

Our theological commitments. Last, but certainly not least, the Fuller Youth Institute (as part of Fuller Theological Seminary) holds particular beliefs and theological commitments that have grounded and guided our research. Undoubtedly, these commitments have influenced the research in ways that those from other traditions may find unhelpful.[17]

Notes

Chapter 1 Growing Young

1. Max De Pree, *Leadership Is an Art* (New York: Doubleday, 1989), 9.

2. Pew Research Center, "America's Changing Religious Landscape," May 12, 2015, http://www.pewforum.org/2015/05/12/americas-changing-religious-landscape/.

3. Pew Research Center, "America's Changing Religious Landscape."

4. Some Pentecostal denominations are seeing great growth outside of the US in Asia, Africa, and especially Latin America. Pew Research Center, "Why Has Pentecostalism Grown So Dramatically in Latin America?," November 14, 2014, http://www.pewresearch.org/fact-tank/2014/11/14/why-has-pentecostalism-grown-so-dramatically-in-latin-america/.

5. Conrad Hacket, "Emerging Adult Participation in Congregations," http://www.faithformationlearningexchange.net/uploads/5/2/4/6/5246709/emering_adult_participation_in_congregations_-_hackett.pdf.

Often cited as one of the most up-to-date repositories of data on US churches, the recent National Congregations Study highlights how quickly congregations are aging. Between 1998 and 2007, the number of regular attenders over age 60 in the 2,740 congregations surveyed jumped from 25 percent to 30 percent. During that same short time period, regular attenders younger than 35 dropped from 25 percent to 20 percent. Mark Chavez, "American Congregations at the Beginning of the 21st Century: A National Congregations Study," http://www.soc.duke.edu/natcong/Docs/NCSII_report_final.pdf.

6. Pew Research Center, "The Shifting Religious Identity of Latinos in the United States," May 7, 2014, http://www.pewforum.org/2014/05/07/the-shifting-religious-identity-of-latinos-in-the-united-states/.

7. Pew Research Center, "Asian Americans: A Mosaic of Faiths," July 19, 2012, http://www.pewforum.org/2012/07/19/asian-americans-a-mosaic-of-faiths-overview/.

8. A 2011 study of young adults indicates that approximately 59 percent of young people with a Christian background report that they have dropped out of church. David Kinnaman and Aly Hawkins, *You Lost Me* (Grand Rapids: Baker, 2011), 23.

According to a Gallup poll, approximately 40 percent of 18- to 29-year-olds who attended church when they were 16 or 17 years old are no longer attending. George H. Gallup Jr., "The Religiosity Cycle," *The Gallup Poll*, June 4, 2002; and Frank Newport, "A Look at Religious Switching in America Today," *The Gallup Poll*, June 23, 2006.

A 2007 survey by LifeWay Research of over 1,000 adults ages 18 to 30 who spent a year or more in youth group during high school suggests that more than 65 percent of young adults who attend a Protestant church for at least a year in high school will stop attending church regularly for at least a year between the ages of 18 and 22. In this study, respondents were not necessarily seniors who had graduated from youth group. In addition, the research design did not factor in parachurch or on-campus faith communities in its definition of college "church" attendance.

Data from the National Study of Youth and Religion indicates that 20 to 35 percent of Roman Catholic and Protestant teenagers who were religious become young adults who are no longer religious. Christian Smith with Patricia Snell, *Souls in Transition: The Religious and Spiritual Lives of Emerging Adults* (New York: Oxford University Press, 2009), 109–10.

In a Pew study of faith transition for US adults in general, roughly half of the US population changed religion at some point in their lives. Pew Research Center, "Faith in Flux," February 2011, http://www.pewforum.org /2009/04/27/faith-in-flux/.

Our estimate that 40 to 50 percent of high school graduates will fail to stick with their faith is based on a compilation of data from these various studies.

9. In the first two stages of our project, we wanted respondents to be anonymous, so we are not including their real names or other identifiable information when we quote or describe them. In the third and final stage of our research, we received permission to use real church names and other identifiable information.

10. When we use the phrase "fall away" from the faith, we don't necessarily mean that students have "lost" their salvation but rather that they have moved away from a faith that places Jesus at the center of all they are and do.

11. One of our nation's leading scholars on young adults, Jeffrey J. Arnett, observes a widespread return to faith after emerging adults become parents. Jeffrey J. Arnett, *Emerging Adulthood: The Winding Road*

from the Late Teens through the Twenties (New York: Oxford University Press, 2004), 177. Previous data studying young adults' religious trajectories indicates that among baby boomers who left the church (overall at slightly higher rates than today), those whose families regularly attended church in childhood returned at rates of 65 percent for mainline Protestants, 72 percent for evangelical Protestants, and 52 percent for Roman Catholics. See Wade Clark Roof and Lyn Gesch, "Boomers and the Culture of Choice: Changing Patterns of Work, Family, and Religion," in *Work, Family, and Religion in Contemporary Society*, ed. N. Ammerman and W. C. Roof (New York: Routledge, 1995), 61–79.

12. Our appreciation for this term increased thanks to the writing of brothers Chip Heath and Dan Heath, who highlight "bright spots" as important data in the search to bring about change. Chip Heath and Dan Heath, *Switch* (New York: Broadway Books, 2010).

13. The exception to this is that even in congregations growing young, it's challenging to build a year-round ministry to college students if there are few colleges located near the church. In those cases, the college ministry is often far more vibrant in the summer, when students who had been part of the church in high school return.

14. The term *emerging adult* was first coined by Jeffrey J. Arnett in 2000. Jeffrey Jensen Arnett, "Emerging Adulthood: A Theory of Development from the Late Teens through the Twenties," *American Psychologist* 55, no. 5 (May 2000).

15. We intentionally started with 15-year-olds (and not 13- or 14-year-olds) because we wanted to focus on high school–aged adolescents, which is when the precipitous faith drop-off seems to gain momentum.

16. Tim Clydesdale, *The Purposeful Graduate: Why Colleges Must Talk to Students about Vocation* (Chicago: University of Chicago Press, 2015), 201.

17. The 13 Protestant denominations are the Southern Baptist Convention, Assemblies of God, Presbyterian Church USA, Evangelical Covenant Church, Evangelical

Lutheran Church in America, United Methodist Church, Church of the Nazarene, American Baptist Churches USA, Church of God in Christ, Lutheran Church—Missouri Synod, Episcopal Church, Christian Reformed Church, and Christian and Missionary Alliance.

18. Most of the nominations from the Fuller Youth Institute were congregations that have participated in our yearlong Sticky Faith Cohort training program.

19. "Noteworthy churches" were primarily those with a high percentage of young people attending the church or participating in specific congregational characteristics, or whose young people had high faith maturity as assessed by church leaders. The FYI research team added a handful of congregations to this "noteworthy" list because of their unique and creative approaches to faith formation. For more details about the research process, see the appendix.

20. Kara has a PhD in practical theology; Brad and Jake have master's degrees and extensive theological training. Obviously, theology matters to us and shapes our research. To get a sense for many of the central theological tenets that have most influenced our research and ministry, see the statement of faith for Fuller Theological Seminary online at http://fuller.edu/About/Mission-and-Values/What-We-Believe-and-Teach/.

21. Defined as "participants."

22. Approximately 14 percent of US congregations are considered "multiracial," so we are pleased by the 31 percent of congregations in Stage 1 that fall into that category. Scott Thumma, "Racial Diversity Increasing in US Congregations," *Huffington Post Blog*, March 24, 2013, http://www.huffingtonpost.com/scott-thumma-phd/racial-diversity-increasing-in-us-congregations_b_2944470.html.

23. The primary reason that diversity increased is that our selection criteria in those two later stages tended to yield diverse congregations. A second and less influential reason that diversity increased is that in a handful of instances, as our team was choosing among churches, we opted for those with greater diversity.

24. Several quantitative and qualitative measures were used to assess spiritual vibrancy and faith maturity of young people, both indirectly (by pastors) and directly (by young people themselves). The primary quantitative measure we used is a nine-item scale utilizing significantly modified items from the Faith Maturity Scale popularized by the Search Institute. See Peter Benson, Michael J. Donahue, and Joseph A. Erickson, "The Faith Maturity Scale: Conceptualization, Measurement, and Empirical Validation," *Social Scientific Study of Religion*, vol. 5 (Greenwich, CT: JAI Press, 1995), 1–26.

25. When we quote our advisors without footnoting a specific source, their comment occurred during a group meeting or one-on-one discussion with our research team.

26. Many of our findings have numbers and statistics to back them up. Others are drawn from on-the-ground observation during site visits. While we don't want to debate the value of quantitative or qualitative research, know that this study utilized multidisciplinary methods to explore church effectiveness in order to provide a panoramic vista from which to take in both statistics and stories.

Chapter 2 Unlock Keychain Leadership

1. In the past few decades, there has been much attention placed on "missional" leadership, which emphasizes the sending nature of God and our "sent" nature as the people of God. Attention has also recently been given to "emergent" leadership, which paints leadership as highly flexible and responsive to our shifting culture. While there is great merit in both of these models, the keychain leaders we studied didn't neatly fit either of these categories. Neither did they fit the "pastor as CEO" model in which leaders dominate decisions and little happens without their consent. In fact, the personality or approach of keychain leaders was difficult to classify with any one existing adjective or profile,

including "purpose-driven," "servant leadership," or being "seeker-sensitive." By naming these as a list of models that we did not find, we are not suggesting they are unhelpful. They all have certain merit and validity.

2. Patrick Lencioni, *The Advantage: Why Organizational Health Trumps Everything Else in Business* (San Francisco: Jossey-Bass, 2012), 190.

3. Robert Wuthnow, *The Crisis in the Churches: Spiritual Malaise, Fiscal Woe* (Oxford: Oxford University Press, 1997), 6–7.

4. Lee G. Bolman and Terrence E. Deal, *Reframing Organizations: Artistry, Choice, and Leadership* (San Francisco: Jossey-Bass, 2008), 13.

5. Ibid., 15–16.

6. The Harvard Business Review Press released a short, practical book that can help you spend one to two weeks tracking your time. See *20 Minute Manager: Managing Time* (Boston: Harvard Business Review Press, 2014).

7. This pastor shared how he was led to pursue greater health through Peter Scazzero's book *Emotionally Healthy Spirituality: Unleash a Revolution in Your Life in Christ* (Nashville: Integrity, 2006).

8. Candace Coppinger Pickett, "Relational Capacity, Personal Well-Being, and Ministry Performance: Consequences of the Evolved Social Brain" (unpublished dissertation, Fuller Theological Seminary, 2014).

9. De Pree, *Leadership Is an Art*, 11.

Chapter 3 Empathize with Today's Young People

1. Walter Isaacson, *Steve Jobs* (New York: Simon & Schuster, 2011), 14–15.

2. Institute of Design at Stanford, "An Introduction to Design Thinking Process Guide," https://dschool.stanford.edu/sand box/groups/designresources/wiki/36873/at tachments/74b3d/ModeGuideBOOTCAM P2010L.pdf?sessionID=9a5d0a2a0cd5fb6c 26a567b2636b19513b76d0f4.

3. Pew Research Center, "Barely Half of U.S. Adults Are Married—A Record Low,"

December 14, 2011, http://www.pewsocial trends.org/2011/12/14/barely-half-of-u-s -adults-are-married-a-record-low/.

4. National Vital Statistics Report, "Births: Final Data for 2013," vol. 64, no. 1, January 15, 2015, http://www.cdc.gov/nchs/data /nvsr/nvsr64/nvsr64_01.pdf; and T. J. Matthews and Brady E. Hamilton, "Delayed Childbearing: More Women Are Having Their First Child Later in Life," NCHS Data Brief, no. 21, August 2009, http://www.cdc .gov/nchs/data/databriefs/db21.pdf.

5. Arnett, *Emerging Adulthood*, 6.

6. Bureau of Labor Statistics, "America's Young Adults at 27: Labor Market Activity, Education, and Household Composition: Results from a Longitudinal Survey," March 26, 2014, http://www.bls.gov/news.release /nlsyth.nr0.htm.

7. Robert Schoeni and Karen Ross, "Material Assistance from Families During the Transition to Adulthood," in *On the Frontiers of Adulthood*, ed. Richard Settersten, Frank Furstenburg, and Ruben Rumbaut (Chicago: University of Chicago Press, 2005), 396–416.

8. Robin Marantz Henig, "What Is It about 20-Somethings?" *New York Times*, August 18, 2010, http://www.nytimes.com /2010/08/22/magazine/22Adulthood-t.html ?pagewanted=all&_r=1.

9. Some scholars actually prefer the term *extended adolescence* to *emerging adulthood*. We find *extended adolescence* a vivid term to describe the delay in transition to adulthood, but as a general rule, we will use the more common term of *emerging adulthood*.

10. Susan Y. Euling et al., "Role of Environmental Factors in the Timing of Puberty," *Pediatrics* 21 (February 1, 2008): S167–S171.

11. See Arlie Hochschild and Anne Machung, *The Second Shift: Working Families and the Revolution at Home* (New York: Penguin, 2012).

12. As a result of this pace, only 15 percent of teenagers are getting 8.5 hours of sleep, which is the minimum amount required to function best. National Sleep Foundation, "Teens and Sleep," http://sleepfoundation .org/sleep-topics/teens-and-sleep.

13. American Psychological Association, "American Psychological Association Survey Shows Teen Stress Rivals That of Adults," February 11, 2014, http://www.apa.org/news/press/releases/2014/02/teen-stress.aspx.

14. American Psychological Association, "2010 Stress in America Findings," November 9, 2010, https://www.apa.org/news/press/releases/stress/2010/national-report.pdf.

15. In a 2014 nationwide study of over 3,000 students, 57 percent of undergraduates and 58 percent of graduate students reported more than average or tremendous stress. Only four years prior, that percentage hovered around 49 percent. University of Michigan University Health Service, "National College Health Assessment," https://www.uhs.umich.edu/ncha.

16. Clydesdale, *Purposeful Graduate*, 109.

17. Tim Clydesdale, *The First Year Out* (Chicago: University of Chicago Press, 2007), 2–3, 39.

18. The 16 percent of young people in our study who confess that their church adds to their stress note that these anxiety-filled seasons occur during times of increased responsibility, usually around a specific event or program. Yet despite the stress added by these roles, young people still celebrate these leadership opportunities because they infuse their lives with greater meaning.

19. Kenda Creasy Dean, *Almost Christian: What the Faith of Our Teenagers Is Telling the American Church* (New York: Oxford University Press, 2010), 10, 18.

20. Psalm 23:4.

21. Pew Research Center, "Teens, Social Media, and Technology Overview 2015," April 9, 2015, http://www.pewinternet.org/2015/04/09/teens-social-media-technology-2015/.

22. danah boyd, *It's Complicated: The Social Lives of Networked Teens* (New Haven, CT: Yale University Press, 2014), 127.

23. Andrew K. Przybylski et al., "Motivational, Emotional, and Behavioral Correlates of Fear of Missing Out," *Computers in Human Behavior* 29, no. 4 (2013): 1841–48.

24. Mark D. Regnerus, *Forbidden Fruit: Sex and Religion in the Lives of American Teenagers* (New York: Oxford University Press, 2007), 85.

25. Ibid., 121.

26. LGBTQ is an abbreviation for a cluster of sexual behaviors and identities including lesbian, gay, bisexual, transgender, and queer/questioning (depending on the source of the designation). See Mark D. Regnerus, *Premarital Sex in America: How Young Americans Meet, Mate, and Think about Marrying* (New York: Oxford University Press, 2011), 8–9. As researchers, we are not taking a particular theological or ethical position about same-sex attraction, identity, and marriage. Throughout this book, we are merely describing what we observed in the churches that grow young, as well as what we've gleaned from additional research. For help on how to talk to young people about this complicated and provocative issue, see Jim Candy, Brad M. Griffin, and Kara Powell, *Can I Ask That? 8 Hard Questions about God and Faith* (Pasadena, CA: Fuller Youth Institute, 2014), and *Can I Ask That? Volume 2*, released in 2015.

27. Bill Albert, Sarah Brown, and Christine M. Flanigan, *14 and Younger: The Sexual Behavior of Young Adolescents* (Washington, DC: National Campaign to Prevent Teen Pregnancy, 2003).

28. Chap Clark, *Hurt 2.0: Inside the World of Today's Teenagers* (Grand Rapids: Baker Academic, 2011), 31.

29. Robert Wuthnow, *After the Baby Boomers: How Twenty- and Thirty-Somethings Are Shaping the Future of American Religion* (Princeton, NJ: Princeton University Press, 2007), 216.

30. According to the Global Enterprise Monitor 2014 Global Report, 18 percent of 25- to 34-year-olds were starting or running new businesses. Babson College, "Entrepreneurship Rebounds Globally in 2014," http://www.babson.edu/News-Events/babson-news/Pages/2015-gem-global-report-shows-ambition-rising.aspx.

31. Smith and Snell, *Souls in Transition*, 72.

32. US Census Bureau, "New US Census Bureau Report Analyzes US Population

Projections," March 3, 2015, https://www.census.gov/newsroom/press-releases/2015/cb15-tps16.html.

33. Pew Research Center, "America's Changing Religious Landscape."

34. Pew Research Center, "Children Under 12 Are Fastest Growing Group of Unaccompanied Minors at U.S. Border," July 22, 2014, http://www.pewresearch.org/fact-tank/2014/07/22/children-12-and-under-are-fastest-growing-group-of-unaccompanied-minors-at-u-s-border/.

35. As Christian Smith, lead researcher of the NSYR, describes, "For most of their lives, from preschool on, most emerging adults have been taught by multiple institutions to celebrate diversity, to be inclusive of difference, to overcome racial divides, to embrace multiculturalism, to avoid being narrowly judgmental toward others who are out of the ordinary." Smith and Snell, *Souls in Transition*, 80.

36. Ibid., 80–81.

37. Andy Stanley, *Deep and Wide: Creating Churches Unchurched People Love to Attend* (Grand Rapids: Zondervan, 2012), 159.

Chapter 4 Take Jesus' Message Seriously

1. Dean, *Almost Christian*, 3.

2. Christian Smith with Melinda Lundquist Denton, *Soul Searching: The Religious and Spiritual Lives of America's Teenagers* (New York: Oxford University Press, 2005), 162–65.

3. Dean, *Almost Christian*, 3. Elsewhere she locates MTD more historically in some of the unhealthy aspects of Western culture: "After two and a half centuries of shacking up with 'the American Dream,' churches have perfected a dicey codependence between consumer-driven therapeutic individualism and religious pragmatism. These theological proxies gnaw, termite-like, at our identity as the Body of Christ, eroding our ability to recognize that Jesus' life of self-giving love directly challenges the American gospel of self-fulfillment and self-actualization" (p. 5).

4. George C. Hunter III, *The Celtic Way of Evangelism: How Christianity Can Reach the West . . . Again* (Nashville: Abingdon, 2000, 2010), 94.

5. Nancy T. Ammerman, "Golden Rule Christianity: Lived Religion in the American Mainstream," in *Lived Religion in America*, ed. David Hall (Princeton, NJ: Princeton University Press, 1997), 196–216.

6. Including terms related to "Son of God" and to the Trinity, or "Father, Son, and Holy Spirit."

7. Another study examining teenagers' articulation of Jesus—who he is, what he has done, and why it matters—concluded that a majority of Christian adolescents hold incomplete images of Jesus when compared with orthodox faith. In fact, only about a quarter of the respondents believe Jesus is fully God and fully human. See Jen Bradbury, *The Jesus Gap: What Teens Actually Believe about Jesus* (San Diego: Youth Cartel, 2014).

8. Seventy-eight percent of college-age young people ages 19 to 23 in our study mentioned Jesus, sonship, or Trinity in their responses, which is notably closer to just 2 out of 10 leaving Jesus out of the gospel. It's also worth noting that in previous research for Sticky Faith, 35 percent of young people did not mention Jesus in their responses to the question, "What does it mean to be a Christian?" The question was slightly different, but in this CEYP study, Jesus-centered responses were 5 percent more common. See Kara Powell, Brad M. Griffin, and Cheryl Crawford, *Sticky Faith Youth Worker Edition* (Grand Rapids: Zondervan, 2011), 29.

9. One resource to help emerging adults develop a redemptive gospel narrative is Craig G. Bartholomew and Michael W. Goheen, *The Drama of Scripture: Finding Our Place in the Biblical Story*, 2nd ed. (Grand Rapids: Baker Academic, 2014). Also see Scot McKnight, *The Blue Parakeet: Rethinking How You Read the Bible* (Grand Rapids: Zondervan, 2010).

10. Nancy Ammerman suggests, "Creating and telling stories of faith is at the heart of how congregations provide a heritage their

children can take with them. Precisely because they will indeed take that heritage to many other places as adults, the stories told and experienced are essential." Nancy Ammerman, "Journeys of Faith: Meeting the Challenges in Twenty-First-Century America," in *Passing On the Faith: Transforming Traditions for the Next Generation of Jews, Christians, and Muslims*, ed. James L. Heft, S.M. (New York: Fordham University Press, 2006), 49.

11. Formation experts David Setran and Chris Kiesling conclude that three things need to happen in order for emerging adults to move beyond MTD: reshape their loves (longings and desires), urge them to costly sacrifice, and call them to a life "with Christ" marked by regular practices and the ongoing work of the Holy Spirit. See chapter 2, "Spiritual Formation: Reversing Moralistic Therapeutic Deism," in David P. Setran and Chris A. Kiesling, *Spiritual Formation in Emerging Adulthood: A Practical Theology for College and Young Adult Ministry* (Grand Rapids: Baker Academic, 2013), 29–53.

12. Willard describes it this way: "History has brought us to the point where the Christian message is thought to be *essentially* concerned *only* with how to deal with sin: with wrongdoing or wrong-being and its effects. Life, our actual existence, is not included in what is now presented as the heart of the Christian message, or it is included only marginally." Dallas Willard, *The Divine Conspiracy: Rediscovering Our Hidden Life in God* (San Francisco: HarperCollins, 1998), 41.

13. Similarly, in their study of congregations identified as exemplary in youth ministry practice, Martinson, Black, and Roberto conclude, "The purpose of youth ministry in the congregations we studied can be summarized in a single goal: making disciples of Jesus Christ. These congregations focus their youth ministries on Jesus Christ and engage young people in discipleship, witness, and service that transforms their lives. Effective youth ministries make a significant impact on the personal faith of young people by deepening their relationship with Jesus, helping them understand the faith better, applying their

faith to daily life and serious life choices, and sharing their faith with others." Roland D. Martinson, Wesley Black, and John Roberto, *The Spirit and Culture of Youth Ministry: Leading Congregations toward Exemplary Youth Ministry* (St. Paul: EYM, 2010), 14.

14. As they run, young people need us running alongside them, balancing challenge with ample support. Challenge without support can lead to toxic pressure to perform and ultimately to burnout. Support without challenge, on the other hand, leaves us coddling young people in their pursuit of self-soothing distractions. Entertainment is what happens when we don't do either well.

15. Our quantitative faith maturity measure included nine items. See the research method and procedures in the appendix and on our website, www.churchesgrowingyoung.org, for further details.

16. For example, the story of David and Goliath becomes an admonition to be brave rather than a story of God's miraculous rescue, or the parable of the sower becomes about our character as "good soil" rather than about God's character as a generous sower.

17. Smith and Snell, *Souls in Transition*, 149.

18. For additional resources on how to explain the Bible within a larger narrative, see Mark Novelli, *Shaped by the Story: Helping Students Encounter God in a New Way* (Grand Rapids: Zondervan/Youth Specialties, 2008); V. Roberts, *God's Big Picture: Tracing the Storyline of the Bible* (Downers Grove, IL: InterVarsity, 2002); and N. T. Wright's For Everyone series.

19. If the liturgical year is unfamiliar in your tradition, a quick online search will yield a number of free introductory resources. Some calendars include more seasons than others, but the most common are Advent, Christmas, Epiphany, Lent, Easter, Pentecost, and Ordinary (or Common) Time. Another helpful resource is Joan Chittister, *The Liturgical Year: The Spiraling Adventure of the Spiritual Life* (Nashville: Thomas Nelson, 2010).

20. For a current version of the Reformation catechisms paired with contemporary

teaching, see the complimentary resources developed by Tim Keller and Sam Shammas at www.newcitycatechism.com.

21. For more of the findings from this study, see Thomas Bergler and Dave Rahn, "Results of a Collaborative Research Project in Gathering Evangelism Stories," *Journal of Youth Ministry* 4, no. 2 (Spring 2006): 65–74, and a related interview with Dave Rahn by Brad Griffin, "Re-Storying Conversion: Listening to Students' Accounts of Coming to Christ," available at https://fuller youthinstitute.org/articles/re-storying -conversion.

22. Richard Peace, *Conversion in the New Testament: Paul and the Twelve* (Grand Rapids: Eerdmans, 1999).

23. Sharon Daloz Parks, *Big Questions, Worthy Dreams: Mentoring Young Adults in Their Search for Meaning, Purpose, and Faith* (San Francisco: Jossey-Bass, 2000), 198.

24. Powell, Griffin, and Crawford, *Sticky Faith Youth Worker Edition*, 143–45.

25. The Fuller Youth Institute created a two-volume small group study to help teenagers and emerging adults explore some of the most common hard questions of faith. See Candy, Griffin, and Powell, *Can I Ask That?: 8 Hard Questions about God and Faith* and *Can I Ask That? Volume 2: More Hard Questions about God and Faith.*

26. See Steve Argue, "From Faith to Faithing: Could Faith Be a Verb?," http://stickyfaith .org/articles/from-faith-to-faithing. Note that the term *faithing* is also used by Sharon Daloz Parks in *Big Questions, Worthy Dreams.*

27. Sociologist Robert Wuthnow similarly describes young people's faithing process as *tinkering*: "The single word that best describes young adults' approach to religion and spirituality—indeed life—is *tinkering*. A tinkerer puts together a life from whatever skills, ideas, and resources that are readily at hand. . . . If specialized skills are required, they have them. When they need help from experts, they seek it. But they do not rely on only one way of doing things." Wuthnow, *After the Baby Boomers*, 13.

Chapter 5 Fuel a Warm Community

1. See for example Exod. 23:9; Deut. 10:18; 14:29; Matt. 25:34–36; Rom. 12:13; Heb. 13:2.

2. Christine D. Pohl, *Making Room: Recovering Hospitality as a Christian Tradition* (Grand Rapids: Eerdmans, 1999), 13.

3. Theologian Andrew Root asserts that this experience of belonging is most deeply felt when a young person senses that they are not the target or object of a ministry leader's efforts but rather a *person* engaging with other persons. Root encourages adults to participate in the act of "place-sharing," in which adults see and enter the reality—and suffering—of young people's lives; in this space of authentic interaction, Christ is present. See Andrew Root, *Revisiting Relational Youth Ministry: From a Strategy of Influence to a Theology of Incarnation* (Downers Grove, IL: InterVarsity, 2007).

4. This approach and phrase were championed by the Young Life movement in the mid-1900s, eventually making their way into church-based youth ministry practice.

5. The lack of mentoring in the church has been noted by others as a significant problem to address related to the retention of young adults. A 2014 Barna report found that young adults who continue their involvement in a local church beyond their teen years are twice as likely as those who don't to have a close personal friendship with an older adult in their church. Seven out of 10 millennials who dropped out of church did not have a close friendship with an older adult, and nearly 9 out of 10 never had a mentor at their church. See Barna Group, *Making Space for Millennials: A Blueprint for Your Culture, Ministry, Leadership, and Facilities* (Ventura, CA: Barna, 2014), 48.

6. Kara Eckmann Powell, Brad M. Griffin, and Cheryl A. Crawford, *Sticky Faith: Practical Ideas to Nurture Long-Term Faith in Teenagers* (Grand Rapids: Zondervan, 2011), 75.

7. This is true across most American churches. Holly Allen and Christine Ross conclude, "Though church leaders endorse intergenerationality in general whenever they cite biblical metaphors such as 'the body of

Christ' or 'the family of God,' in practice American mainline and evangelical churches generally conduct many of their services and activities . . . in age-segregated settings. Consequently, in the second decade of twenty-first-century America, all generations of the faith community—babies through nonagenarians—are seldom together." Holly Catterton Allen and Christine Lawton Ross, *Intergenerational Christian Formation: Bringing the Whole Church Together in Ministry, Community, and Worship* (Downers Grove, IL: IVP Academic, 2012), 30–31.

8. Miroslav Volf, *After Our Likeness: The Church as the Image of the Trinity* (Grand Rapids: Eerdmans, 1998), 11.

9. See Warren S. Brown and Brad D. Strawn, *The Physical Nature of Christian Life: Neuroscience, Psychology, and the Church* (New York: Cambridge University Press, 2012), 125.

10. Chap Clark also uses the helpful Pauline metaphor of adoption to encourage the enfolding of young people into the community. Adoption forces us to change when we become family. When you adopt a child, the family system itself must change so the child can become part of the system. Adopting people (of any age) into the church is the call of the gospel. Clark urges, "Adoptive ministry mandates that it is the responsibility of those in power to draw in, to include, and to equip all those who feel like outsiders so that they feel included in the very center of the family of God." See "Adoption: Re-envisioning Youth Ministry and the Family of God," in Chap Clark, *Adoptive Youth Ministry: Integrating Emerging Generations into the Family of Faith* (Grand Rapids: Baker Academic, 2016), 2.

11. It's worth noting here that despite the fact that we studied churches that are pretty warm, 10 percent of our interview respondents still wish that they had even more warmth and community! This highlights just how important warmth is for young people.

12. Brad's church was one of 363 churches identified by 35 nominators as engaging young

people well. While his church participated as one of 259 churches in Stage 1 and 41 churches in Stage 2, Brad never participated directly in any research communication or data gathering via surveys or interviews from his congregation. All data was analyzed anonymously and with names and other identifiers removed, including for the process of inclusion in Stage 2. See the research method in the appendix and at www.churchesgrowingyoung.org for more details about the selection method.

13. In the provocative book *Slow Church*, the authors explore connections between the "slow food" movement and Scripture's vision of the church community embedded in a local neighborhood. While they offer a number of critiques and counternarratives to the "fast church" movement (akin to fast food), they conclude with a pair of remedies that sound a lot like warmth: eating together and sharing in conversation. See chapter 11, "Dinner Table Conversation as a Way of Being Church," in C. Christopher Smith and John Pattison, *Slow Church: Cultivating Community in the Patient Way of Jesus* (Downers Grove, IL: InterVarsity, 2014), 208–22.

Chapter 6 Prioritize Young People (and Families) Everywhere

1. First Baptist's changes model what immigration researchers Alejandro Portes and Ruben G. Rumbaut call "selective acculturation," where first-generation immigrant parents and second-generation children adapt to culture positively, "embedded in a co-ethnic community of sufficient size and institutional diversity to slow down the cultural shift and promote partial retention of the parents' home language and norms." Their research finds that selective acculturation is "closely intertwined with preservation of fluent bilingualism and linked, in turn, with higher self-esteem, higher educational and occupational expectations, and higher academic achievement." Alejandro Portes and Ruben G. Rumbaut, *Legacies: The Story of the Immigrant Second Generation* (Berkeley: University of California Press, 2001), 54, 274.

2. Sticky Faith has been part of this shift, but we also applaud the influential work of our friends at Orange for pioneering incredible momentum within children's and youth ministry toward more intentional partnership between families and churches. See www.orangeleaders.com.

3. "The best general rule of thumb that parents might use to reckon their children's most likely religious outcomes is this: 'We'll get what we are.'" Smith and Lundquist Denton, *Soul Searching*, 57. The importance of parental example is confirmed in a number of studies, including Pam E. King and Ross A. Mueller, "Parental Influence on Adolescent Religiousness: Exploring the Roles of Spiritual Modeling and Social Capital," *Marriage and Family: A Christian Journal* 6, no. 3 (2003): 401–13.

4. Note that these findings were based on Stage 1 surveys of pastors assessing parent participation and young people's vibrancy and faith maturity, not the later interviews of parents and groups of young people.

5. Leaders regularly cite the statistic that 50 percent of all marriages in the US end in divorce. New data suggests this is inaccurate. According to the Census Bureau, 72 percent of those who have ever been married are still married to their first spouse. Included in the remaining 28 percent who are not married to their first spouse are those whose spouse has passed away. Given this data, one reliable estimate concludes that 20 to 25 percent of first marriages end in divorce. Shaunti Feldhahn, *The Good News about Marriage: Debunking Discouraging Myths about Marriage and Divorce* (Colorado Springs: Multnomah, 2014), 19–22.

6. Elizabeth Marquardt, *Between Two Worlds: The Inner Lives of Children of Divorce* (New York: Three Rivers Press, 2005), 48, 59, 85.

7. Arnett, *Emerging Adulthood*, 60–61.

8. Marquardt, *Between Two Worlds*, 155.

9. This saying is popularly attributed to Peter Drucker, though he did not include the direct statement in his own writings.

10. Italics added in this version but not in the original survey.

11. One midwestern Roman Catholic cathedral in particular stirs reverence, awe, and a sense of rootedness in tradition that matters deeply to both young and old.

12. Judith M. Gundry-Volf, "The Least and the Greatest," in *The Child in Christian Thought*, ed. Marcia J. Bunge (Grand Rapids: Eerdmans, 2001), 34.

13. Mary Ann Hinsdale, "'Infinite Openness to the Infinite': Karl Rahner's Contributions to Modern Catholic Thought on the Child," in Bunge, *The Child in Christian Thought*, 428.

14. See www.orangeleaders.com for more resources and a detailed look at the Orange strategy.

Chapter 7 Be the Best Neighbors

1. See Andy Crouch, *Culture Making: Recovering Our Creative Calling* (Downers Grove, IL: InterVarsity, 2008), 23. Crouch credits cultural critic Ken Myers for this phrase as used in Albert Louis Zambone, "But What Do You Think, Ken Myers?," *re:generation quarterly* 6, no. 3 (2000).

2. Timothy J. Keller, *Center Church: Doing Balanced, Gospel-Centered Ministry in Your City* (Grand Rapids: Zondervan, 2012), 22.

3. By using these terms, we mean joining God in "righting wrongs" in the world so that all people might have the opportunity to flourish or to experience the *shalom* (holistic well-being) that God intends.

4. Quote from Kuyper's inaugural address at the dedication of the Free University. Found in *Abraham Kuyper: A Centennial Reader*, ed. James D. Bratt (Grand Rapids: Eerdmans, 1998), 488.

5. Makoto Fujimura, *Culture Care: Reconnecting with Beauty for Our Common Life* (New York: Fujimura Institute and International Arts Movement, 2015), Kindle edition, location 7041.

6. Gabe Lyons, *The Next Christians: The Good News about the End of Christian America* (New York: Doubleday Religion, 2010), 59.

7. Pew Research Center, "The Most and Least Racially Diverse U.S. Religious Groups," July 27, 2015, http://www.pewresearch.org/fact-tank/2015/07/27/the-most-and-least-racially-diverse-u-s-religious-groups/.

8. Soong-Chan Rah, *The Next Evangelicalism: Releasing the Church from Western Cultural Captivity* (Downers Grove, IL: InterVarsity, 2009), 12.

9. Specifically, statistically significant correlations were found between diversity at this level and emphasizing social justice and serving others in need; teaching people how to interact with cultural and societal issues; helping people understand that faith is about more than behaviors or following rules; having engaging worship services; faith influencing friendships; and having young people who take time to read and study the Bible.

10. For more helpful discussion on this topic, see chapter 5 on vocation in Setran and Kiesling, *Spiritual Formation in Emerging Adulthood.*

11. We found a positive relationship between churches being intentional in engaging cultural issues and both vibrant faith in young people and overall church participation in identified measures of church health.

12. Crouch, *Culture Making*, 67.

13. US Census Bureau, "Most Children Younger Than Age 1 Are Minorities, Census Bureau Reports," news release, May 17, 2012, https://www.census.gov/newsroom/releases/archives/population/cb12-90.html.

14. While we've heard of this idea from multiple sources, it can be found in Chris Heuertz and Christine Pohl, *Friendship at the Margins: Discovering Mutuality in Service and Mission* (Downers Grove, IL: InterVarsity, 2010).

15. For more reflection on approaching service, mission, and justice with more reciprocity, see Chap Clark and Kara Powell, *Deep Justice in a Broken World: Helping Your Kids Serve Others and Right the Wrongs around Them* (Grand Rapids: Zondervan, 2007) and David A. Livermore, *Serving with Eyes Wide Open: Doing Short-Term Missions with Cultural Intelligence*, updated ed. (Grand Rapids: Baker, 2013).

16. Kara Powell and Brad M. Griffin, *Sticky Faith Service Guide: Moving Students from Mission Trips to Missional Living* (Grand Rapids: Zondervan, 2016), 17.

17. For example, see Gen. 12:1–9; 1 Sam. 3:1–21; Isa. 6:1–13; Jer. 1:1–10; Matt. 4:18–22; 16:24–28; 20:20–28; 1 Pet. 2:9–10.

18. Mark Labberton, *Called: The Crisis and Promise of Following Jesus Today* (Downers Grove, IL: InterVarsity, 2014).

Chapter 8 Growing Young in Your Context

1. This work has taken place through our Sticky Faith Cohorts, which are learning communities of churches that participate in a yearlong dynamic interplay between research and the implications of research for specific church contexts. The cohort process includes a church/youth ministry assessment, monthly online webinars, two three-day summits in Pasadena, a strategic plan for implementing change, and customized coaching.

2. Ronald A. Heifetz and Marty Linsky, *Leadership on the Line: Staying Alive through the Dangers of Leading* (Boston: Harvard Business School Press, 2002), 14.

3. Scott Cormode, "Leadership Begins with Listening," Fuller Theological Seminary, http://leadership.fuller.edu/Leadership/Classes/CF565/Wk01-03/Leadership_Begins_with_Listening.aspx.

4. Appreciative Inquiry is an effective approach to listening well in order to bring about change. Our colleague at Fuller Seminary, Dr. Mark Lau Branson, has successfully applied this approach to congregations. See Mark Lau Branson, *Memories, Hopes, and Conversations: Appreciative Inquiry and Congregational Change* (Lanham, MD: Rowman and Littlefield, 2004).

5. To better understand how pastors can respond to "longings and losses" and "the things that keep people awake at night," please see D. Scott Cormode, *Making Spiritual Sense: Christian Leaders as Spiritual*

Interpreters (Nashville: Abingdon, 2006), xiii–xvi.

6. Scott Cormode, "A Shared Story of Future Hope," Fuller Theological Seminary, http://leadership.fuller.edu/Leadership/Re sources/Part_2-Three_Ways_to_Lead/IV _The_Cultural_or_Interpretative_Ap proach_to_Leading/D_Meaning_Making _Leaders_Proclaim_Vision/1_A_Shared _Story_of_Future%C2%A0Hope.aspx.

7. Ammerman, "Journeys of Faith," 49–50.

8. Heifetz and Linsky, *Leadership on the Line*, 102–16.

9. Scott Cormode, "Leading for Transformative Change," Fuller Theological Seminary, http://leadership.fuller.edu/Leadership /Resources/Part_4_Leading_for_Transfor mative_Change.aspx.

10. Ronald A. Heifetz and Donald L. Laurie, "The Work of Leadership," *Harvard Business Review*, December 2001, 135.

Appendix

1. For example, in the Stage 1 survey, church leaders were asked to think of a young person with vibrant faith in Jesus Christ and then describe three to five characteristics of what that young person's faith looks like. The leader then rated (based on that description) what percentage of the young people in their church have a vibrant faith. A youth leader was also asked to select the percentage of young people in the congregation who participated in particular faith practices or actions believed to correlate with mature faith. In Stage 2 interviews, participants were asked to rate how true particular statements were of their congregation, such as, "My congregation effectively equips people to grow as followers of Jesus Christ." Young people themselves were asked to rate how true particular statements were that might describe their own faith practices. These statements comprised a nine-item scale utilizing significantly modified items from the Faith Maturity Scale popularized by the Search Institute.

See Benson, Donahue, and Erickson, "The Faith Maturity Scale," 1–26. Finally, during Stage 3 site visits, the research team assessed vibrant faith through observation and asking interview and focus group participants for their perspective on the spiritual vibrancy of the church. While none of these measures alone were comprehensive or gave the team a full picture, they provided a sufficient understanding to accomplish the goals of this project.

2. While multiple scholarly works formed the basis for the research design, the research team found Anne Colby and William Damon, *Some Do Care: Contemporary Lives of Moral Commitment* (New York: Free Press, 1992); and Pamela Ebstyne King, C. E. Clardy, and J. S. Ramos, "Adolescent Spiritual Exemplars: Exploring Spirituality in the Lives of Diverse Youth," *Journal of Adolescent Research* 29, no. 2 (2014): 186–212, to be particularly helpful in the development of an exemplar methodology. The work of several sociologists of religion, including Nancy Ammerman, Christian Smith, and Robert Wuthnow, were also invaluable to the overall research design.

3. In addition to submitting names of 15 noteworthy churches, nominators were also invited to submit the names of up to 10 churches that are "more typical in their engagement of young people." This group of more typical churches was not central to the project's exemplar methodology but was pursued as a matched comparison sample in order to examine if any significant differences would be found between the more typical and noteworthy churches.

4. Nominators were provided with the project's working definition of an *effective church*.

5. While designing this nomination process, the research team considered providing more specific criteria. However, after much discussion the decision was made to leave the criteria somewhat open to the interpretation of the nominator. This allowed the team to identify and learn from a wide variety of churches that the expert nominators believed to be noteworthy, including those that might

not fit the initial expectations of what the research team thought it meant for a church to be effective. This resulted in nominated churches that were *perceived as effective* in their engagement of young people.

6. For example, one question in this scale was, "How intentional is your congregation in planning activities that cultivate relationships where peers can share honestly with each other?"

7. For example, "What percentage of the young people in your congregation take time to read and study the Bible?"

8. To view the survey instruments used in each stage of the research, please visit www.churchesgrowingyoung.org.

9. Since the Stage 1 analyses demonstrated a relationship between these characteristics and church effectiveness, the research team found them to be viable selection criteria.

10. The team determined that this characteristic was the most broadly stated of the eight and most widely interpreted by Stage 1 participants. Therefore, the team sought to understand the topic better in Stages 2 and 3 rather than use it as selection criteria for inclusion in Stage 2.

11. The research team determined to wait to conduct interviews and focus groups with minors (ages 15 to 17) until the church site visits in Stage 3. This decision was made so that the project could be explained and informed consent could be obtained from parents in person.

12. For example, one question in this scale was, "How true is it that your church teaches people how to interact with cultural and societal issues?"

13. For example, one question in this scale was, "How true is it that you talk about your faith with others who are not Christians?" An example of an open-ended question about faith maturity is, "In a few sentences, how would you describe the central message of the gospel, or Good News, of Christianity?"

14. Participants were asked to indicate their household income as compared to their perception of the national norm.

15. For example, one church was going through a significant staff change as three of its paid leaders had left the church since the time the Stage 2 interviews began. This change would have made it difficult for the FYI research team to conduct the necessary research.

16. These composite scores were calculated based on average ratings for each church of the statements, "My church effectively equips people to grow as followers of Jesus Christ," "My church equips people to follow Jesus in their job, at school, or the other daily activities of life," and "My church helps people know and understand the gospel, or Good News, of Christianity."

17. Fuller's statement of faith can be found online. To better understand our beliefs, please visit http://fuller.edu/About/Mission-and-Values/What-We-Believe-and-Teach/.

Kara Powell, PhD, is the executive director of the Fuller Youth Institute (FYI) and a faculty member at Fuller Theological Seminary (see FullerYouthInstitute.org). Named by *Christianity Today* as one of "50 Women to Watch," Kara serves as a youth and family strategist for Orange and also speaks regularly at parenting and leadership conferences. Kara is the author or coauthor of a number of books, including *The Sticky Faith Guide for Your Family*, *Sticky Faith Curriculum*, *Can I Ask That?*, *Deep Justice Journeys*, *Essential Leadership*, *Deep Justice in a Broken World*, *Deep Ministry in a Shallow World*, and the *Good Sex Youth Ministry Curriculum*. Kara lives in Pasadena, California, with her husband, Dave, who is a medical device engineer, and their children, Nathan, Krista, and Jessica. Twitter: @kpowellfyi

Jake Mulder, MDiv, is the director of strategic initiatives at the Fuller Youth Institute (FYI), where he oversees business administration, coordinates new research, develops resources, and helps the team think strategically. He is a graduate of Fuller Theological Seminary (master of divinity) and Western Michigan University (bachelor of business administration in finance) and is currently a PhD candidate at Fuller. Jake is passionate about helping individuals and organizations achieve their full potential. He has worked in a variety of ministry and professional roles, including as a financial analyst, youth pastor in the

Reformed Church of America, ministry director with Youth for Christ, and missionary with Youth With A Mission (YWAM) in Europe and Asia. Originally from Michigan, Jake lives in Pasadena, California, with his wife, Lauren, a nutritionist, and their son, Will. Twitter: @jmulderfyi

Brad M. Griffin, MDiv, is the associate director of the Fuller Youth Institute (FYI), where he develops research-based training for youth workers and parents. A speaker, blogger at Fuller YouthInstitute.org, and volunteer youth pastor, Brad is the coauthor of several Sticky Faith books (see StickyFaith.org), *Right Click: Parenting Your Teenager in a Digital Media World*, *Can I Ask That? 8 Hard Questions about God and Faith*, and *Can I Ask That? Volume 2: More Hard Questions about God and Faith*. He has also authored a number of youth ministry book chapters and journal articles. He is a graduate of Fuller Theological Seminary (master of divinity in youth, family, and culture) and Asbury University (bachelor of arts in psychology). Originally from Kentucky, Brad now lives in Southern California with his wife, Missy, and their three children and leads the youth ministry at Mountainside Communion. Twitter: @bgriffinfyi

READY TO BEGIN?

TAKE THE GROWING YOUNG
ASSESSMENT

How well is your church currently positioned to grow young?

Where should you focus your time and energy?

Our comprehensive online diagnostic test sheds light on areas for growth and guides your first steps.

Take it on your own, with your leadership team, or with members of your congregation.

Both free and paid versions of this assessment can be found at:

churchesgrowingyoung.org

JUMP-START FULL-SCALE
CULTURE CHANGE

THROUGH A
**GROWING
YOUNG**
COHORT

Effective ministry with young people elevates *every* ministry in your church. Our advanced training model invites you to journey together for one year through:

IN-PERSON SUMMITS

WEBINARS

CUSTOMIZED COACHING

CONGREGATIONAL ASSESSMENT

TO **LEARN MORE** VISIT:

churchesgrowingyoung**.org**

The cohort will help your church craft a plan to implement Growing Young and shift your congregational culture.

FIND ANSWERS

to your toughest questions

Research into Resources

Here at the Fuller Youth Institute, we transform breakthrough research into practical resources for leaders, parents, and young people worldwide. For over a decade, we have studied teenagers and emerging adults in the contexts of their churches and families, creating tools such as the Sticky Faith series and the Urban Youth Ministry Certificate. Our model has empowered hundreds of thousands of leaders and parents. We look forward to partnering with you too!

Equipping

Leaders • Parents • Young People

fulleryouthinstitute.org

LIKE THIS
BOOK?
Consider sharing it with others!

- Share or mention the book on your social media platforms. Use the hashtag **#GrowingYoung**.

- Write a book review on your blog or on a retailer site.

- Pick up a copy for friends, family, or strangers! Anyone who you think would enjoy and be challenged by its message.

- Share this message on Twitter or Facebook: **"I loved #GrowingYoung** from **@FullerFYI //@ReadBakerBooks"**

- Recommend this book for your church, workplace, book club, or class.

- Follow Baker Books on social media and tell us what you like.

 Facebook.com/ReadBakerBooks

 @ReadBakerBooks